D1391837

ISAAC WATTS

ISAAC WATTS

HIS LIFE AND WORKS

Arthur Paul Davis

Virginia Union University

LONDON:

INDEPENDENT PRESS LTD

MEMORIAL HALL, FARRINGDON STREET, E.C.4

COPYRIGHT, 1943, BY
ARTHUR P. DAVIS

English edition 1948

PRINTED IN GREAT BRITAIN BY
JARROLD AND SONS LIMITED, NORWICH

To

Clarice and Arthur Paul

ACKNOWLEDGMENTS

To the following publishers I am deeply indebted for permission to quote from copyrighted material: The Columbia University Press, New York City, for H. N. Fairchild's *Religious Trends in English Poetry,* William Haller's *Rise of Puritanism* and *Tracts on Liberty in the Puritan Revolution,* Amy Reed's *The Background* of Gray's Elegy, and William York Tindall's *John Bunyan Mechanick Preacher;* Grafton and Company, London, for James P. R. Lyell's *Mrs. Piozzi and Isaac Watts;* the Macmillan Company, New York City, for F. J. Harvey Darton's *Children's Books in England* (Cambridge University Press, England) and A. E. Housman's *The Name and Nature of Poetry* (Cambridge University Press, England); Longmans, Green, and Company, Inc., New York City; for J. Hay Colligan's *Eighteenth Century Nonconformity;* G. P. Putnam's Sons, New York City, for Leslie Stephen's *English Thought in the Eighteenth Century;* and the *Nation,* New York City, for material from an editorial on Watts. I am also grateful to Mr. Malcom N. Stone for permission to quote from Wilbur M. Stone's *The Divine and Moral Songs of Isaac Watts* and Professor V. de Sola Pinto of University College, Nottingham, England, for permission to quote from his article, "Isaac Watts and His Poetry" in *Wessex,* Vol. III (Southampton, 1935).

PUBLISHER'S NOTE

A Life of Isaac Watts has long been desired, and it is interesting that a well-documented one comes from the United States from the pen of Arthur Paul Davis (Virginia Union University).

Mr. Davis shows a sound understanding of Watts and his times, and he does not make the mistake of thinking of him as a writer of hymns only. His influence on the life of his times—once we bear in mind his services to theology and education as well as to worship—was nothing less than profound.

It was extremely desirable that an authoritative biography should appear in this year when the bicentenary of Watts' death is being celebrated. The only way to secure this, in the conditions of to-day, is to photograph the text and print as it stands and we are grateful to Mr. Davis for permission to do this.

British readers will notice the American idioms and perhaps one or two slips—Thos. Wright, e.g., was not a minister—but they will be swept along by the narrative. For the first time Isaac Watts has an adequate modern biography and Independent Press is glad to introduce the book to Britain.

PREFACE

THAT ISAAC WATTS was a famous hymn-writer is generally known; but that he was considered by his contemporaries a popular and respected author in the fields of education, theology, philosophy, and poetry is a fact too often overlooked by layman and literary historian alike. I shall not attempt to paint Watts as a forgotten genius in any of these fields, but I do hope to show that he is more significant in his century than has been commonly thought.

Since four full-length biographies of Watts have already appeared in print, one may well ask why another is necessary at this late date. A brief consideration of the four lives will, I am sure, answer this query. The first, *Memoirs of the Rev. Isaac Watts, D.D.,* was written by Thomas Gibbons (1720-85), dissenting minister, friend of Watts, and associate of Boswell and Johnson. Appearing in 1780, it was based, the author claims, on manuscripts given him by Watts and by certain members of the latter's immediate family. This book has naturally become the fountain-head of all subsequent study of Isaac Watts, and yet in spite of its genuine usefulness and importance, it is an unsatisfactory piece of work. Gibbons did not select his material wisely or arrange it effectively, and he overlooked much that was extremely important. Taking everything that he could find on his subject, he placed it somewhere in the book. The result is a clumsy compilation of ill-digested matter, much of which could well have been omitted or relegated to an appendix.

The second full length biography, *The Life, Times and Correspondence of the Rev. Isaac Watts, D.D.,* was written by Thomas Milner and published in 1834. It is a 734-page volume based primarily upon Gibbons but containing also a great deal of additional material. Unfortunately the work is likewise awkwardly arranged. Milner has placed at the end of each chapter the letters written by and to Watts during the period treated in the chapter. These letters, making up one-third of the book, are frequently trivial and without pertinence to the matters discussed; they retard rather than advance the narrative. Much of the other material is also not pertinent to the subject; some of its details are inaccurate, and the work is far too long and too unwieldy to appeal to the ordinary reader.

The third biography, *Isaac Watts; His Life and Writings, His Homes and Friends,* was written by E. Paxton Hood and published in 1875. Writing for the Religious Tract Society, Mr. Hood was content to produce a readable and popular version of the material found in the first two works.

The fourth and most recent work, *The Life of Isaac Watts,* was written by Thomas Wright and published in 1914. In spite of a statement in the preface that the work is founded largely on materials which were inaccessible to his predecessors, Mr. Wright has added nothing of importance to our knowledge of Watts's life. The work is insufficiently documented and occasionally quite inaccurate.

Not one of these biographies has given the correct dates of the first publication of Watts's various works. Not one has pointed out in any convincing manner his importance as an educator and as a poet. Not one has attempted to trace the sources of Watts's literary, philosophical, and theological beliefs or to show his significance as a transitional figure.

I do not mean to be too severe with the efforts of Gibbons, Milner, Hood, and Wright. I realize that their objectives were different from those which I have in view. Writing as ministers and writing therefore primarily for a religious public, they have made their works too largely evangelical and inspirational. They have dwelt at length upon "Watts the hymnwriter" and "Watts the saint" and, as a consequence, have neglected to show with any degree of thoroughness their subject's relations with the past and his place in his own age. In short they have made of him an isolated phenomenon. The inadequacy of this interpretation and the structural and biographical faults mentioned above have persuaded me to attempt a re-statement of Watts's life and a new evaluation of his works.

I am deeply indebted, of course, to the works of Gibbons, Milner, and Wright; and I consider this life in the nature of a supplement to their efforts. It has been my privilege, however, to have access to several collections not available to my predecessors. Among them are a series of letters now in the possession of Basil Cozens-Hardy, Esq., Norwich, England; the letters and other material left by Watts's secretary, now owned by the Reverend Mr. Wilton Rix, Ealing, London; and the magnificent collection of manuscript letters found in both the archives of the Massachusetts Historical Society and in their published *Proceedings*. Although this material has given no startling new facts about Watts's life, it has been of great value in clarifying many small issues. It has helped me to correct several minor errors found in the earlier lives, to add a considerable number of new letters to Watts's correspondence, and to give new data on his relations with several important figures, including Cotton Mather, Jonathan Edwards, George Whitefield, and John Wesley. I feel that I have given a simpler and more accurate account of Watts's life than has formerly been given; showed for the first time in this type of book his importance as educator and poet; and, above all, traced to some extent the sources of his literary, philosophical, and religious beliefs. My ultimate purpose has been to present Watts as a typical and significant eighteenth century minor transitional figure whose works transmitted to that century the evangelical tendencies inherent in seventeenth century Puritanism.

Of the members of the faculty of Columbia University who have helped me in this work, I am especially indebted to Professor Ernest Hunter Wright, who suggested the subject, and who has directed my study through all of its stages, aiding me in more ways than I need record here. I am also grateful to Professor Hoxie Neale Fairchild (now of Hunter College), to

Professor William Haller, and to Professor William York Tindall for reading the work in manuscript. Their criticisms of the manuscript and their suggestions for its improvement have been of inestimable value. My thanks are likewise due to Professor Jan Schilt who was kind enough to read and appraise for me Watts's *Astronomy*.

I want to thank Dr. William John Clark, President-Emeritus of Virginia Union University, and Dr. John M. Ellison, President, for their patience and understanding during the course of my research. For encouragement and help in publishing this work, I am indebted to my brother, Dr. John A. Davis.

To the General Education Board through whose grants I was enabled to pursue my studies at Columbia and in England, and to the Trustees of Columbia University whose award of the Proudfit Fellowship made it possible for me to continue my work during the summer of 1937, I wish to express my deepest gratitude.

The following persons have been of special help to me in the gathering of material for this work, and I wish to acknowledge my appreciation: Mr. Robert F. Metzdorf, Curator of the Rush Rhees Library, University of Rochester; Basil Cozens-Hardy, Esq., Norwich, England; and the Reverend Mr. Wilton Rix, Ealing, London.

To the officers and staffs of the following libraries, I offer sincere thanks for unfailing kindness and helpfulness: the British Museum; the Union Theological Seminary Library; Columbia University Library; Dr. Williams' Library, London; Memorial Hall Library, London; the Bodleian; the National Library of Scotland; the University of Edinburgh Library; the Widener Library of Harvard University; the Massachusetts Historical Society Library; and the Public Library of Southampton, England.

Virginia Union University   A. P. D.
Richmond, Virginia

CONTENTS

Chapter		Page
I.	Child of Dissent	1
II.	Saints' World	20
III.	Later Life	39
IV.	Educator: Religious and Secular	73
V.	Controversies	103
VI.	Sermon and Essay	127
VII.	The Adventurous Muse	156
VIII.	System of Praise	188
IX.	Character and Influence: A Summary	216
	Appendix	231
	Notes	243
	Bibliography	271
	Index	297

CHAPTER I

Child of Dissent

ISAAC WATTS was born in Southampton,[1] July 17, 1674. He was descended from two well known and "respectable" dissenting families of that town, the Wattses and the Tauntons. Both families seem to have been good, successful nonconforming folk, active in the business and religious life of Southampton; but we are not able to trace the history of either very far. The earliest member of either family of whom we have record is the grandfather. And in each case the record narrows itself to practically a single biographical fact.

We learn from a footnote to a poem written by Watts in 1693 that:

My grandfather Mr. Thomas Watts had such acquaintance with the mathematics, painting, music, and poesy, etc. as gave him considerable esteem among his contemporaries. He was commander of a ship of war 1656, and by blowing up of the ship in the Dutch war he was drowned in his youth.[2]

Watts's maternal grandfather, Alderman Richard Taunton, was an affluent and distinguished citizen of Southampton. The Tauntons claimed Huguenot ancestry. Their family had been driven from France during the reign of Elizabeth by the St. Bartholomew Massacre. Alderman Taunton, like so many of the dissenters whom we shall touch upon in the course of this work, was a philanthropist. Through the terms of his will he left money to set up a school in Southampton for the training of boys for a seafaring life.[3] The school is still in existence, though not used for its original purpose.

Biographical data on Watts's father are fuller than for any other member of the poet's family. The elder Isaac Watts was born in 1650-1, presumably in Southampton. He married Sarah Taunton September 11, 1673, and the following year he was imprisoned for nonconformity. This was the year of the poet's birth, and tradition reports that Watts was often suckled on the steps of Old Town Gaol, Southampton, when his mother made her daily visits to the prison.

There is some confusion concerning the nature of the father's occupation. Gibbons states that the elder Watts was master of a "flourishing boarding school" to which gentlemen's sons from America and the West Indies came.[4] He is supposed to have taken to teaching because of family losses at the Restoration. The records of the Above Bar Congregational Church, of which the father was deacon, refer to him in 1700 and in 1719 as a "clothier," that is, a cloth-maker or cloth-factor. But in 1736, he is mentioned in these records as "Isaac Watts, of the Town and County of Southampton, Gentleman,"[5] the latter designation probably meaning that he had retired from business, for he died the following year. Watts's father may have been both teacher and clothier. Many dissenters of the period combined trade with preaching or teaching.[6] But whatever business he followed, he became quite early in his career a prosperous and influential member of the dissenting group in his town.

The Watts family were affiliated with the Independents[7] or Congregationalists;[8] and, as I shall mention the group quite often in the course of this work, a word concerning its origin and growth is necessary here. The Independents, like the other Puritan sects, had their origin in the stirrings of religious protest which occurred during the reign of Queen Mary. After the unsatisfactory Elizabethan settlement of the church, these stirrings developed into the Puritan reform movement.[9] In the course of time, the entire movement fell roughly into three general types of dissent—the presbyterian, the separatist, and the independent. The first comprised the main body of Puritan preachers. It was this group that wished to take over the Establishment and run it "according to the scheme of the *Book of Discipline*." The Independents were a minority group engendered from the first by the Presbyterians' insistence upon a strict and uniform church government. The early Independents were not separatist in character; they were interested primarily in two things: the restriction of the particular church to an approved "communion of saints" and a larger freedom for the individual congregation and preacher.[10]

Independency as a sect was not important until the time of the Westminster Assembly. In 1644 the Presbyterians were ready to reorganize the church according to their scheme. It was then that the Independents and the other more radical sects "suddenly came forward to oppose the majority in the Assembly, disrupt its plans, . . . fill Cromwell's army, push forward a revolution far more sweeping than any which the original Puritan reformers had conceived, ..."[11] "The logic of events," Professor Haller asserts, "drove them in the direction of a larger freedom than they could approve, and, when the time came, they retreated willingly to the Cromwellian compromise, which tolerated only such quiet, respectable, law-abiding groups as would support the existing government."[12]

The Independents had never been "enthusiastic" or fanatic in either religion or politics. Their great leaders in the last three decades of the seventeenth century were respected and learned divines like Thomas Goodwin, Philip Nye, Joseph Caryl, Theophilus Gale, and John Owen. Their chapels and meetings were composed largely of respectable middle-class persons. With the Presbyterians, they constituted the conservative, dignified, and strongly Calvinistic element of Protestant dissent. The group in Southampton with which the Wattses were connected was typical of the Independents at large.

There were two Congregationalist pastors in the town after 1662: Giles Say (1632-92), the ejected vicar of St. Michael's, and Nathaniel Robinson (d. 1696), the ejected rector of All Saints'. The Says and the Wattses were closely associated for many years. Giles Say and the elder Watts suffered persecution together; Samuel Say and Isaac Watts were schoolmates and lifelong friends.[13] But the Watts family evidently did not belong to Giles Say's meeting. All of the records available connect the family with Robinson's group. Say left Southampton sometime before 1688.

Nathaniel Robinson was in Southampton as early as 1643, for the court records of that year show that he was warned to discontinue preaching without legal ordination. In 1646-7 he was summoned again on the same charge, but the officers were unable to find him.[14] He evidently must have been ordained by October 1648, for at that time he was rector of St. Lawrence's Church. From there he moved to All Saints', from which he was ejected in 1662. Robinson was a man of some learning and eminence. He was a "lecturer" [15] in 1647 at Holy Rood church, and so great was his popularity among the "well affected" in the town that the mayor and aldermen were unable to stop his preaching.[16] He was also a friend of Oliver Cromwell and acted as an intermediary for the latter in the marriage settlement of Richard Cromwell and Dorothy Mayjor, the daughter of a Southampton alderman.[17]

After his ejection, Robinson became leader of a little group of Independents meeting in Above Bar. On August 24, 1688, the group combined with one from Romsey and organized themselves into a "distinct and separate church." The land for the chapel was leased from the elder Watts.[18] As secretary of the new meeting, he entered his son Isaac's name as the first on the baptismal register. He was also elected deacon and appointed one of the original trustees of Thorner's Charity.[19] Deacon, leaseholder, trustee—all of these positions show Mr. Watts as a prosperous and respected figure in his community.

A man of strong convictions, he was willing to suffer for the sake of conscience. He was twice imprisoned for nonconformity, once in 1674, as already noted, and again in 1683. The exact cause of the first punishment is not known, but as Watts's father was closely associated with Say and Robinson, both of whom were persecuted for violation of the Act of Uniformity, one assumes that the elder Watts suffered along with them. In 1674 there occurred one of the several outbreaks of violence against dissenters which marked the reign of Charles the Second. By the Act of Indulgence (1672) Charles had granted religious liberty to all groups in England. The act, however, antagonized the High Church Tories because it gave too much freedom to dissenters; and the Commons in 1673 forced the king to withdraw it. As a result, all of the penal laws directed against dissent were enforced with renewed vigor and great violence.

The second imprisonment was recorded by Isaac Watts himself, then a boy of nine, in an autobiographical document entitled "Memorable Affairs in My Life":[20]

1683. My father persecuted and imprisoned for nonconformity 6 months. After that forced to leave his family and live privately in London 2 years . . .

The restraint of this entry adds to its effect. It is not hard to imagine the distress of the wife of the persecuted man and the impression made on the mind of the child.

The specific cause of this imprisonment is again not known, but 1683 was the high point in Charles' fight with Parliament over the Exclusion Bill. The Tories were in power, and the dissenters' stand on the bill added fuel to the fires of persecution. The years 1683 to 1685 saw the execution of Russell and Sydney and the Bloody Assizes of Jeffreys. These were terrible years for dissent, and Watts's father was simply one of the many hundreds who suffered.

There is extant a letter[21] which the father wrote to the children from his London exile. He commented only briefly on his own condition; his great concern was the religious welfare of his family. He urged them to read the Scriptures with delight, to understand their "sinful state", to pray, "to worship God in God's own way", that is, according to the rules not of men but of the Gospel, and above all, to spurn all "popish doctrine" of salvation through works. The letter, dated May 21, 1685 (James II had become King in February), was an effective lesson in the "School of Dissent" for young Isaac, to whom it was principally addressed. One can understand the strong dislike for the House of Stuart which Watts bore throughout his life and the passion of his later Whig panegyrics on the Prince of Orange.[22]

The elder Watts lived to see his eighty-fifth birthday, an event which he celebrated with an appropriate poem on "The Soul's Desire of Remove."[23] With his duties as deacon of Above Bar, with his business interests, and with a famous son devoting his life to the service of God and to the cause of dissent, his old age must have been far more peaceful and serene than his earlier years of persecution and exile. Watts was in his sixty-third year when his father died.

Data concerning the lives of Watts's brothers and sisters are scarce. Isaac, born in 1674, was the oldest child. There were eight children in all, six of them living to maturity. Richard, the second son, was born July 17, 1676 and died in 1750. He became a prosperous London physician and will appear again in this work. Enoch was born March 11, 1678 and lived to help Gibbons, the first biographer of Watts, with materials for the life of his brother. The date of his death is unknown. Thomas was born January 20, 1680, and the only further reference we have to him is a note in Watts's "Memorable Affairs" stating that he married in 1706. Watts also left 150 pounds in South-Sea stock in his will to "my nephew Thomas Watts, of Chichester", probably the son of this Thomas. Sarah, the "Sarissa" of Watts's poems and apparently his favorite of the children, was born October 31, 1681, and married in 1707-8 a Mr. Brackstone, a draper of Southampton. Her son appears later in this account in a none too favorable light. Watts left to her and Enoch the bulk of his estate. Sarah, too, helped Gibbons with materials for the first life. There were also Mary, born February 13, 1684, buried January 1, 1686; a second Mary, born April 10, 1687, died March 4, 1715; and Elizabeth, born August 15, 1689, died November 11, 1691.[24]

Very little is known concerning the home life of this family and practically nothing about Watts's mother. There are, however, two anecdotes from the period which give obliquely some insight into her character. It was her custom to make the boys in the school write verses as a diversion. A farthing prize was offered for the best work. Isaac Watts at the age of seven submitted this bit of childish egotism as his prize poem:

> I wrote not for a farthing, but to try
> How I your farthing writers can outvie.[25]

The other anecdote of Watts's early life reveals, as one would expect, the strong religious influence on his childhood. The mother, so the story goes, found one day some verses of her son Isaac. Surprised at their excellence she hinted some doubt concerning their authorship. In order to prove that he was the author and could produce other verses just as good, Watts composed for her the following acrostic:

> I am a vile polluted lump of earth,
> S o I've continued ever since my birth,
> A lthough Jehovah grace does daily give me,
> A s sure this monster Satan will deceive me,
> C ome therefore, Lord, from Satan's claws relieve me.
>
> W ash me in Thy blood, O Christ,
> A nd grace divine impart,
> T hen search and try the corners of my heart,
> T hat I in all things may be fit to do
> S ervice to thee, and sing thy praises too.[26]

For a child of seven, these verses are not contemptible. To the modern reader, the religious sentiment expressed may seem

surprising in one so young, but it was a perfectly normal view
and attitude for any intelligent boy of seven in that era. It was
also quite normal for Watts to fall, as he phrases it, "under
considerable convictions of sin" and to become converted at the
age of fourteen.[27]

At first glance, the record of Watts's early education strikes
us as showing definite precocity:

> Began to learn Latin of my father 1678
> To Latin School and Writing 1680
> Began to learn Greek .... 1683 or before
> Learned French 1684, 1685
> Learned Hebrew .... 1687 or 8.[28]

Latin at four, Greek at nine, and Hebrew at thirteen—this
sequence is impressive to those of us accustomed to the modern
procedure in language study. But Watts's course of study, with
one exception, was orthodox for his age. Sir Henry Wotton's
An Essay on the Education of Children (1672) outlines the
same order of study—that is, from Latin to Greek to Hebrew—
for the education of his son. Incidentally, William Wotton also
began Latin at four and, even earlier than Watts, Greek and
Hebrew at five.[29]

The one incongruous note in Watts's memorandum is the
statement that he learned French in 1684-85. The study of
French in the elementary and public schools of the seventeenth
century was not customary. One can only hazard a guess that
the French refugee influence was strong in Southampton; and
the Tauntons, Says, and other families with French ancestry
influenced the curriculum to the extent of including the
language.

It should be noted here that Watts's Latin schoolmaster was
a minister of the Establishment, the Reverend Mr. John Pinhorne, Rector of All Saints' and master of the Free-School at
Southampton. There was a close bond of affection between
Watts and Pinhorne. When Watts was ordained in 1702, he

sat for a portrait which he sent to Pinhorne.[30] In 1694 he attempted a Latin Pindaric ode of appreciation dedicated: "Ad Reverendum Virum Dominum Johannem Pinhorne, fidum Adolescentiae Meae Praeceptorem." [31] Feeling it beyond his ability at the time, Watts abruptly ends the poem with the following apology:

> Forgive Rev. Sir, the vain attempt, and
> kindly accept this poetical fragment,
> though rude and unpolished, as an
> expression of that gratitude which has
> been so long due to your merit.[32]

The fragment however shows just how deeply Pinhorne influenced his student's poetical beliefs. It was he who first opened to Watts the works of Casimire, the modern Latin poet. The extravagant praise of Casimire and the many translations of his poetry that Watts produced later show that he never lost his schoolboy regard for the writer. Pinhorne also impressed upon his student the importance of dedicating his muse to the service of religion. The idea became the guiding principle of Watts's literary life. The preface to *Horae Lyricae* is an important eighteenth century statement of this attitude.[33]

By 1690 Watts was ready to leave Pinhorne and to begin his university training. The whole community, Anglican and dissenter alike, seems to have been proud of the young scholar. Dr. John Speed, a physician of Southampton, with the help of other interested persons, offered Watts a scholarship if he would matriculate at one of the universities. Preferring to continue with the dissenters, Watts declined the offer.

The decision was not surprising. His family had been so closely allied with dissent in its days of persecution that a change in the relatively tolerant age of William III would be not only traitorous to principle but somewhat pointless. But there were obvious advantages in the Establishment, and many dissenters were conforming. The Act of Toleration had lifted the pressure of persecution from dissent, and the result had been a tendency towards disintegration. Samuel Wesley left the movement during this time; it was but a short while later that Watts's schoolfellows, John Hughes and Josiah, afterwards Archbishop, Hort, conformed. It would not have been unusual if Watts had accepted Speed's offer.

Watts, then in his sixteenth year, went to Thomas Rowe's Academy in London. The term "academy" requires explanation here. Dissenters found themselves barred by the Act of Uniformity (1662) from attendance at Oxford or Cambridge, because entrance to either meant subscription to the Articles of the Church of England. They therefore had to create for their own group schools which would give equivalent training. These institutions were called academies; the name was probably taken from John Calvin's famous school in Geneva.[34] The first academy opened in 1663.

The academies in the first period of their development, that is, from 1663 to 1690, were usually one-man institutions.[35] The tutor was in most cases an ejected minister who had turned to teaching for a livelihood. He would gather in his home from twenty to thirty boys, ranging in age from fourteen to twenty-one years. In many instances the tutor and his school had to make frequent removals to escape persecution. The academy which Watts attended, for example, started in Newington Green, moved to Clapham, from there to Little Britain, and finally returned to its original location. These schools generally ended with the death of the tutor. They prepared students for the ministry primarily, but other types of training were also given. The course of study required four years.

It should be emphasized that Watts went to the academy for *university* training, for these schools provided advanced scholastic training. Most of the tutors in the first-period academies were university men. They used the methods and the standard texts of Oxford and Cambridge, and they tried to give a conventional education. The elder Wesley, who attended Morton's Academy at Newington, states that he was advised by his tutor to register also at one of the universities in the hope that the subscription bars would soon be let down, and he could obtain a degree from Oxford or Cambridge for work done in the academy.

What did Watts study? Unfortunately we do not have an outline of the courses offered by Thomas Rowe, but there are extant two fairly good descriptions of work done in these schools. Toulmin[36] gives an account of the curriculum at Sheriffhales, an academy in existence from 1663 to 1697. The subjects taught were Latin, Greek, Hebrew, mathematics, history, geography, natural science, rhetoric, ethics, metaphysics, anatomy, law, and divinity. The students were trained in scholastic disputations in the syllogistic form. They practiced English composition through the writing of letters and speeches. The theological students had to analyze chapters and verses from the Bible, to draw up outlines for sermons, to pray at the Lord's-Day evening service, and to set Psalms to different tunes. There were daily reviews of the preceding day's work and a Saturday review of the whole week's work. Once a year the whole grammar was publicly recited. Practical exercises accompanied the lectures, and the students were employed at various times in surveying land, composing almanacs, making sun dials, and dissecting animals.

The following authors were studied at Sheriffhales: Galtruchius, Gassendi, Gunter, Leybourn, Moxon, and Euclid (Elements) in mathematics; Descartes (*Principia*), De Stair, Heereboord, Magirus, Rhegius, and Robault in natural science; Burgersdicius (with Heereboord's *Commentary*), Wallis, Ramus, and Downam in logic; Quintilian, Radeau, and Vossius in rhetoric; Baronius, Facchaeus, Frommenius, Blank (*Theses*), and Ward (*Determinationes*) in metaphysics; Eustachius, Heereboord, More, and Whitby in ethics; Euchard in

geography; Puffendorf in history; Gibson, Bartoline and Blan-
cardi (*Anatomia Reformata*) in anatomy; and Bythner
(*Grammar* and *Lyra Prophetica*) in Hebrew.[37]

Samuel Palmer, who went to Morton's Academy at Newington Green, describes in some detail the work done there.[38] The
students began the day with logic, for which they read Heereboord, the text used at Cambridge. "Ethics was our next study,
and our system Heereboord: in reading which our tutor recommended to our meditation Dr. Henry More, Marcus Antonius,
Epictetus, with the comments of Arrian and Simplicius, and
the morals of Solomon; and under this head the moral works
of the great Puffendorf." In natural philosophy they used the
system of Le Clerc which they compared with that of Aristotle,
Descartes, De Stair, and other philosophers. They disputed
every other day in Latin upon the "several philosophical controversies." Every Saturday the classes declaimed by turns on
some "noble and useful subject." Latin and Greek writers
were read daily but not in the "pedantic method of common
schools." The Greek Testament was read through once a year.
Mondays and Fridays were given to divinity lectures; and for
practical divinity the students were advised to read Baxter,
Tillotson, Charnock, "in a word, the best books, both of the
Episcopalian, Presbyterian, and Independent divines." [39]

The books and methods used at these two schools were
typical. Different tutors, however, emphasized different aspects
of the general program. Thus at Newington Green Morton
seems to have stressed natural science, for both Defoe and
Samuel Wesley mention especially their experiments in the
subject. At Sheriffhales English essay-writing was stressed, as
noted above, and students were required to set the Psalms to
English metre. In all cases the individuality of the tutor was
the important spiritual and educational force of the school. This
was particularly true of Rowe's Academy at Newington Green.

This academy had been founded about 1666 by Theophilus
Gale,[40] who taught there until his death. He was succeeded

by his former student, Thomas Rowe, pastor of the Independent group meeting in Girdlers' Hall, Basinghall Street,[41]
(Watts joined this church in 1693). Although only twenty-one
when he took over Gale's work, Rowe was excellently qualified for the task. "To extensive learning he united great ur-
banity of manners and a most amiable, conciliatory disposition." [42] Few tutors have been more successful in turning out
useful and famous students. To have Henry Grove, Dr. John
Evans, Dr. Jeremiah Hunt, Samuel Say, John Hughes, Daniel
Neal, Archbishop Hort, David Polhill, Lord Barrington, and
Isaac Watts as alumni of a one-man school is certainly an enviable achievement. Through the lives and works of these men,
Rowe became a potent force in shaping the thought of eighteenth century nonconformity.[43]

Alexander Gordon states that Thomas Rowe was an early
liberal in education and philosophy. He was a Cartesian in
physics and an exponent of Locke in "mental science"; he was
among the first to desert the traditional textbooks and to introduce his students to what Watts called "Free Philosophy," [44]
that is, philosophy which, asserting the liberty of enquiry,
based its foundation upon reason rather than upon implicit
authority.[45]

In religion, Rowe was a "doctrinal Calvinist," and there is no
doubt that he inculcated the same principles in his academy.
But he "possessed a noble and generous mind, free from the
shackles of a party, and utterly averse to all impositions in the
concerns of religion. . . . To his pupils he allowed the most
enlarged freedom of enquiry, and it is well known that some of
them followed a path in controversy very different to that of
the tutor." [46]

Isaac Watts's academy notebooks[47] bear out this statement.
The dissertations contained in them show that Watts at the
time was an orthodox but inquiring Calvinist. They also show
that Rowe was a thorough and capable teacher. Samuel Johnson, after seeing some of these academy exercises, felt that they

revealed "a degree of knowledge both philosophical and theological, such as very few attain by a much longer course of study." [48]

Rowe died prematurely August 18, 1705, and the academy was dissolved. Watts paid him a fitting tribute in a poem, "To the much honored Mr. Thomas Rowe, the Director of my youthful Studies," entitled "Free Philosophy":

> Custom, that tyranness of fools,
>   That leads the learned round the schools,
> In magic chains of forms and rules!
>   My genius storms her throne:
> No more, ye slaves, with awe profound
> Beat the dull track, nor dance the round;
> Loose hands, and quit th' inchanted ground:
>   Knowledge invites us each alone. [49]

The poem was not schoolboy rhetoric. At the academy Watts learned to storm the "throne" of custom in his private thoughts on religion. A letter which he sent in 1696 to Pocyon, an unknown correspondent, expressed this attitude:

In matters of the christian faith, I would make the scripture my guide . . . My reason should be used as a necessary instrument to compare the several parts of revelation together, to discover their mutual explication, as well as to judge whether they run counter to any dictates of natural light. But if an inquisitive mind overleap the bounds of faith, and give the reins to all our reasonings upon divine themes in so wide and open a field as that of possibles and probables, it is no easy matter to guess where they will stop their career. I have made experiment of this in my own meditations; when I have given my thoughts a loose, and let them rove without confinement, sometimes I seem to have carried reason with me even to the camp of *Socinus;* but then *St. John* gives my soul a twitch, and *St. Paul* bears me back again (if I mistake not his meaning) almost to the tents of John Calvin. [50]

Two phrases in the letter attract attention: "even to the camp of Socinus" and "almost to the tents of John Calvin." In later life Watts was accused of Socinianism; and although the accusation was not just, he was, as we shall see, definitely un-orthodox in his explication of the Trinity.[51] Even at this period, he was obviously not a rigid Calvinist. As Watts's Calvinism will be discussed later in some detail, it is sufficient here to note that in 1696 he had already begun that examination and ques-tioning of the mysteries of religion which were to disturb his declining years.

The poetry that Watts wrote while attending the academy foretokens his later and increasing concern with the "person" of Christ in his treatment of the Canticles, in his Trinity essays, and in his "experimental" preaching. This poetry is predominantly Latin, much of it Pindaric in form. Most of the poems have the same theme: Christ's love, suffering, and dying for sinful man. Watts's rapturous depiction of Christ's love and passion reminds one of Crashaw's poetic treatment of the Virgin.[52] The poems show traces of that mystical eroticism for which he apologized in later editions of *Horae Lyricae*.[53]

Watts was not the only poet at Newington Green. Two of his closest friends, John Hughes[54] and Samuel Say, also wrote verses; and the three of them carried on a poetical and critical correspondence during their school career and for several years after their graduation. The letters[55] exchanged among the three are an excellent index to the intellectual life of the academy. One finds that all were writing Latin poetry; all were interested in Pindarics and in correct çanons of criticism. All, too, seemed to be firmly convinced that the function of poetry was moral. "In all times and in all places of the world," Say dogmatically asserted to Hughes, "the moral poets have ever been the great-est, and as much superior to the others in wit as in virtue."[56]

The attitude of this group towards the authorized transla-tion of the Psalms foreshadows Watts's later strictures. Hughes wrote to Say in 1697:

But, ceremony apart, I give you my hearty thanks for your in-genious paraphrase, in which you have so generously rescued the noble Psalmist out of the butcherly hands of Hopkins and Stern-hold.[57]

Watts sent his poems to Hughes for criticism, but the latter refused to act the part of a critic because he had "neither judg-ment nor ill-will enough." [58] Say and Hughes discussed the use of Sapphics in English. They commented on the rarity of the measure in the language, showing, incidentally, that they knew about Sir Philip Sidney's attempts in "hexameters based on Latin Measure." [59] They all paid excessive compliments to one another's poetry.

One letter,[60] written by Hughes to Watts, throws some light on the latter's character. All friends are agreed, says Hughes, that Watts has one trait in perfection, modesty. The quality certainly grew with age. In later years it became so extreme as to arouse suspicions concerning its genuineness.[61] The same letter mentions another characteristic of Watts which was evi-dently sternly suppressed in later years, his ability to write a "witty and diverting letter." The witty and diverting Watts of 1696 soon became the "pious and learned Dr. Watts" and with this change came his gradual withdrawal from intimacy with Hughes.

Hughes was educated for the ministry; but Watts, it is said, persuaded him not to preach because he was too gay for that profession.[62] Hughes later conformed and became an associate of Addison, Pope, and others in the polite world. The breach between the two friends was therefore considerably widened, for this world did not often touch the circumscribed one in which Watts moved. Hughes died in 1734. His works were published by his brother-in-law, who sent Watts a "ticket" for a complimentary copy. The latter's note of thanks was touch-ing:

My acquaintance and intimacy with that ingenious gentleman [Hughes] was in the younger years of life chiefly; our later situa-tions in the world divided us so far as to prevent frequent conversation, though not to destroy mutual esteem. . . . While I write this, methinks I recall youth, and revive some buried ideas. But eternity lies before me, and appears in a much nearer view. May I be found ready for the important summons! . . .[63]

Samuel Say, on the other hand, stayed within the bosom of dissent. He and Watts remained intimate to the end,[64] and it was through the latter's influence that Say finally succeeded to Calamy's church at Westminster. Say died in 1743. His works were published posthumously in 1745. He is best known for his two essays: "On the Harmony, Variety, and Power of Numbers, whether in Prose or Verse" and "On the Numbers of *Paradise Lost*." The first is an interesting study in prosody; the second, an early and remarkable analysis of the prosodic excellences of Milton.[65]

Josiah Hort was another friend of the school years. Watts designated him the "first genius in the academy" and dedicated one of his early poems to him.[66] Hort, like Hughes, conformed. Although his dissenting background was used against him, he rose to the Archbishopric of Tuam in 1742. He and Watts remained friendly and corresponded until the latter's death.

Academies were looked upon with extreme disfavor by the High Church-Tory group. Perhaps the most famous of the Anglican attacks on the institutions was Samuel Wesley's *A Letter from a Country Divine to his Friend in London concerning the Education of the Dissenters in their Private Academies, in several Parts of the Nation* (1703). Wesley, who had gone to Morton's school in Newington Green, afterwards conformed. His pamphlet was obviously a bid for preferment. The crux of Wesley's criticism may be found in the following lines:

We almost universally entertained a mortal aversion to the Episcopal Order, and very few but equally abhorr'd monarchy itself, on either of which, notwithstanding our Tutor's contrary Advice and Commands, nothing too satyrical or Reflecting could, we thought, be spoken. The King-killing doctrines were generally received and defended; . . . . The Established clergy, Liturgy,[67] Discipline, treated with the height of disgrace and ridicule; . . . . Nothing more common than to hear the Publick Prayers and Established Liturgy ridiculed, and the Words and Expressions therein, as well as the Persons officiating, made the constant subject of all the bad Jests could be invented. . . .[68]

Wesley admitted that the tutors did not encourage a spirit of sedition, but the charge of teaching "defection" in these schools was the constant refrain of the High Church-Tory group. This Tory agitation culminated in the Schism Act of 1714[69] which, but for the death of Queen Anne, would have led to the extermination of the academies. The act was repealed in 1718.

Space does not permit a résumé of the debate[70] between the dissenters and the Tories concerning the academies. Moreover, it is really little to the purpose, for time has amply vindicated the staunch loyalty of the dissenters, even to Queen Anne. But it is safe to generalize here and admit that Wesley's statements were essentially true. There was freedom of discussion in the academies, and one would expect segregated groups of this sort to talk satirically about their oppressors. They probably held Calves-Head Feasts "under the rose" on January 30 at which they attacked the memory of the Royal Martyr. But that they were "hotbeds of faction and revolution" is a charge not supported by fact. The dissenters of the academies were largely sons of Whig, middle-class business men. They wanted revolution least of any group in England. They wanted and helped to give the country a strong, stable shopkeepers' government.

Watts left the academy in 1694. In his autobiographical memoranda, he wrote:

> I went into ye country   June 1694
> Dwelt at my father's house two years and a quarter.

He was now twenty years old. Like Milton he returned to his father's house for a sort of breathing spell before attempting a career. It was during this period, tradition reports, that Watts wrote his first hymn. Upon complaining to his father about the harshness and uncouthness of the Psalm-version used at their meeting-house, Watts was advised by the latter to compose something better. Taking the advice seriously, he wrote "Behold the Glories of the Lamb."[71]

The reasons for Watts's retirement are not known. He probably considered himself too young to preach. Twenty years is certainly not the ideal age to begin the work of ministering to a flock of sober-minded dissenters. In later life Watts warned the academies against sending out immature pastors. He felt that the practice hurt dissent. Whatever his reasons were, his hesitancy interested the members of the Congregational Fund Board,[72] as the following entry shows:

9th March 1695/6. Mr. Larner, Chairman
Seventeen present. [Inter alia] Mr. Gouge is desired to speak with Mr. Shallet to endeavor that Mr. Watts do now go out to the ministry.[73]

The two persons commissioned to see Watts are worthy of notice. They were two of the best known dissenters of the day. Thomas Gouge (1665?-1700),[74] Merchants' Lecturer at Pinners' Hall, was a very popular London Preacher (Watts classed him, Stennett, and Howe as the three greatest preachers of his youth). It was Gouge who, by his own experiments with the poor in London, inspired Thomas Firmin, the father of the work-school system, to undertake his great experiment in philanthropy.[75] The other was Arthur Shallet, an extremely rich London merchant and a powerful figure in the political life of the city. It was Shallet who founded in 1687 the first dissenting charity-school in England.[76] One wonders whether these men knew Watts's father or whether Watts's record at the academy had called attention to him. In either case they were sponsors of the kind with which all of his subsequent life was to be led —the rich, upper class element of London dissent.

CHAPTER II

Saints' World

"WHEN LIFE is given or continued to the saints, it is for their advantage."[1] Slightly altered in meaning, this theme of a sermon by Watts could easily be applied to the attitude of the group into which Watts moved in 1696. On October 15 of that year, he left his father's house in Southampton to come to London as tutor for the son of Sir John Hartopp, who lived in Newington, the residential section of London's richest dissenters. The Hartopps were one of the first families of London dissent. They were typical "saints"—rich, pious, Whiggishly minded nonconformists of the kind who made their money in trade and who became the aldermen, members of Parliament, and Lord-Mayors of London. These persons possessed neither the democratic Bibliolatry of Bunyan's group nor the highly emotional religion of the later Methodists. A "stately, learned, wealthy society, they were the aristocracy of Puritanism. These were the men who would have ruled if Cromwell had accepted the Crown in 1656 and founded a Puritan dynasty."[2]

These men, however, did not possess the religious ardor of their forbears. Up to the Revolution of 1688, dissent had to fight for existence. When the pressure was removed by the Toleration Act (1689), "zeal cooled as the polemic tension slackened."[3] Membership in the cause tended to decline, and the children of wealthier dissenters began to drift to the Establishment. "I believe it would be difficult to find," Mrs. Bar-

bauld has said, "an instance of families who for three generations have kept their carriage and continued dissenters."[4]

The Revolution gave the nonconformists toleration, not complete freedom. That was enough, however, for they were no
longer as zealous and uncompromising as their parents had
been. They had freedom enough to do business and to become
rich. Through the loophole of occasional conformity, they
could become aldermen and Lord-Mayors of London, and as
Professor Fairchild observes, "London was worth a mass."[5]

During the reign of Anne a brief glimmer of the old fighting
spirit of dissent was invoked by High Church persecution, but
it was no longer accompanied by deep religious feeling. It was
merely a fitful awakening; and with the coming of George I
in 1714, nonconformity returned to the unctuous, decorous, and
profitable contentment of the reign of William III. It was to
this world that Watts at the age of twenty-two came as tutor
to young John Hartopp.

Sir John Hartopp (1637?-1722) was the only son of Sir John
Hartopp, Bart., of Freeby, Leicestershire, and Mary, daughter
of Sir John Coke of Derbyshire. He succeeded in 1658 as third
baronet. Marrying Elizabeth, daughter of Sir Charles Fleetwood, he inherited the latter's home in fashionable Stoke Newington. His life as a dissenting politician ran true to form. He
represented his county, Leicestershire, in the Parliament of
1678-9, 1679, and 1680-1; he zealously supported the Bill of
Exclusion in his last year. During the reign of James II, he was
fined over £7,000 for nonconformity. In later life he became
an alderman of the city of London.[6]

Sir John was an excellent representative of the old order of
Puritanism carrying over into the eighteenth century. His religious life was centered in the meeting in Mark Lane which
Watts was to serve, but he had been a member when the great
and venerable Owen was pastor. Like so many of his generation, he took down in shorthand the sermons which he heard,

and read them at the Lord's-Day evening service in his home.[7] His house was always open to ministers with whom he liked to discuss moot points of theology. He was so zealous for the word of God that he began the study of Hebrew when past fifty in order to read his Bible in the original. At his death he left £10,000 for the instruction of youth as dissenting ministers.[8]

Sir John must have been an interesting study for the young Watts. When he died in 1722, his funeral sermon was preached by Watts, who said, among other things, that he considered it among the "blessings of heaven" that he had received "five years of pleasure and improvement" in the Hartopp family. "I found much instruction myself, where I was called to be an instructor." [9]

Not much is known concerning Watts's activities as tutor to young John Hartopp. He evidently took his work seriously, for the *Logic* (1724) and sections of the *Improvement of the Mind* (1741) were written during his teaching experience with the Hartopps. He also found time to continue his university studies and to prepare for an active ministry. Watts was evidently fond of his pupil. Two poems in *Horae Lyricae* are dedicated to John Hartopp as is also the *Logic,* written for his instruction.[10]

It is quite likely that Watts preached at the Lord's-Day evening services held in the Hartopp city and country homes.[11] But according to his memoranda he did not deliver his first public sermon until his twenty-fourth birthday, July 17, 1698. In August of the same year he went home and "preached there several times" to his friends; and by "Feb.1698/9," he had become assistant to Dr. Chauncy at Mark Lane, an enviable position for a young minister. Unfortunately, Watts's "fever and weakness" began soon after the appointment, and he spent the next five months in trips to Southampton, to Bath, and to Tunbridge Wells in search of health. The "Memorable Affairs" is confusing here, but apparently he did not return permanently to Mark Lane until November, 1701.

The meeting in Mark Lane[12] was one of London's most exclusive congregations. It had been founded probably in 1662 by Joseph Caryl, the author of the famous *Commentary on the Book of Job*. Caryl, dying in 1673, had been succeeded by John Owen, the acknowledged leader of Commonwealth and Restoration Independency. Under the pastorship of the latter, Mark Lane became the most aristocratic dissenting meeting in London. Among its members were Sir Thomas Overbury, Sir John Hartopp, Lady Tompson, the Countess of Anglescy, Lady Vere Wilkinson, and the remnant of the Cromwellian clan—Lord Charles Fleetwood, Major-General Desborough (Cromwell's brother-in-law), Major-General Berry, and Mrs. Bendish,[13] Cromwell's eccentric and "enthusiastic" granddaughter. The dignity and sanctity of a lost cause hovered over this group at Mark Lane, and the meeting possessed a tone unlike that of any other in the city.

When Watts came to Mark Lane in 1701, only a few of Owen's congregation were alive. But the Abneys, the Pickards, the Shutes, William Steele, sergeant at law, Mrs. Polhill (wife of Kentish-Petition Polhill), Arthur Shallet, and other wealthy and influential dissenters continued the aristocratic tradition. And Richard Cromwell,[14] though not a member, was a friend of Watts and an associate of this group. Watts, even as a young man, must have impressed his hearers with learning and piety, for both were required of the minister who came to the pulpit once graced by Caryl and Owen and now held by Dr. Chauncy, who, though not popular, was certainly learned and able.

Dr. Isaac Chauncy, son of Charles Chauncy, president of Harvard College (1654-71), was an ejected minister who had come to London in 1687 to practice medicine.[15] Mark Lane had called him upon his arrival, but the church had not prospered under his leadership. His troubles with the group came as the result of stubbornness in a controversy and an unbending attitude towards church discipline. In the words of Wilson:

[He] was a Divine of considerable learning; but rigid in his principles, and very unpopular as a preacher. He greatly distinguished himself in the controversy that followed the publication of Dr. Crisp's work, by his zeal against Dr. Williams, and what was then called the Neonomian doctrine. This he frequently made the subject of his ministry. But what rendered him chiefly unpopular, was his frequent preaching upon the order and discipline of gospel churches, by which he, at last, preached away most of his people. This determined him, at length, wholly to quit the ministry, and no entreaties could prevail with him to the contrary. He resigned his charge, April 15, 1701, ...[16]

After giving up the charge, Chauncy became a tutor at Homerton Academy, but remained a member of the church under Watts's pastorship.

Chauncy resigned in April, 1701, but it was not until January 15 of the following year that Watts was called to the pastoral office. The *Register*[17] of the church gives a fascinating, almost humorous, depiction of the fencing between the "callers" and the "called" which occurred in the interim. This fencing seemed the correct thing in church politics of the time, for the procedure used here was observed again when Watts made Price co-pastor of Mark Lane.

On April 21, 1701, a church meeting was called at which the members decided that, since Mr. Chauncy insisted on leaving, it was necessary to seek a new pastor. An effort was made to secure the services of one of their own members, the elderly Mr. Bereman, the ejected rector of St. Thomas, Southwark; but Mr. Bereman refused on the grounds of age. The group met again on April 28 and was still unable to decide upon a suitable person. One notes that these first efforts were to get another pastor and leave Watts as assistant.

On May 5 it was resolved that Watts be considered as "a

fit person to be called to the Pastoral office among us." [18] But on June 9 Watts left for the country because of ill health, and the entry under September 7 states that Watts, "being under continued indispositions of Body and weakness in the country," has "given us but little encouragement to expect his return among us."

At the same meeting the members resolved to call Thomas Bradbury,[19] who was then in Newcastle. Bradbury had preached among them to their satisfaction, and inasmuch as he was having trouble with his people at Newcastle, they felt that he was available. Bradbury, however, put them off with indefinite promises, and efforts to secure him were discontinued.

The pendulum now swung again towards Watts. On September 21, the members appointed October 10 as a day of fasting and prayers for the "restoration of Mr. Watts's health and for the provision of a pastor for this Church." They had done this before in August, and, so the *Register* states, God had answered their prayers by "restoring and recovering Mr. Watts from his great weakness."

On November 1, Watts returned to Mark Lane, but conditions remained as they were through the whole of November and December. On January 14, 1702, however, after a day of fasting and prayer, all "with one consent" agreed to call Watts to the pastorship. Four brethren were deputed to carry the news to him, but Watts "urged them to fix on one who might more constantly preach amongst them (viz.) twice a day which his health would not permit him to do, and made many other objections which were in some measure answer'd, and then he desired time to consider of it, and to ask counsell of God and his Friends." [20]

Watts's next move was to ascertain whether all of the brethren who had a voice had been for him. The answer was, "all except two or three." Chauncy wanted Watts; Bereman had no objection save Watts's health. Watts's reply to this report was to insist again that he was too weak in body to accept. But a month later he wrote a letter to the church stating his views on Independent church discipline:

To the Church of Christ Assembling
in Mark Lane, London

Beloved in our Lord,

When you first called me to minister the word of God among you, I took the freedom to acquaint you, that in the chief doctrines of Christianity I was of the same mind with your former reverend pastor, Dr. John Owen, who being dead yet speaketh; and I have been glad to find, by three years' experience, that you retain the same principles that he preached among you. Now, since, through your great affection and undeserved respect to me, you have thought fit to call me to the great and solemn office of a pastor, I cannot but take the same freedom to hope, that you are of one mind with him in the chief points of *church discipline*. Though I call no man master upon earth, nor confine my belief to the judgment of another, yet I cannot but own, that, in the study of gospel order, I have found much light and assistance from his works, and from those of your late reverend pastor, Dr. Isaac Chauncey: but being desired by you to give some hints of my principles in writing, in order to future satisfaction, and continuance of peace and love (if the Lord shall fix me with you), I have here briefly written a few things, whereby you may discover something of my knowledge in the mind and will of Christ concerning his churches.[21]

The rest of the letter was a conventional statement of Independent church discipline.[22] Christ, Watts felt, had empowered and commanded his saints to form spiritual societies. Every society whose members covenanted to walk with one another and with God was a church. When this church chose a pastor who had been "ordained by their public call," by his "public acceptance," and by "solemn separation of him to the work by fasting and prayer," the church was then complete. It had power to administer all ordinances necessary to religious worship. The power of the pastor, however, did not come to him *from* the people but *through* the people from Jesus Christ, the only king and head of the church. The pastor must also remember that his ordination placed him at the head of a group of persons who freely but not blindly submitted to his guidance. He must be guided in all things by the will of the people.

Among the Independents, the church was a closed voluntary association of men and women who had been "truly drawn to Christ." Membership was not to a universal but a particular church, and communion was open only to members. Persons seeking admission to a particular church had to make a public confession of faith and be voted upon by the congregation. The officers of such a church were usually the pastor (or, in some cases, pastors), who had the general guidance of the church and whose primary duty was exhortation; a teacher (or as in Watts's church, assistant pastor), who was generally less gifted than the pastor and who acted as the latter's subordinate in the work of the church; elders, who constituted a sort of advisory council; and deacons, who gathered and distributed the charity of the church.[23]

Watts's letter was read twice to the congregation. They decided that it was agreeable and sent two church officers to "call" him. But Watts asked for more time to consider their call. On February 15, he told the group "that it had pleased God to answer many of his objections and make his way somewhat clearer." He promised to secure a letter of dismissal from Thomas Rowe's church which he had joined in 1693 and to which he still belonged. It is worthy of note that Watts, though assistant-pastor of Mark Lane, was not a member. On March 8 he confessed to the group "that God had removed at last mighty difficulties out of his way and inclined his heart unto them." [24] He wrote the following letter of acceptance:

Brethren,

You know what a constant aversion I have had to any proposals of a pastoral office for these three years, ever since the providence

of God called me first among you. You know also that, since you
have given me a unanimous and solemn call thereto, I have heartily
proposed several methods for your settlement without me, but your
choice and your affections seemed still to be settled and unmoved.
I have objected warmly and often, my own indispositions of body,
. . . and I have pointed often to three *reverend divines* that are
members of this church, whose gifts might render them more
proper for instruction, and whose age for government. These things
I have urged till I have provoked you to sorrow and tears, and till
I myself have been almost ashamed. But your perseverance in your
choice and love, your constant profession of edification by my ministry, the great probability you show of building up this famous
and decayed church of Christ, if I accept the call, and your pre-
vailing fears of its dissolution if I refuse, have given me ground to
believe that the voice of this church is the voice of Christ by you;
and to answer this call I have not consulted with flesh and blood:
I have laid aside the thoughts of myself to serve the interest of our
Lord. . . . I accept your call, promising in the presence of God
and his saints, my utmost diligence in all the duties of a pastor,
so far as God shall enlighten and strengthen me; and I leave this
promise in the hands of Christ our Mediator, to see it performed
by me unto you through the assistance of his grace and Spirit.[25]

March 8, the day of Watts's acceptance, was a "dread day"
for the dissenters, for King William died that morning. Nonconformists felt that with the return of a Stuart to the throne,
persecution would begin anew. Their fears were justified, but
only in part. Other forces larger than Anne's personal allegiance to the High Church intervened to prevent most of the
persecution feared by the dissenters. Nevertheless Watts must
have had serious thoughts concerning the future of dissent
when on that day he accepted the pastorship of Mark Lane, a
meeting so definitely associated with the lost cause.

A day of fasting and prayer was appointed for Watts's ordination or "separation into pastoral office" and his "approbation" as a "fit person" by other ministers. On March 18 the
Reverend Mr. Thomas Rowe, Matthew Clark, Thomas Collins,

Robert Bragg, Thomas Lloyd, and Thomas Ridgley publicly stated their approbation. Mr. Clark began the meeting with prayer; Deacon William Pickard put the question to the church: "Do you all agree to choose Mr. Isaac Watts to the office of a Pastor in this Church and promise to submit yourselves accordingly to him in the Lord?" Every brother (women had to remain silent in God's house) answered, "aye." Watts gave his acceptance; the Rev. Mr. Collins prayed; Thomas Rowe preached a proper sermon; Mr. Benoni Rowe[26] prayed; then Mr. Ridgley prayed; and Watts "as entering upon his office, finish'd the duties of the day with Prayer, Singing, and the Blessing." [27]

Sometime during 1702, the year he assumed the pastorate of Mark Lane, Watts moved from the home of Hartopp to that of Thomas Hollis "in the Minories." [28] The cause of this removal is not known, and one can only surmise that his pastoral duties required his presence in the city. Thomas Hollis, like Sir John Hartopp, was a wealthy saint. He, too, was interested in the education of the dissenting group and left at his death in 1732 a considerable sum of money to Harvard College.[29] Watts was named a trustee of the fund. Hollis also founded the first professorship of mathematics and natural philosophy at Harvard and with Watts's aid picked Isaac Greenwood as the first occupant of the chair. It was in the home of Hollis that Watts lived from 1702 until 1710.

We do not know very much concerning Watts's activities during these years. The facts to be found in his "Memorable Affairs" are few and tersely stated, but one can glean from them certain impressions. First of all, one finds that the church under the guidance of Watts was growing rapidly. In 1703, an assistant pastor, Samuel Price[30] (uncle of Richard Price), was added to the staff. In 1704, the size of the congregation made necessary its removal from Mark Lane to Pinners Hall,[31] and four years later it had to move once more, this time to the group's own building newly constructed in Bury

Street.[32] This new meeting-house seated 428, whereas Watts had received only about sixty members from Chauncy in 1702. The remarkable growth during the six-year interim may be attributed almost solely to the increasing popularity of Watts.

The second impression one receives is that Watts was fast becoming a prominent and influential London divine. In 1707 he published his first prose work, an *Essay Against Uncharitableness,* and also *Hymns and Spiritual Songs,* a work which was to make his name famous throughout the Protestant world. In the same year the Societies for the Reformation of Manners in London and in Westminster invited him to deliver their annual "Reformation Sermon" at Salters' Hall. It was a signal honor to be chosen for this occasion.

Watts's "Memorable Affairs" for the period shows that the old order was dying out. One by one his Puritan friends and sponsors were passing away. The widow of John Owen died in 1704; Thomas Rowe, Watts's tutor, in 1705; Benoni Rowe in 1706; Arthur Shallet and Lady Hartopp in 1711; and Richard Cromwell in 1712. One notes also that the Owens, the Goodwins, and the Howes of the last age have been replaced in the dissenting pulpits by good but definitely lesser men: Daniel Burgess, who amused the actors in Covent Garden; Joseph Stennett, the Baptist hymn-writer; Dr. Williams, the wealthy founder of the famous library in Gordon Square; Thomas Bradbury, the political preacher; Samuel Pomfret, the enthusiast of Gravel Lane; and Edmund Calamy.

Watts was also gaining literary fame. *Horae Lyricae* (1706) and *Hymns and Spiritual Songs* (1707) placed him among the foremost writers of divine poetry. John Dunton's "The Dissenting Doctors" (second edition, 1710), although a bit too extravagant in its praise, at least tells one that Watts was a known literary figure:

> The next Dissenter that does preach in Town
> Who has no titles got, nor Doctor's Gown   [33]
> (But merits more than any Doctor can),

Is pious, learned, rhyming, modest Watts:
"He that did tune his harp by Chloris' notes;
"Nay, was all ear, when on the banks of Thames
"He listen'd to her sweet harmonious strains;
"Listen'd!—and well might; for when she sings,
"His zeal did rise on her seraphic wings." [34]

No wonder then his Muse so well indites,
That all his Lyricks have such noble flights;
For whosoe'er does hear that Angel sing,
Is straight a Doctor, Wit, and every thing.
At least a Rhyming Doctor we will call
The famous Watts, he's so poetical.[35]

In 1710 Watts left Thomas Hollis, with whom he had lived
for eight years, and moved to the home of Mr. Bowes in
Bishopgate Street.[36] The reason for moving may possibly be
intimated in a letter to Say, dated November 1, 1709, in which
Watts complains that his servant had in some instances "in-
commoded" the Hollis family.[37] Mr. Bowes kept an academy,
and it was here that Watts first met Thomas, afterwards Archbishop Secker, who came as a student in the same year. Watts
subsequently secured admission for the brilliant lad to Mr.
Jones' Academy at Gloucester and helped him financially. Although Secker later conformed, the two remained friends
through life.

In 1712 Watts suffered a particularly severe attack of illness.
He was seized with a violent fever which left his nerves permanently affected. During the early stage of this sickness, Sir
Thomas Abney invited Watts to his home, Theobalds, near
Cheshunt in Hertfordshire, for rest and quiet. The illness
lasted four years, but Watts remained in the various Abney
homes[38] until his death in 1748.

There is an interesting anecdote told concerning this extended visit. Lady Huntingdon, calling on Watts at Stoke
Newington, was told by him: "Madam, your Ladyship is come
to see me on a very remarkable day." Upon Lady Hunting-

don's request for an explanation, Watts answered: "This very day thirty years ago I came hither, to the house of my good friend Sir Thomas Abney, intending to spend but one single week under this friendly roof: and I have extended my visit to the length of exactly thirty years." Lady Abney then interrupted to say: "Sir, what you term a long thirty years visit, I consider as the shortest visit my family ever received." [39]

Sir Thomas Abney, [40] alderman and one-time Lord-Mayor of the city of London, was a typical saint, and his life epitomized all that sainthood meant to Watts's group. The younger son of an old Derby family, Sir Thomas was born of Puritan parents in 1639. He suffered as a boy along with his family during the period of civil war. His mother died when he was very young, and he was reared by his aunt, Lady Bromley, relict of Sir Edward Bromley, Baron of the Exchequer under Elizabeth and James I. An extremely religious woman, Lady Bromley labored successfully to instill piety and virtue in her young nephew.

Sir Thomas was twice married. His first wife was Sarah, daughter of the Reverend Mr. Joseph Caryl, founder of Watts's church. Of this union there were seven children, six of whom died in infancy. The first Lady Abney died in 1698. His second wife was Mary, the oldest daughter of Sir Thomas Gunston, a very rich London dissenter. [41] With this marriage Sir Thomas Abney received a beautiful manor at Stoke Newington, not yet completed, but destined to become a show place. There were three daughters, only one of whom married; the last of the three died in 1782 at the age of seventy-eight. She left all the remaining Abney fortune to charity.

Sir Thomas was a successful saint. One found in him that same mixture of business acumen, philanthropy, and piety which seemed to characterize all of the group. He was one of the original directors and promoters of the Bank of England and was, during the later years of his life, president of St.

Thomas' Hospital (for the poor) in Southwark. Sir Thomas
was one of the Hospital's most munificent benefactors. He
loved ministers and entertained them often at his house. Like
Hartopp, he took down notable sermons in shorthand and read
them to his family on Lord's-Day evenings. He was also an
important political figure in London. In 1693 he was elected
sheriff of London and Middlesex and before his year expired
was chosen alderman of Vintry Ward and knighted by King
William. In 1700 he was chosen Lord-Mayor—some years before his turn—and in 1701 he became a member of Parliament
for London. In later life he was again an alderman.

Sir Thomas' protestantism, however, was put to the test by
the furore which was created during his mayoralty by the
occasional conformity controversy. Sir Humphrey Edwin, elected Lord-Mayor in 1697, had started a debate on the matter
of occasional conformity by leaving church dressed in his re-
galia of office and going to worship in a chapel at Pinners
Hall. After this flare-up, matters had remained dormant until
Abney came to office. As a member of the meeting of the
venerable John Howe, Abney revived the practice of occasional
conformity, thereby precipitating the famous controversy between Defoe and John Howe on the question.

Defoe had attacked Sir Humphrey Edwin in 1697. In 1701
he returned to the question with a pamphlet entitled *An Enquiry into the Occasional Conformity of Dissenters in Cases
of Preferment. With a Preface to Mr. Howe,* . . . .[42] The object of this second attack was Sir Thomas Abney, and Howe
as Abney's minister was singled out for special treatment by
Defoe. Howe's answer to Defoe need not concern us here.
There is, however, one aspect of the controversy between Abney and Defoe which does interest us. Practically all scholars
who write on either Defoe or Watts identify the latter as the
figure satirized in Defoe's incidental comment on Abney in
the *Shortest Way with the Dissenters* (1702):

But a lady now sits on the throne, who . . . would have your Sir
Tom sing psalms at Highgate-Hill, and split texts of scripture with
his *diminutive figure of a chaplain*. . . .

Was Watts the chaplain referred to in the above passage?
First of all, according to Watts's own statement, he did not
move from the home of Hartopp until 1702, and he moved
then to that of Thomas Hollis in the Minories. He was therefore obviously not in the Abney home at the time. Moreover,
from June, 1701 to November 3, 1701, that is, half of the year,
Watts was at Tunbridge Wells, Southampton, and Bath seeking health. In his state of health, he could hardly have preached
at Mark Lane, taught the Hartopp children, and acted as
chaplain to Abney at the same time. Can it be that Watts was
often seen in the company of Abney? The Hartopps and Abneys both lived in Newington, and Lady Abney's brother was
a close friend of Watts. Can it be, then, that a wrong conclusion was drawn from some such association? Could not Abney
have had another chaplain who was *diminutive?* Whatever
the answer, one is led to believe that Watts was not Abney's
chaplain in 1701-2.

After 1712 Watts did act as chaplain, but he was not called
to the house for that purpose. Though he went, one is constantly reminded by Watts, for only a week's visit, he stayed
the rest of his life. He voluntarily took up the duties of tutor to
the Abney children, but he considered this a labor of love.[43]
It was only after his stay took on a permanent aspect that he
assumed a chaplain's duties, if one can designate Watts's activities there as duties, for he was a guest and in no way an em-
ployee of the Abney household. He gradually became a member of the family just as Cowper later "grew" into the Unwin
home. Watts was famous in his own right in 1712, and there
was no condescension or patronage on either side.

For the present, it is necessary to note Watts's relations with
his church during this trying period of illness. He seems to
have sent periodical letters to the congregation advising his

members on all kinds of matters from the election of Price
to co-pastorship to the dismissal of members for misbehavior
and non-attendance. But running through all these letters one
finds pathetic descriptions of his suffering, physical and mental, and heart-rending requests that his people pray for him.[44]
This they did regularly, and on one occasion all of the dissenting churches in London set aside a day (November 20, 1716)
for public prayer in his behalf.

But into these letters there creeps now and again a hint of
irritation. Some members had evidently intimated that if
Watts was well enough to preach to the Abneys, he should be
able to return to his charge. Although he never stated the
issue directly, Watts answered the veiled accusation by constant and almost extravagant praise of the Abneys. The nearest
that he ever came to an open discussion of the situation may
be found in the following lines from the regular church letter
of November 21, 1716:

Shall I tell you the little health which I have received is chiefly
owing to the perpetual change of place and air and travelling for
which I enjoy such conveniencys in this worthy family. Had I
stay'd in London till this time I had not been able to have minis-
tered to you again. My moments of ease and strength are so few
and incertain that I cannot appoint any hour or day, and sometimes my indispositions seize me when I most earnestly desire an
hour of service as they have lately done. The last two attempts of
any thing like preaching that I have made in private in this family
[illegible] unexampled friendship. I would not give you any sus-
picion that I deprive you of my strength by employing it another
way; Tho some of my friends are of opinion that such private attempts would rather encourage and hasten me towards the publick. However these last two Lord's days I did desyre to try again
in the family and that in the Evening which is my best hour. But
God was pleased to disappoint me both days by the return of the
weak'ning fits of the headache each morning. My kind ffriends
around me saw the hand of God, submitted to the disappointment,
and made no Reflexion on what I had done lately in publick. They

rejoyced heartily that God had indulged me so far as to serve you twice together tho' I was prevented serving them at all: And they take more sensible satisfaction in any ability God bestows upon me to minister among you than to worship in this household. I am sure they deserve a large share in my Thanks and Prayers, and I think also they zealously and sincerely seek your Interests, if my Health and Publick Ministry may be so esteemed. Tho I owe my life under God to their care and kindness, yet they desire no manner of service from me that may prevent or cut short my labours among you. It is God who cuts them short and it is God who prevents them. He is Wise and Holy, and I would learn to be patient and humble.[45]

NOTE: This which is enclosed in these lines was not transcribed in the copy I sent the church.

The note on the original draft of the letter shows that Watts saw the unpleasant possibilities inherent in the issue, and he had too much sense to stir up trouble.

Watts tried to serve his congregation in yet another manner during this interval of illness. He sent them his publications as they appeared. The following letter (dated August 6, 1715) accompanied the presentation of *Divine Songs:*

While I am thus waiting his will, I would be doing some work, as I told you in my last letter; and review some of my former Labours to make them publick for your profit. As I lately made your selves a small present of a Treatise of Prayer, so I now desire your acceptance of a few Divine Songs for your young children for whom they were written. Every person that hath children under fifteen years of age capable of reading a verse will receive of my Brother Price a book for each. And may God even your God cause your family's [sic] to flourish in grace & build the church in the next generation! [46]

The next paragraph states that the kindness of the Abneys to him makes possible his paying this "respect to my ffriends

[sic] of giving such small presents to themselves or their children while I cannot preach." During this illness Watts requested that the church stop his salary. The group refused this offer and gave him additional money to pay his doctor's fees. Watts's salary during his later years was £100 a year.

Thus by 1716 Watts had become a permanent addition to the family of Sir Thomas Abney. As with Shallet, the Hartopps, the Hollises, so now above all with the Abneys, Watts lived and moved in a middle-class world of security, culture, piety, and refinement. His work, his character, and his whole outlook were conditioned by this environment. These saints were highly equipped for success in this life even though they kept their eyes on the world to come. No better example of the psychology and philosophy which motivated their kind can be found than in Jeremiah Smith's funeral sermon on Sir Thomas Abney. Smith tells us that Abney was calm and sedate, reticent, temperate, honest, and just. "He sought no gain, but with a good conscience; nor made haste to be rich; yet did God own, and bless his fair and righteous methods with considerable increase." "He was very charitable, both in his judging and speaking of others; and in ministering to the necessities of the saints." "Only open-enemies of virtue and piety would raise warmth in him, who had always a just zeal for God, and the good of mankind; against all corrupters of morality and true religion." [47]

These men prospered in spite of proscription and the occasional persecution meted out to them. And their success proved that they were beloved of God. Max Weber[48] thinks that protestantism of the type held by Watts's associates had a tendency to encourage business success. One mark of a saint was to do well the work of the Father and to be an example in the world of sinners. God's work had to go on in the world; the saints had to do it. Failure meant that the person was slack, dishonorable, unchristian. Bankruptcy was not only a disgrace, but almost a sin; witness this letter to Watts from Doddridge:

It is the unanimous Judgment of this church that the frequent acts of Bankruptcy which have happened in dissenting congregations as well as elsewhere, have brought so great a Dishonor on Religion, . . . that we are obliged in Duty to enter our publick protest and caution on this head. And we do hereby declare that if any person in stated communion with us shall become a Bankrupt or as it is commonly expressed *fail in the world,* he must expect to be cut off from our Body. . . .[49]

The world of the saints laid its definite impress on Watts. It added to that breadth acquired through his academy education. His association with the rich occasional conformers like the Abneys and the Hartopps showed him that too great a sectarian zeal was impracticable in a world of wealth, influence, and position. Watts acquired a certain innocent worldliness which lifted him above religious fanaticism. He also acquired a certain amount of business shrewdness. He handled his own publications in a profitable manner; and though never wealthy, he acquired a satisfactory competence. His will showed that he made good investments. He, too, was a successful saint.

CHAPTER III

Later Life

WHEN WATTS came to the Abneys to live, he was thirty-eight. The remaining years until his death in 1748 were passed quietly in the sanctuary of this home, unmarred by any disturbing incidents save a misunderstanding with Bradbury and some minor difficulties with his nephews. Sir Thomas Abney died in 1722, but Watts remained with the family. There are no exciting experiences to record. He never traveled further than to Bath or Tunbridge Wells; he preached at the same meeting during the whole course of his ministry; he was a bachelor; and he was a chronic invalid, staying as much as possible out of the city.

But the course of dissent during the same period was not so smooth. The age of George I found the movement at its lowest spiritual level. In 1723 Walpole gave £500 to help the widows of dissenting pastors and to augment the salaries of the poorer dissenting ministers.[1] The money came from the private purse of the king, and Walpole used it as a bribe to silence nonconformist agitation for the repeal of the Test and Corporation acts. The bribe worked.

The decline of spiritual integrity shown in the acceptance of the "regium donum" was also evident in the Salters' Hall Controversy of 1719. On this occasion a reactionary group led by Thomas Bradbury tried to force subscription to the Athanasian creed on dissent. The effort failed, but after the debates the power of dissent both politically and spiritually waned appreciably. Both ministers and members left the movement.

A survey[2] of nonconformity in London made in 1731 showed that fifty ministers had conformed since 1714. There were fewer meeting-houses than in 1695; yet the population of London had increased by one-sixth.[3] Heterodoxy became more open and popular. Arianism, Arminianism, and Socinianism, especially among the Presbyterians, were growing in an alarming degree. Of thirty-nine Presbyterian churches surveyed in 1731, eleven were Arminian, twelve were unwilling to declare themselves, and only sixteen were orthodox Calvinist. The maker of this survey felt that dissent was decaying primarily because of two things: occasional conformity and the "growth of error" which was given impetus by the "Synod of Salters!"

The most sensational notice of nonconformity's decline came in 1730 when Strickland Gough (?-1752) published *An Enquiry into the Causes of the Decay of the Dissenting Interest*. Gough likewise felt that dissent had lost its spiritual heritage. It had become bigoted, and "of all the Tories, dissenting Tories are the most inconsistent." [4] Liberty is the fundamental principle of dissent, and when that is lost, dissent must perish. Among the numerous answers to Gough was one by Isaac Watts, *An Humble Attempt towards the Revival of Practical Religion among Christians* (1731), which will be discussed later in this work.[5]

The leaders of dissent sought to rehabilitate the cause by a revival of the spirituality of old Puritanism. They established lectures in which the content and the manner of the preaching would quicken the hearts of the people. In 1723 a lectureship was started at the Old Jewry for the purpose of stating and defending the evidences of natural and revealed religion. The Merchants' Lecture was continued with new and able ministers. Thomas Bradbury began a lecture at Lime Street in 1730 for the defense of the Gospel scheme. The King's Head Society was founded in 1730 for the purpose of restoring religion to the theological type of John Owen. In 1733 Isaac Watts started a lecture at Bury Street.

These were efforts in the right direction, but they lacked the sweep, fervor, and vitality necessary to stop the decay of dissent. The real revival of religion was effected by the Methodists who began their work at the time. With the mass-appeal of its emotional approach, Methodism achieved results more far-reaching than the dissenters could conceive. Nevertheless, the spiritual foundation upon which Methodism flourished was laid in part by right-wing nonconformity.[6]

The period was also transitional for left-wing dissent. Seventeenth century Anti-Trinitarianism after Salters' Hall became the Unitarianism of Lardner, Price, Priestley, and other eighteenth century dissenters. Watts's essays on the Trinity brought him into forced contact with this group, but he was essentially of the opposite camp as later chapters will show. It is sufficient to point out here that in these crucial years Watts was London's most important dissenting minister.

The years brought to Watts greater and greater popularity as a writer,[7] an ever-widening circle of friends, and deeper veneration from persons in all walks of life. He became a national figure; and though laughed at on occasion by the wits, he was genuinely respected by Anglicans and dissenters alike. The dissenting ministers elected him to preach the "Charity School Sermon" for the year 1727, an honor conferred only upon its ablest preachers. In the same year he helped to found the London Congregational Board. In 1728 both Aberdeen and Edinburgh universities conferred upon him the degree of doctor of divinity.[8]

His general importance in Protestant London brought flattering responsibilities. He helped the Reverend Mr. Frederick Michael Ziegenhagen, chaplain to George II, to raise money to move the persecuted Salzburgers from Germany to the American colony of Georgia. Ziegenhagen, on the other hand, supplied material for the prefaces of Watts's works translated into German. Watts knew and corresponded with Zinzendorf and his Moravian Brotherhood. His works were used and translated by the Pietist Franke of Halle. He kept up a voluminous correspondence with many of the New England religious leaders. The early decades of the eighteenth century thus found this little stay-at-home London dissenter in vital contact with the Evangelical movements in three countries—England, Germany, and America.

A consideration of Watts's friends and correspondents affords another index to his popularity. It is of course impossible to mention all of the persons whom Watts knew or to whom he wrote, for his range of friendship was wide.[9] Only those who in some way influenced or were influenced by Watts and those of intrinsic importance will be treated here. For the sake of convenience, these friends are divided into three groups: Anglican, American, and dissenter. This period of Watts's life will be discussed, even at the expense of slight chronological distortion, as a résumé of his relations with these important friends and correspondents.

Many well-known and influential Anglicans were attracted to Watts by his efforts to evangelize the age. Josiah Hort, Archbishop of Tuam, and Thomas Secker, Archbishop of Canterbury, had both been dissenters originally and had known Watts in their younger days. Their friendship naturally carried over into later life. But Watts courted contact with other Anglican divines. Edmund Gibson, Bishop of London, was one whose acquaintance Watts had definitely sought. Watts read Gibson's "Charge" for the year 1727; and, finding the sentiments expressed so congenial to his own, he wrote to the author.[10] This note started an exchange of compliments and opinions that lasted in extant letters until 1745. Bishop and dissenter were at one in their belief that a reformed preaching in the Church would help rid the age of irreligion. They were also agreed in their condemnation of Whitefield.

James Hervey, George Whitefield, and John Wesley all knew Watts, and their acquaintance marks an interesting relation among three different but fundamentally similar movements. Hervey the Evangelical, Wesley and Whitefield the Methodists, and Watts the dissenter were drawn into friendship through the recognition of their common problem. One could add to these names those of two famous women, the Countess of Huntingdon and Frances, Countess of Hertford. This little group of strongly religious souls, all connected in one way or another with the Evangelical movement, honored Watts as a pioneer and as a fellow-worker. All (with the possible exception of Hervey) came at some time to visit him.

Hervey's letter to Watts, written December 10, 1747, typifies the attitude of this group:

> To tell you, worthy Doctor, that your works have long been my delight and study, the favorite pattern by which I would form my conduct and model my style, would be only to echo back in the faintest accents what sounds in the general voice of the nation.[11]

Hervey was the author of the popular *Meditations and Contemplations* (1745-6). Perdeck feels that Hervey is the "link that connects Methodism with literature." [12]

John Wesley's visit to Watts is concisely described in the *Journal*:

Wednesday 4 Oct. 1738 . . . 1:30 at Dr. Watts', conversed; 2:30 walked, singing, conversed; . . . .[13]

Charles Wesley was also present. It was an interesting occasion in the field of hymnody—the two greatest English hymn-writers joining their voices in song. The Wesleys had used Watts's hymns in their student meetings at Oxford, and both were close students of the latter's works throughout the course of their lives. Although John Wesley sharply criticized Watts on occasion, he had a profound respect for the dissenter. Writing in 1765, he designated Watts one of the "Children of God" and expressed pleasure that, though differently ordered, Watts had not been against him.[14] Wesley made constant use of Watts's hymns in the Revival.[15] One-third of the pieces in

Wesley's first hymnal, published in 1737, came from Watts. In 1757 Wesley published *The Doctrine of Original Sin*,[16] incorporating in the work forty-four pages taken from Watts's *Ruin and Recovery* (1740). In 1769 he abridged the latter's *Treatise on the Passions,* and in 1778 he produced *Serious Considerations concerning the Doctrine of Election and Reprobation extracted from a Late Author* [*Watts*].

The Countess of Hertford (1699-1754) was a generous and admirable person. Her character is nowhere more vividly portrayed than in her correspondence with Watts from 1729 to 1748. Although Lady of the Bed-Chamber to Queen Caroline, she was not the usual court noblewoman. Religiously inclined, she was given to melancholy and to a love of retirement. She was a devoted and exemplary wife and mother, but found time to dabble in poetry and to cultivate the acquaintance of literary persons. Thomson, as is well-known, spent a spring in her house. She interposed with the Queen for Savage, favored Shenstone and Duck, and was a patroness of Elizabeth Carter. Among the dissenters she formed an intimate friendship with Elizabeth Rowe and Isaac Watts. Her regard for the latter is shown in the following extract from a letter written in 1739:

. . . though I have not written to you, you have shared my time with her [a visitor], for almost all the hours I passed alone, I have employed in reading your works, which for ever represent to my imagination the idea of a ladder or flight of steps, since every volume seems to rise a step nearer the language of heaven, and there is a visible progression toward that better country through every page; . . . for I must believe that the manner in which you treat divine subjects is more likely to reform and work upon the affections of your readers than that of any other writer now living.[17]

Other letters show that the Countess had sent her son to visit Watts. In return the latter presented to the boy books which Lady Frances used in his education. On March 4,

1744-5 she wrote Watts a heart-rending letter telling him of the death of her son.[18] In her sorrow, she confessed, she had turned to Watts's sermons for consolation. And she had sought some little relief from sadness in writing poetry.

Watts included in *Reliquiae Juveniles* (1734) four of the Countess' earlier poems: "A Rural Meditation," "A Penitential Thought," "A Midnight Hymn," and "The Dying Christian's Hope." They are all in the typical religious vein of the melancholy school and are neither very good nor very bad. She was not an "enthusiastic" writer; and in spite of her friendship with Mrs. Rowe, she would not allow Watts (who edited the work) to dedicate to her Mrs. Rowe's *Devout Exercises of the Heart* (1737). In the matter of literary decorum she was typical of her age and her class.

Watts dedicated *Reliquiae Juveniles* to Lady Frances, and as an introduction to her four pieces he wrote a poem fittingly entitled "Piety in a Court":

> Is there a soul so temper'd, so refin'd,
> That pomp nor feeds her sense, nor fires the mind,
> That soars above the globe with high disdain,
> While earth's gay trifles tempt her thoughts in vain?
> . . . Angels, speak her name,
> Consign *Eusebia*[19] to celestial fame.[20]

The last of this group was the great revivalist George Whitefield (1714-1770). The co-founder of Methodism was at one time more intimate with Watts than is commonly known. The intimacy did not last very long, because Watts soon became cool to the young man. Although Watts realized that he and Whitefield were fundamentally at one in their religious attitude, he was appalled by some of the excesses of the latter. He was unable to tolerate gracefully the indecorous and enthusiastic behaviour of the Methodists.[21]

It is interesting to trace the course of this friendship. In 1739 Whitefield, then twenty-four, visited Watts, probably for the first time.[22] In the same year Watts, writing to Bishop Gibson of London on the subject of the "extraordinary influence of the Spirit," told the bishop that Whitefield had visited him and had confessed that he felt divinely inspired but could give no proof of it. Watts then added:

I said many things to warn him of the danger of delusion, and to guard him against the irregularities and imprudences which youth and zeal might lead him into, and told him plainly, that though I believed him very sincere and desirous to do good to souls, yet I was not convinced of any extraordinary call he had to some parts of his conduct; and he seemed to take this free discourse in a very candid and modest manner.[23]

The rub here is the horror of enthusiasm, and it is amusing to see bishop and dissenter both so complacent in their condemnation. Bishop Gibson in his answer to Watts's letter dryly remarked: "It had been happy for Mr. Whitefield, if he had taken the wise advice and caution you gave him." [24]

For a period of seven years, the letters of Watts to Benjamin Colman of Boston contain comments on the activities of Whitefield. On May 23, 1740, Watts wrote: "Mr. Whitefield had been several times to see me, ..." He had reminded Whitefield that the latter's principles were the same as those found in many of the dissenting churches. Watts told the young evangelist to "go on and prosper." He informed Colman that Whitefield was far more popular than the Wesleys.[25]

On March 18, 1740-1, Watts wrote that the Methodists had gone into "some odd opinions," but that he still believed that Whitefield was doing a great work. He then mentioned the rumor that Whitefield would "propose himself to the Dissenters for admittance." [26]

In May 1740 he wrote Colman that Whitefield had visited him six weeks earlier, and that they had discussed the "strange unscriptural and enthusiastical notions" of the Wesleys. Whitefield was still considering joining the dissenters,[27] but Watts was distressed because Whitefield had attacked Bishop Tillotson.[28] He tried to get the evangelist to retract his statements concerning the great divine but was unsuccessful.[29]

In February 1742, Watts saw Whitefield and gave him money for an orphanage in Georgia.[30] Whitefield visited him again on April 7 while still a member of the Church of England. Watts was secretly glad, because he felt that Whitefield could do a greater service within the Church than he could in dissent.[31]

In 1742 we begin to see signs of the rift. Whitefield, writing to Benjamin Colman of Boston, referred to the dissenters as his "cooler friends". Colman sent the remark to Watts, who answered rather sharply:

. . . I believe he speaks the truth, and perhaps this expression is a word I have used concerning ye behaviour of us Dissenters towards him more than once, because his narrow zeal for the Church of England as a party, and some imprudencys, made him less accepted here in ye beginning of his publick preaching. . . . I must confess also there are severall of us who rather despise than honor him: our sentiments about him are different.[32]

Watts added that, since Whitefield's success in America, the dissenters thought better of him, but they did not wish to "discover it too much, lest we should seem to invite him amongst us which we think will attain no good end."

News of the rift between the two great divines reached New England in the same year, and we find Watts writing to an unknown American correspondent:

You urge me very much to give you my sentiments of Mr. Whitefield, because 'tis spread abroad amongst you, that *I have* given you a friendly caution not *to encourage him.* Now Sir, *how great a falsehood this is,* will appear by the letter which I sent to you with my Book of the *Improvement of the Mind.*[33]

The letter referred to by Watts stated: "I think he [Whitefield] has been wonderfully assisted, and greatly honoured of

God, as an instrument to call home Souls by Jesus Christ the Saviour." [34]

The letter is dated April 7, 1742. The next day Watts wrote in a similar vein:

Tho' I do not fall in with him in all his conduct, yet I cannot but think him a man raised up by Providence in something of an uncommon Way to awaken a stupid and ungodly World to a Sense of the important Affairs of Religion and Eternity. You may show these letters of mine to what persons you please, and let *my opinion* of Mr. Whitefield even notwithstanding all his Imprudences, be known where you think fit.[35]

But on September 20, 1743, Watts, in spite of these reassuring letters to his American following, remonstrated with his protégé, Doddridge, for taking part in Whitefield's service:

I am sorry that, since your departure, I have had many questions asked me about your preaching or praying at the Tabernacle, and of sinking the character of a minister, and especially of a tutor among the Dissenters, so low thereby. I find many of your friends entertain this idea; but I can give no answer, not knowing how much you have been engaged there. I pray God to guard us from every temptation.[36]

The language of this letter shows Watts's true conception of the Methodist program. It is also indicative of his real attitude towards Whitefield.

On February 28, 1744, Watts curtly replied to an inquiry about Whitefield from Colman:

I am sorry Mr. Whitefield acts in such a manner as to expose himself to so many reproaches, ... He preaches about London. I seldom see him.[37]

On March 20, 1744-5 he replied to another Colman inquiry: "As for Mr. Whitefield, we hear he went to Philadelphia. Some say he is dead . . . ." [38]

These last reports[39] to Colman were a strange contrast to

the long and glowing accounts of the great evangelist found in the earlier letters. In them Watts dismissed Whitefield as briefly as possible; he was simply telling Colman that he was no longer interested in the revivalist. It is a pity that this friendship could not have flourished. Both men were trying hard to accomplish the same mission. Save the reference to "cool friends" quoted above, we have no evidence of a changed attitude on the part of Whitefield.[40] He devotes the greater portion of his *Hymns for Social Worship* (1753) to hymns by Watts; and, though the latter probably never realized it, part of the success of the "System of Praise" may be attributed to the prominence given it by Whitefield both in England and in America.

Watts's coolness towards Whitefield was characteristic of the dissenters' first reaction to the Methodist movement. Although the new Puritanism was doing magnificently what they were attempting in the third and fourth decades of the century, it was not until after 1750 that the dissenters were finally won over to any considerable degree of reconcilement. Doddridge was almost alone in his recognition of the common bonds between dissent and Methodism, and the letter which he received from Watts noted above was one of several sent him by members of the Coward Trustee Board of which he was a member.[41] The enthusiasm of the Methodists shocked the staid Independents of the 1740's. Watts tried to be tolerant but was not completely successful.

Isaac Watts was keenly interested in New England. In later life he came to know all of the leaders of the colony, and his home in London became a sort of clearing house for American problems. He acted as literary agent for Benjamin Colman, Elisha Williams, and others; sent books to the libraries of Harvard and Yale; collected money for missionary work among the Indians; found donors for Harvard; acted as trustee for two of her important funds; helped to pick her text-books and professors; counselled New England's governors; wrote catechisms, hymns, and other texts which were used in the New England churches and schools; and took part in the Great Awakening Controversy. Without a doubt Watts entered as fully into the life of New England as any Englishman of his day.[42]

Three major figures stand out in this mass of American correspondence: Benjamin Colman, Cotton Mather, and Jonathan Edwards. The first, Colman (1673-1747), was pastor of Brattle Street Church in Boston and an overseer of Harvard. From 1695 to 1699, however, he had been pastor of a fashionable meeting in Bath, and it was probably then that Watts met him. Colman and Watts were very similar in physique and temperament, and held similar beliefs concerning evangelical religion. They were close friends; and the letters which Watts wrote to Colman were, with the possible exception of those to Doddridge, franker, more gossipy, and more wasplike on occasion than any others that he wrote. Colman acted as an agent for Watts in Massachusetts. Most of the latter's contributions to the colonies were disbursed by Colman. In these letters one finds Watts a very generous and unselfish friend of New England and particularly of Harvard College.

Watts deeply revered Cotton Mather (1663-1728) and corresponded with him frequently.[43] Mather, on the other hand, was very much taken with the efforts of Watts to evangelize the age. In his diary for 1711, Mather mentioned with pleasure the receipt of Watts's hymns[44]; in 1713 he sought to use the hymns to counteract the singing of profane ballads.[45] In 1717-18 Watts sent Mather portions of the *Psalms of David Imitated* (1719) in manuscript for critical comment.[46] The following year he sent a long account of the Salters' Hall Controversy.[47] During the same period he secured Mather's consent for Neal to use the *Magnalia* in the writing of the *History of New England* (1720). When Mather became incensed over Neal's treatment of the witchcraft material in the *Magnalia,*

Watts tried to smooth out the differences between the two men.[48]

But when Watts published *The Arian Invited to the Orthodox Faith* (1724),[49] Mather lost all of his former respect. His letter on the occasion (quoted elsewhere in this work)[50] charged Watts with being too shallow and too much led away by a spurious and criminal charity toward Arians and other "Idolators" to write on the Trinity. Watts probably never saw the above-mentioned letter. In 1743 he prevailed upon his friend, David Jennings, to write an abridgment of Samuel Mather's life of his father. Watts wrote the "Recommendation" to the work. Fifteen years after Mather's death, Watts commented to Doddridge that, when he compared himself with Mather, he felt "hardly worthy to be called a servant of Christ." [51]

Jonathan Edwards (1703-58) studied seriously Watts's sermons, texts, and poems when he was at Yale;[52] but the first direct contact with the latter came as a result of the London publication by Watts and Dr. Guyse[53] of *A Faithful Narrative of the Surprizing Work of God in the Conversion of Many Hundred Souls in Northampton* (1737).[54] Colman sent the work to Watts and Guyse; but the two London ministers, feeling that the *Narrative,* because of its enthusiasm, would be severely criticized by the polite world, had been reluctant about publishing it. Since they could not refuse Colman on this score, they took the liberty of toning down certain over-enthusiastic sections of the work. In the process of editing they made one or two errors. Edwards protested strongly through Colman, but Watts answered with spirit:

. . . we can bear with satisfaction all the reproaches we sustain here, both in conversation and in newspapers, but we hope we shall receive no addition from New England of anything that should make us uneasy.[55]

5

Watts believed that the Great Awakening was a true manifestation of the spirit of God in spite of its "raised affections" and irregularities. When Charles Chauncy of Boston's First Church attacked Edwards in 1743 because of these follies and irregularities, Watts came to the defense of the latter in a series of letters to Colman and Chauncy.[56] Edwards' work in the Great Awakening became for Watts a sort of laboratory verification of all that he had preached concerning the "extraordinary visitation of the spirit";[57] and though he was embarrassed by some of its enthusiasm, he became a stout defender of Edwards and the whole movement.

Watts's position finally as leading Independent minister of London brought him into close contact with practically all of the important figures of London dissent. Among the broadest of the eighteenth century nonconformists was Daniel Neal (1678-1743), author of the *History of New England* (1720) and the *History of the Puritans* (1732-8). Neal, like Watts, was a graduate of Thomas Rowe's Academy, but he had continued his studies at Utrecht and at Leyden. He was pastor of a well-known meeting in Jewin Street, and he and Watts were closely associated throughout life. Both were trustees of the Coward Trust Fund; both were important members of the London Congregational Board. Neal, like Watts, was one of the few ministers who stayed out of the Salters' dispute.

Henry Grove (1684-1738), Watts's first cousin, is best remembered for four papers contributed to the revived *Spectator* in 1714. The third of these papers (November 29) was the ingenious essay on the love of novelty which Samuel Johnson praised as the finest he had ever read. The fourth, that on a future state, closed the *Spectator*. Grove criticized Watts for the "overdrawn theology of his hymns," but he also wrote a good dedicatory poem to *Horae Lyricae* which was inserted in all editions after 1709. At his death, Grove was working on a life of Elizabeth Rowe.

Two of London's wealthiest and most interesting dissenters

of the period were William Coward (d. 1738) and John Hopkins (d. 1732). Coward, when Watts came to know him, was living at Walthamstow, where he kept a magnificent home open always to preachers, but where he also insisted that all doors be locked at eight p.m., often to the embarrassment of inmates and visitors alike. Coward was highly orthodox and in 1733 financed the publication of the *Bury Street Collection of Sermons* as his share in the effort to stem heterodoxy among the dissenters. It was Coward also who financed Doddridge's Academy at Northampton.

Coward honored Watts highly all during his life and named him an executor of his estate. But at one time there arose some doubt in his mind concerning Watts's orthodoxy. We find Hugh Farmer writing in 1737 to Doddridge: "Mr. Coward begins to think Dr. Watts Baxterian, and is almost come to an open rupture with you" [perhaps because of the friendship of Doddridge for Watts or else because both held the same opinions].[58]

Coward left at his death £150,000 to charity, a considerable amount of which was allocated to the training of young men for the dissenting ministry. The income from the Coward Trust is now used for the maintenance of New College, St. John's Wood, London.[59]

John Hopkins was perhaps even richer than the eccentric Coward. The *Gentleman's Magazine* (Vol. II, p. 725) gave the following informing notice of his death:

April 25th, 1732, John Hopkins, Esq., died at his house in Broad-Street, worth £300,000, bequeathing £500 to be distributed by Dr. Calamy, Dr. Watts, Dr. Evans, and Dr. Wright, to poor widows of dissenting ministers; and £1,000 to poor dissenting ministers in the country, not exceeding £10 each.

Pope has a line on Hopkins in his *Moral Essays,* III, 85:

What can they give? to dying Hopkins, heirs?

with the following appended note:

A citizen whose rapacity obtained him the name of Vulture Hopkins. He lived worthless, but died worth three hundred thousand
pounds, which he would give to no person living, but left it so as
not to be inherited till after the second generation.

One notes that the Hopkinses and Cowards have taken the
place held by the Hartopps and Abneys at the turn of the century. The wealth of these dissenters is astounding, but even
more noteworthy is their constant concern for the continuance of dissent. Their charity was certainly biased, but it was
nevertheless charity.

John Shute,[60] first Viscount Barrington (1678-1734), lawyer,
Christian apologist, and political leader of dissent, was also an
intimate friend of Watts. Shute was educated at Rowe's Academy but studied afterwards at Utrecht and at the Inner Temple. His mother was the daughter of Joseph Caryl and the
sister of the first Lady Abney. His father was a wealthy London merchant.

Shute made his mark early in Augustan politics. He was sent
to Scotland to win Presbyterian support for the Union. Highly
successful in this mission, he was rewarded for his services in
1708 by an appointment as commissioner of the customs.
Swift's letter to Archbishop King of Dublin, dated November
30, 1708, describes Shute as

a very young man, but reckoned the shrewdest head in England,
and the person in whom the Presbyterians chiefly confide; and if
money be necessary toward the good work (that is, the repeal of
the sacramental test) in Ireland, it is reckoned he can command as
far as £100,000 from the body of Dissenters here.[61]

Swift also described Shute as "moderate in principles" and
as one "frequenting church and meeting indifferently." Shute
was considered the political head of English dissent, and his
efforts to keep the dissenting vote intact made him leader of
the liberal element in the Salters' Hall Controversy. His allegiance to the House of Hanover went so far as to make him a

voluntary scapegoat for the Prince of Wales (the future George II) in the Harburgh Lottery Scandal, but Shute had by this time been created Baron of Newcastle (County of Dublin) and Viscount Barrington of Ardglass in the Irish peerage. Consequently, it did not greatly matter that he was expelled from Parliament because of his "bubble speculation" activities.

Shute was a typical "worldly saint", successful and opportunistic in his religio-political life. Like so many of his group, he dabbled in theology; he corresponded with Watts, Lardner and others on theological subjects. The letters to Watts are highly evangelical. Shute looked upon Watts as a saint and seer. He promised the latter to read the *Logic* at least once a year as others do Cicero. He regarded Watts's letters to him as valuable spiritual oracles and solemnly promised to model his life on the precepts contained in them. Watts preached at his house, and the two prayed with and for each other.

After his political downfall, Shute spent the latter years of his life in revising his theological treatises, which were originally published in 1725 under the title, *Miscellanea Sacra*. They were issued finally in a posthumous edition by Shute's son in 1770. It is ironical to note that Dr. Shute Barrington, the son of dissent's political leader, was in 1770 the Bishop of Llandoff.

The name of Elizabeth Rowe (1674-1737), the author of *Letters from the Dead* (1728) and *Devout Exercises of the Heart* (1737), and that of Isaac Watts have been long associated in a sentimental fashion. The tradition persists that Watts was at one time a lover of Elizabeth Singer (Mrs. Rowe's maiden name) and an unsuccessful suitor for her hand. The first hint of this romance comes from Edward Young's Satire V ("On Love of Women"):

> *Isaac,* a brother of the canting strain,
> When he has knock'd at his own skull in vain,
> To beauteous Marcia often will repair
> With a dark text to light it at the fair.
> O how his pious Soul exults to find

> Such love for holy men in woman-kind!
> Charm'd with her learning, with what raptures he
> Hangs on her bloom, like an industrious bee;
> Hums round about her, and with all his power
> Extracts sweet wisdom from so fair a flower! [62]

The rejected-suitor part of this tradition takes on curious ramifications in the hands of two of Watts's New England friends. Belcher, the governor of Massachusetts Colony, tells us that when Watts proposed to Miss Singer she told him that "though she loved the Jewel she could not admire the casket which contained it." [63]

Dr. Colman of Boston, who knew Miss Singer in England, stated that

after long hesitation and delay, Dr. Watts ventured to declare to Miss Singer his affection for her and to ask her hand; to which he received an answer that must have mortified him extremely; that she had long expected his address, but had on the preceding day given her consent to the solicitation of Mr. Rowe. [64]

Miss Singer evidently possessed a varied charm, for it is hard to conceive of two lovers so dissimilar as Watts and Prior, the other person with whom her name has been romantically and poetically linked. Prior included Miss Singer's poem—"Love and Friendship: A Pastoral"—among his works and answered it in the role of

> . . . . the mournful swain,
> Who loving much, who not beloved again,
> Feels an ill-fated passion's last excess;
> And dies in woe; that thou mayst live in peace. [65]

Mrs. Barbauld also links the name of Miss Singer and Prior:

> Thynne, Carteret, Blackmore, Orrery approved
> And Prior praised, and noble Hertford loved,
> Seraphic Ken, and tuneful Watts were thine,
> And virtue's noblest champions filled the line. [66]

It is somewhat difficult to imagine Watts a lover, even an unsuccessful lover, but if he was repulsed by the rhapsodic Miss Singer, their friendship was evidently not impaired; for we find Watts publishing in his *Reliquiae Juveniles* (1734) a letter to her concerning the character of their mutual friend, Lady Hertford.[67]

Mrs. Rowe died in 1737, leaving the manuscript of her *Devout Exercises* (the title was supplied by Watts) to him to edit. Watts was embarrassed with the charge, and he admitted to his friend Colman of Boston:

> I cannot but say 'twas a peece of nice and dangerous work put into my hands to recommend a book to the world wherein I knew some expressions would awaken the ridicule of the age; . . . .[68]

But he loyally edited the work, supplying an interesting preface by way of half-apology to the "polite world" both for his earlier and Mrs. Rowe's posthumous enthusiasm. He had to perform the task, for there was no denying the request contained in the following letter:

> Sir:—The opinion I have of your piety and judgment is the reason of my giving you the trouble of looking over these papers, in order to publish them; which I desire you to do as soon as you can conveniently; only you have full liberty to suppress what you think proper.
>
> I think there can be no vanity in this design, for I am sensible such thoughts as these will not be for the taste of the modish part of the world; and before they appear, I shall be entirely disinterested in the censure or applause of mortals. . . .
>
> Through the blood of the Lamb I hope for an entire victory over the last enemy; and that before this comes to you, I shall have reached the celestial heights; and while you are reading these lines, I shall be adoring before the throne of God, ... Adieu.[69]

Thomas Gibbons (1720-85), the first biographer of Watts, must be added to this group of intimate friends.[70] He was a sincere admirer of Watts on whom he largely modeled his own life and works.[71] And he tried hard to protect the name of his friend from the accusations of heterodoxy and insanity which were brought against it shortly after Watts's death.[72] From the *Diary*[73] which he left and from other contemporary material, we find that Gibbons succeeded Watts as leader of London Independency. He was evidently a man of unusual charm. Samuel Johnson attests this, confessing:

I took to Dr. Gibbons. I shall be glad to see him. Tell him, if he'll call on me, and dawdle over a dish of tea in an afternoon, I shall take it kind.[74]

On May 17, 1784 Gibbons dined with Johnson, a noteworthy fact considering the latter's antipathy toward dissenters.

Thomas Bradbury (1677-1759), the stormy petrel of early eighteenth century dissent, must also be placed in this circle of friends even though he later became Watts's one important enemy. Bradbury was an interesting character; though argumentative and vindictive, he was a fearless preacher. A strict Calvinist, he was the leader of the reactionary element in dissent. Although constantly belabored in pamphlet and pulpit by his colleagues, Bradbury had a strong following in London and was nonconformity's most representative political preacher.

Anecdotes concerning the man abound. The Queen herself is supposed to have given him the name "Bold Bradbury" because of his presumptuous attacks on the house of Stuart. At her death, it is rumored that he preached from the text: "Go see now this cursed woman, and bury her, for she is a king's daughter." [75] His November 5 sermons were notorious for their violent attacks on the Stuart pretenders. On these occasions he preached on such subjects as "The Lawfulness of Resisting Tyrants," "Non-resistance without Priestcraft," and "The Sons of Tabeal." After these sermons he would go to a nearby tavern and, eating and drinking heartily, would bellow loudly "The Roast Beef of Old England." Both Watts and

Whitefield remonstrated with him on the impropriety of such behavior in a minister.

On the accession of George I, nearly one hundred dissenting ministers dressed in black Genevan cloaks presented an address to the King. Bradbury was among them. "Pray, sir, what is this, a funeral?" asked a nobleman of the latter. "Yes, my lord", Bradbury answered, "it is the funeral of the Schism Bill and the resurrection of Liberty." [76]

The mob pulled down his meeting house in the Sacheverell Riots. Defoe attacked him in a pamphlet, *A friendly Epistle by way of reproof from one of the people called Quakers to T. B. a dealer in many words* (1715), and many of his dissenting colleagues criticized him for his attacks on Watts and Barrington.[77] But nothing silenced him. He gloried in a fight whether with his own deacons over trivial money matters or with Lord Barrington over the spiritual and political policies of dissent.

In 1708 Watts and Bradbury were friends. Watts invited him to preach at the opening service of the new church on Bury Street and inscribed a poem to him, "Paradise":

> Divine attention held my soul,
>   I was all ear!
> Thro' all my pow'rs the heavn'ly accents roll.
>   I long'd and wish'd my Bradbury there; . . . .

But after the publication of Watts's *Psalms* (1719) relations became strained, although in all probability these two dissimilar men had been drifting apart before this. The Salters' Hall Dispute of 1719, Watts's Trinity essays of 1722, and the Barrington scandal of 1723-4[78] brought to an open rupture this feud between the two divines. Moreover, for some unknown reason, Bradbury disliked two other friends of Watts —Price, his co-pastor, and Neal, the author of *The History of the Puritans*. Watts was loyal to his friends and on one occa-

sion "shut up" Bradbury at a Fund Board meeting when he
arose to attack one of them. All of these differences combined
to produce a series of letters between the two which, for pet-
tiness and spitefulness on both sides, is hard to equal.

These letters are to be found in Vol. II of the *Posthumous
Works,* and though it would be obviously impossible to repro-
duce here all of the recriminations hurled between the two in
this dispute, extracts from one letter in particular will give a
running outline of the dispute from Watts's point of view.
This letter is dated February 26, 1724-5. Watts opens with the
salutation, "Dear Brother," and then rather pointedly adds:

> Though your late conduct in several instances seems to have re-
> nounced the fraternal bonds and duties of love, yet charity per-
> suades me to give you that appellation.[79]

He then reproaches Bradbury for attacks both in the press and
from the pulpit:

> Among other things I could not but be surprised that you should
> fall so foul both in preaching and in print upon my books of
> Psalms and Hymns;[80] when, while I was composing the Book of
> Psalms, I have consulted with you particularly about the various
> metres, and have received directions from you in a little note under
> your own hand, which was sent me many years ago by my brother,
> wherein you desired me to fit the fiftieth and one hundred and
> twenty-second Psalms to their proper metre: though I cannot say
> I am obliged to you for the directions you then gave me, for they
> led me into a mistake in both those Psalms with regard to the
> metre, as I can particularly inform you if desired.[81]

Watts then reminds Bradbury that one of his relatives had
been helped to an education through Watts's efforts. Watts
confesses that it is a "pain" to throw this in Bradbury's face,
but he feels that it is necessary to show the man's ingratitude.
And then Watts becomes even smaller. He says that in return
for all of his works sent to Bradbury as soon as they came off
the press, he has received only a few "Fifth of November"

speeches. The good Doctor ends his list of grievances with remarks on Bradbury's attacks on the Trinity essays:

one would have thought, that you should at least with decency and gentleness have argued against the notions which you disapproved . . . and not have cited them on purpose to make a jest of the author without the least attempt toward a refutation.[82]

After this letter there followed a long series of quibbles and denials on both sides—Bradbury insisting that he respected Watts but that Watts had "picked a quarrel" with him, and Watts insisting that Bradbury's attitude was unfair and insulting. But in answer to Watts's statement concerning Bradbury's former stand on the Psalms, the forthright Bradbury stated that he merely advised the insertion of two measures which Dr. Patrick had omitted. And he continued more insultingly:

But you are mistaken if you think I ever knew, and much less admired, your mangling, garbling, transforming, etc. so many of your songs of Sion, . . .[83]

It is useless to follow these letters further. Again and again they argue over the same ground. But it must be said that one gets from the series a new light on Watts. We find him here just as stubborn and uncharitable as Bradbury, and not as forthright. In these letters, granting even that Bradbury provoked the controversy by his ridicule, we find Watts strangely unwilling to forgive and make up. One holds no brief for Bradbury. He was by nature a most cross-grained and provoking person, but Watts was also surprisingly vindictive in his attack. Here he is definitely not the "saintly" Watts so familiar to us in all other places. And one cannot help having a sneaking admiration for the thumping downrightness of Bold Bradbury in this dispute.

It is a relief to turn from the unpleasantness of the Watts-Bradbury relations to a consideration of those with his closest friend, Philip Doddridge (1702-51). Author, teacher, poet, hymn-writer, Doddridge was a protégé of Watts in each of these activities.[84] His best known work, *The Rise and Progress of Religion in the Soul* (1745), was originally planned by Watts and executed by Doddridge because of the former's weakness. Doddridge's hymns and poetry belong to the School of Watts, and his whole struggle to preserve nonconformity after 1730 was influenced by the philosophy of dissent for which Watts preëminently stood. Moreover, they were intimate friends, and Watts felt that Doddridge was the one person on whom his mantle should fall when he departed. In a letter of recommendation to Mr. David Longueville, minister of the English Church in Amsterdam, vouching for Doddridge's orthodoxy, Watts gives a flattering estimate of his beloved friend:

I have no need to give you a large account of his knowledge in the sciences, in which I confess him to be greatly my superior; . . . He hath a most skilful and condescending way of instruction, nor is there any person of my acquaintance, with whom I am more entirely agreed in all the sentiments of the doctrine of Christ. . . . Since I am now advanced in age beyond my seventieth year, if there were any man to whom Providence would permit me to commit a second part of my life and usefulness in the church of Christ, Dr. Doddridge should be the man.[85]

Doddridge was very much like Watts in background and temperament. Both had the same family tradition of persecution for conscience's sake. Doddridge's paternal grandfather was an ejected vicar and his maternal grandfather an exiled German minister. Like Watts, Doddridge was offered by the Duchess of Bedford the choice of going to either university, and like Watts he unhesitatingly cast his lot with dissent. Both possessed extraordinary energy and were in spite of physical weakness, tireless workers. Both were highly tolerant and disliked controversy, and both, above all, were convinced that dissent needed for its renovation a greater emphasis on "experimental" preaching and living.

Watts met Doddridge while engaged in the activities of the Fund Board. When John Jennings, tutor of an academy at Hinckley, Leicestershire, died in 1723, Watts, in looking for a successor to him, happened upon a scheme for academy teaching written by Doddridge. He liked the scheme so well that he asked to meet the author. Though unknown to him, Doddridge had long revered the great Doctor. This he frankly states in his first letter to Watts:

I can truly say, that your name was in the number of those dearest to me, long before I ever saw you; yet since I have known you, I cannot but find a still more tender pleasure in the thought of your valuable and successful services for the advancement of practical Christianity.[86]

Watts became both a spiritual and literary father to Doddridge. He secured money from the Fund Board and Coward Trust for Doddridge's students. He recommended him to his position as tutor of the famous academy in Northampton; he secured students for Doddridge, sending him among others his biographer, Job Orton. Watts counseled Doddridge on matters of style and evidently reviewed the younger man's works before they went to press. The only intimation of a difference between these two friends came when Doddridge allowed Whitefield the privilege of his pulpit and in return preached in that of the evangelist.[87]

Doddridge was a rebel both in religion and in educational methods. He sponsored Whitefield, he organized a charity-school, he was among the first to devise a plan for a foreign mission project.[88] His first work, *Free Thoughts on the Most Probable Means of Reviving the Dissenting Interest* (1730), published in answer to Gough's *Enquiry,*[89] was one of the sanest and most spiritual contributions to the cause of dissent in the century. All in all, Doddridge probably did more than any other man in his age to preserve orthodox nonconformity. J. Hay Colligan thinks that:

There is no minister of eighteenth century Nonconformity who approaches nearer the modern ideal than Philip Doddridge. His theological views were broader than those of traditional orthodoxy. He gave a new setting to Evangelicalism, and he placed the Christian mysteries in a light that was both rational and reverent.[90]

The last years of Watts's life were plagued by continual illness accompanied with increasing weakness, by worry over the subject of the Trinity,[91] and by two family disturbances which we do not fully understand, but one of which temporarily unbalanced his mind. In 1738 he had to stop writing long letters even to his closest friends and turn over this function to an amanuensis. In 1739 he suffered a paralytic stroke which left him permanently feeble. For many years, he had been a victim of nervous insomnia, unable to sleep without the use of drugs. This weakness naturally became accentuated with worry and the passing of years. The care of the Abneys became more necessary as he got older.

Along with ill-health came trouble from his own family. There were two disturbances, but the details of neither are known. Doddridge, writing to his wife on August 16, 1746, tells her that:

His nephew, once so great a favorite, has done something to vex him, and his poor weak spirits cannot bear it; so that he is quite amazed, and even stupefied with it to such a degree as hardly to take notice of anything about him, insomuch that tho he knew my chief reason for coming from Bath was to see him, he hardly took any notice of me; and instead of those tears and embraces with which he has often dismissed me, parted with me, though probably for the last time, as coldly as he did with young Mr. Lavington, who happened to be there, and who is entirely a stranger to him.[92]

This nephew was young Brackstone, son of Watts's sister Sarah. He was a bookseller for whom Watts had once assiduously solicited business from Lady Hertford, Doddridge, and his American friends. We are not told by any of the contemporary letter-writers just what Brackstone did. Whatever it was, it was serious enough to arouse grave thoughts in the mind of Doddridge, for he wrote to his wife again on August 22:

Poor Dr. Watts is no more himself; what I heard from Mr. Jennings concerning his late behavior made me more sensible of it than what I saw.[93]

Gibbons violently attacked Augustus Toplady because the latter insinuated that Watts had suffered some derangement before his death.[94] But it is plain from these extracts that both Doddridge and Jennings felt that Watts was "no more himself" in 1746. Watts, of course, recovered, but the trouble which caused the shock continued for some time. We find John Barker writing to Doddridge on February 3, 1747:

The behaviour of Dr. Richard Watts and the wretch Brackstone towards Dr. Watts is a most marvelous, infamous, enormous wickedness. Lady Abney, with inimitable steadiness and prudence, keeps her friend in peaceful ignorance, and his enemies at a becoming distance; so that, in the midst of this cruel persecution of that righteous man, he lives comfortably; and when a friend asks him how he does, answers, "Waiting God's leave to die." [95]

On February 11 of the same year, Watts wrote to Benjamin Colman of Boston:

As for my nephew, James Brackstone, I would have you for the future neither send nor write any thing to him relating to me, he has dealt so wickedly and shamefully with me that our church has cast him out a great while ago and I have done with him entirely. . . .[96]

The whole problem of this Brackstone-Watts difficulty is challenging, but there is so far not enough information to solve it. The contemporary letter-writers who mentioned it studiously avoided particulars.

One of the letters quoted above mentions also the "behaviour of Dr. Richard Watts." This was the brother of Watts who became a rather well-to-do London physician. In 1725-6 we find him "roughing" and insulting Bradbury[97] because of the latter's attacks on Watts, but in 1745 we find his son, "Jemmy," also swearing and cursing against his uncle and being threatened with excommunication. The second generation of the family seems strangely addicted to "cursing and swearing" against the saintly Isaac. One cannot even hazard a guess as to the cause. There is extant one letter which discusses the matter, but it does not throw any light on "Jemmy's" original misdemeanor. It was written by Watts to his brother Enoch:

My last by the pen of Joseph Parker gave you notice of our last conference with Dr. R. W. and his son in which Lady Abney told him that there were yet further accusations against him. Jemmy conscious of his guilt got his father to come with him to Newington on Monday morning and there acknowledged to me what dreadful curses he had uttered agt. me ye Tuesday sennight before in Jo Parkers hearing. This by my Ladys persuasion was all reserved to have been publisht to our Church till his wife was out of her childbed; but ye Dr. was impatient to know what it was and to ask my forgiveness, and yt his son might not be so publickly exposed; Jemmy showed as far as words and tears could go, great signs of repentance. So I told him that as far as I could then see, I would not expose him to the Church who would certainly have cast him out of ye church, but since he had so far complyed with the rule of ye gospel Matt. 18:15 I would be silent at present; at his Earnest request and many promises of better carriage both toward God and toward me and the church and with many entreaties of his father I lett it go for the present upon his better behavior for time to come; so far as he had injured me.[98]

Fortunately for Watts there was a Lady Abney to keep his "enemies at a becoming distance." Far too little is known about this dissenting lady, but the few facts that we do have convince us that she was fully capable of protecting her friend during his life. After Sir Thomas' death in 1722, she carried on much of his public charity. We learn from the pages of Gibbons' *Diary* and from the "list of subscribers" to several of the evangelical works published at the time that she too was a figure of importance in London dissent. Until her death in 1750, she was active personally and financially in promoting through publications and charity-schools the cause of non-conformity.

Though a daughter of dissent, she knew well enough the fashionable world of Bath and Tunbridge Wells and saw to it that her daughters were properly presented both at court and in the world. Watts tells us that these daughters were not immured in the "Walls of a Mother's House" but had the "polite diversions" of youth agreeable to rank and not forbidden by reason.[99] Lady Abney's attitude in this matter was typical of that of rich dissent of the period. These persons were somewhat less gay than the fashionable world, but they were by no means like the past generation of Puritans. They were rich and, within decorous limits, worldly.

The household of the Abneys included also Mr. Joseph Parker, Lady Abney's steward and Watts's secretary for the last twenty-one years of his life. Parker was a remarkably efficient and remarkably pious worker. There is extant a collection of his letters (together with some valuable Wattsiana) from which one can see how highly Parker venerated Lady Abney and Watts.[100] Parker in return was held in high esteem not only by Watts and the Abneys but also by Doddridge and other friends of his employers. He was present with Watts at the end.

And there were the Abney daughters, three in all: Sarah who died in 1732, Mary who married Mr. Jocelyn Pickard and died without issue in 1738, and Elizabeth who died in 1782, aged seventy-eight.[101] The funeral sermon of Sarah Abney, preached by Watts in 1732, gives a brief glimpse of the life of these dissenting maidens. Sarah kept a diary of her improvement in piety in which she placed a "conscientious Recollection of the Sermons she heard in publick from her tender years." They all aided their father during his Lord's-Day evening services in reading the Scriptures or the sermon. Even on sightseeing trips these ladies had the pious letters of Watts to follow them. A letter to them at Oxford, dated August 4, 1730, is a typical and to us amusing example of Watts's endeavors to offset the glamor of the world and to keep his spiritual wards ever on the path to heaven:

. . . Has Oxford and the theatre of the Muses there anything to entertain you with, but what is infinitely exceeded by the Buildings, the Sciences, and the Songs of the Upper World, where there are colleges of Saints ever increasing and Abraham and David and Paul are the Tutors and Jesus himself the Sovereign President or Vice-chancellor?

With the Abneys, Watts's last days, save for his illness and family troubles, were as pleasant as they could possibly be. There came to Watts's door the religious leaders of the Protestant world. With these friends, with his correspondence (maintained practically to the end), with his hobbies of painting and collecting portraits and autographs of famous persons, Watts's life moved quietly to a close which came November 25, 1748. At his death, he was the oldest Independent minister in London and one of the most highly revered Protestant ministers in the English-speaking world.

The death of Watts has been the occasion of much evangelical rhapsody on the part of biographers. Gibbons glows with religious emotion when he describes the death-scene and becomes rhetorically happy over it. This attitude fascinates one, this love of the funereal, this morbid concern with every detail of the last moments of a saint. Death to the eighteenth century dissenter was not only the "last enemy" but the first friend. It was a glorious adventure, an experience to be envied by others and not feared by the saint. The Puritan fear of death had softened by this time to a sentimental semi-Calvinistic concept. The "inner witness" plus outward well-doing were more or less accepted as definite assurances of sainthood. One frankly asked the dying person all sorts of "improving" questions, questions which to our taste seem a trifle too pointed. This attitude is excellently shown in the exchange of notes between Doddridge and Joseph Parker, Watts's secretary, just before and after Watts's death.

On November 20, 1748, Doddridge wrote to Parker from Kettering:

I write from abroad in a great hurry but could not persuade myself to delay it as I heard by last post that my ever honoured and beloved friend, Dr. Watts, stood just on the verge of Eternity. perhaps he is already ascended to that distinguished seat of glory which has so long awaited him. but if he yet lives tell him my heart feels a flame of friendship for him which I am fully persuaded will burn for ever. Beseech him to bless me with his dying breath. . . . Scarce can I forbear from saying Oh that mine [spirit] were as near its flight but I shall soon follow him.[102]

On November 22, Parker answered this letter, giving the details of Watts's illness for the preceding three weeks and informing Doddridge of the success of the mission given him:

I fulfilled your request last night at five o'clock; he took notice of it, but in such broken language that I cannot inform you in what manner.[103]

Parker also tells Doddridge that Watts will last only a few hours, but on November 24 he has to write again to say that Watts is not yet dead. He adds more minutiae of the last two days and then reports his conversation with the Doctor:

I told him this morning that he had taught us how to live, and was now teaching us how to die. He replied, "Yes." I told him I hoped he experienced the comfort of those words: "I will never leave thee nor forsake thee." He answered in these words, "I do so."[104]

Parker reports many more of the last religious sentiments of Watts which he took down in shorthand. He promised Doddridge to transcribe them for later use. Doddridge answered on November 25:

Me thinks my heart is attracted towards his dying bed by a kind of irresistable [sic] magnetism.[105]

Watts's plans for his own funeral were very simple. He asked to be buried in Bunhill Fields, the dissenting burial ground, and requested in his will that there be no pomp and show. Tolerant to the end, he asked that his attendants consist of six ministers—two Independent, two Presbyterian, and two Baptist. He composed his own unostentatious epitaph:

Isaac Watts, D.D., Pastor of a Church of Christ in London, successor to the Rev. Mr. Joseph Caryl, Dr. John Owen, Mr. David Clarkson, and Dr. Isaac Chauncy, after fifty years of feeble labours in the Gospel, interrupted by four years of tiresome sickness, was at last dismissed to his rest. In uno Jesu Omnia. 2 Cor. v. 8. Absent from the body, and present with the Lord. Col. iii. 4. When Christ who is my life shall appear, then shall I also appear with him in glory.[106]

The contemporary press, both dissenter and non-dissenter, was kind in its eulogies of Watts. *The General Advertiser* (November 26, 1748) is typical in its comment on Watts but also includes praise of Mrs. Abney:

Yesterday died, Sunk under bodily Infirmities and the weight of Years, the Ingenious and truly Venerable Isaac Watts, D.D.; a man of Exalted Piety and of the most amiable and Exemplary Virtue. In intellectual Endow'ts he was surpassed by few; in moral ones by none; So that it is hard to say whether his capacity for doing Good or his delight in it was greater. His Sentiments as a Divine were so moderate and pacifick as to forbid his being a Favorite with the warm men of any Party: his excellencies so various and eminent as to gain him the Esteem of the best men of all Parties. He was made happy for many years and even to the end of his life

by the generous and honorable Entertainment afforded him in
Lady Abney's Family at Stoke Newington: where Affluence of
Wealth is chiefly distinguished by Acts of the most wise and dis-
interested Beneficence.[107]

On December 11, 1748, the funeral sermon[108] was preached
by David Jennings; Price, the co-pastor, was too moved to
do it. The funeral oration was preached by Samuel Chandler.
Caleb Ashworth[109] and John Milner[110] also preached sermons
on the death of Watts. The dissenter practice consisted of a
sermon and an oration at the grave. The funeral sermon was
given oftentimes as late as two or three weeks after the death
of the person. Such discourses occasionally included a sketch
of the deceased person's life, but they more commonly presented a eulogistic appreciation of the person's character. David
Jennings' sermon included a brief memoir which was affixed
to the authorized edition of Watts's works. The death of
Watts, of course, occasioned many other unofficial sermons of
the type of the two mentioned above.[111]

Jennings and Chandler each received a sum of £2.2.0 for
sermon and oration respectively. According to the Deacons'
Record Book of the Church, the funeral cost all told £17.6.0.[112]
The itemized account shows that this money was wholly for
mourning and for the public discourses. Evidently Watts's
estate paid for the other funeral expenses.

Watts's will[113] shows first of all that though not a rich man
he died well beyond the reach of poverty. He left bequests
amounting to approximately £2900, exclusive of his books,
his household effects, and his copyrights on works.[114] This
sum includes only actual money and stocks. Watts's will is,
moreover, eloquent testimony to his tolerance. He left money
not only to poor dissenting preachers but also to the poor of
the Established Church of Southampton.

The death of this good man called forth a host of elegaic
poems, which paid to him sincere if not always highly poetical
respect. The Reverend Mr. Moses Browne, vicar of Olney and

friend of Cowper and Newton, the Reverend Mr. Benjamin
Snowden, minister of the English Church at Rotterdam, and
Thomas Gibbons all composed rather long poems to the memory of Watts.[115] There were also a Latin epitaph by Daniel
Turner, M.A. of Abingdon, Berks,[116] a *Poem to the Memory
of Isaac Watts, D.D.* by one John Missing, and several anonymous poems. In one of the latter the author makes the typical
request that:

> Next, my Urania shew his sacred Life,
> (Oh could I imitate the Life I sing!)
> Like Angels fair, himself like them divine.
> The heavenly likeness shone with Radiance Bright
> O'er the dull Vail of Clay, and Shewed the Saint.
> The godlike features all with lovely Grace
> In Triumph sat, Majestic on his Soul;
> Virtue enthroned in Grace, Meekness and Love,
> Patience and Hope, Humility and Peace,
> Dwelt in his Heart and form'd a Seraph there! [117]

The concise but all-inclusive eulogy of the *Gentleman's
Magazine* is an appropriate conclusion to this chapter:

Isaac Watts, a truly ingenious and accomplished person as well in
polite literature as in Divinity and the Sciences of which his writings as well poetical as prosaic abundantly testify, and no less exemplary for candor, piety, and solid virtue. He was a Dissenting
Minister but honored by all parties.[118]

CHAPTER IV

Educator:
Religious and Secular

FROM YOUTH to old age, Watts was deeply interested in the art of teaching. He began his career in London as a tutor in the Hartopp family. When he became assistant to Dr. Chauncy at Mark Lane, he organized the younger members of the church into a class for religious instruction. He taught the Abney children. And from each of these experiences he produced a creditable text. Though a busy pastor, holding one of London's most important dissenting pulpits, he still found time to assist students in their preparation for the academy, to write textbooks, and to compose catechisms. His interests ranged from the infant level to that of the university. He wrote catechisms for three-year-olds and a logic which was used by students at Oxford and Cambridge. Watts has a place of some significance as a secular educator in the eighteenth century; as a religious educator, he is without an equal.

Watts published during his lifetime the following educational works: *Guide to Prayer* (1715), *Divine Songs* (1715), *The Art of Reading and Writing English* (1721), *Logic* (1724), *The Knowledge of the Heavens and the Earth* . . . (1726), *Prayers Composed for . . . Children* (1728), *An Essay towards the Encouragement of Charity Schools* (1728), *Catechisms* . . . (1730), *A Brief Scheme of Ontology* (appended to *Philosophical Essays*, 1733), *Questions proper for*

Students in Divinity (1740), and the *Improvement of the Mind*—Part I (1741). Part II of the *Improvement* was published posthumously in 1751 and *A Discourse on the Education of Children and Youth*[1] appeared in the authorized edition of collected works (1753).

Here we have a list of thirteen publications dealing with education, religious and secular, produced between 1715 and Watts's death in 1748; but a catalog of titles by no means tells the whole story. A work like *Catechisms,* for instance, contains six catechetical items each of which was published separately and incorporated into some other work of a like nature. To trace the publications of the various editions and segments of these works would be a considerable bibliographical task, for the popularity of Watts continued far past the middle of the nineteenth century in both England and America. For the sake of convenience these various works have been grouped under the following four heads: Children's Poetry, Textbooks, Religious Educational Texts, and Theory of Education.

Watts's first and most famous essay in the field of children's literature, the *Divine Songs* (1715), was written during his first years with the Abneys and was dedicated to the Abney children.[2] He wrote the book at the request of a friend who wanted some children's hymns to accompany catechisms. In 1715 Watts was working on his imitations of the Psalms, and the friend's request could have reminded him that a renovation of children's devotional poetry was just as much needed as a renovation of adult Psalmody.

Divine Songs has become a landmark in the field of children's literature, and its immense popularity has tended to obscure the fact that Watts was not really pioneering in this sphere. After 1662 there was a definite Puritan tradition of "good godly books"; and *Divine Songs,* though the best and most famous of them, followed in general the pattern set by earlier and cruder works. These books were all written upon the plain, dogmatic belief that there is a heaven and a hell, and the authors purposed to frighten the child out of the latter place.

Among the most popular of the "good godly books" was that by James Janeway (1636?-74): *A Token for Children: being an Exact Account of the Conversion, Holy and Exemplary Lives, and Joyful Deaths of several Young Children, To which is now added, Prayers and Graces, fitted for the use of Little Children* (date uncertain). Janeway's work consisted largely of a series of morbid case-histories of highly religious children and youths. A typical admonition from the original Preface to the work will give some idea of the contents:

Get by thyself, . . . and fall upon thy knees, and weep and mourn, and tell Christ thou art afraid that he doth not love thee . . . .[3]

Janeway was extremely popular between 1670 and 1720. He was being read by children as late as 1874.[4]

William Penn (*The Spiritual Bee*, 1662), Thomas White (*A Little Book for Children*, 1702), Nathaniel Crouch (*The Young Man's Calling*, 1685) and (*Youth's Divine Pastime*, n.d.), William Jole (*The Father's Blessing Penn'd for the Instruction of his Children*), William Ronksley (*The Child's Week's Work*, 1712), Henry Jessey (*A Looking-glass for Children*, 2nd ed., 1673) and Benjamin Keach (*War with the Devil*, 1673) are but a few of the late seventeenth century authors and works for children and youth. These books contained riddles, primers, rhymed alphabets, catechisms, graces, prayers, poems, and hymns, all designed to entertain the young reader and at the same time keep him on the road to heaven.[5] And they were immensely popular. Benjamin Keach, for instance, was practically a professional children's author; and another Baptist, Abraham Cheare, the fuller-preacher of Plymouth, whose poems appeared in Jessey's *A Looking-glass for Children*, wrote some rather good child's verse. The following lines by him are characteristic and often quoted:

> Tis pity, such a pretty maid
> As I should go to hell.[6]

But the most popular of all of these Puritan children's books before *Divine Songs* was John Bunyan's *A Book for Boys and Girls; or, Country Rhymes for Children* (1686). This work remained in ordinary use as *Divine Emblems* until the middle of the nineteenth century.[7] *A Book for Boys and Girls,* written in the tradition of Baptist children's poetry, was "at once an alphabet, a reader, and a guide to doctrine."[8] It contains seventy-four poems, most of them resembling in form and in subject-matter the popular emblem of the early seventeenth century. A typical example of Bunyan's poetic style is found in "Upon the Frog":

> The frog by nature is both damp and cold
> Her mouth is large, her belly much will hold;
> She sits somewhat ascending, loves to be
> Croaking in gardens, though unpleasantly.

> Comparison

> The hypocrite is like unto the frog,
> As like as is the puppy to the dog.
> He is of nature cold, his mouth is wide
> To prate, and at true goodness to deride . . . .

One notes the formal division into description and comparison characteristic of the emblems. Professor Tindall thinks that Bunyan was influenced not only by Keach, Cheare, and other Baptist writers, but also by his "reading of George Wither or one of the many other emblematists."[9]

Watts also knew the works of Wither and other emblematists,[10] but his immediate model in writing *Divine Songs* seems to have been Bunyan's work. One cannot dismiss as accidental the similarity in titles and subject-matter of the following pairs of poems (the first in each instance by Bunyan, the second by Watts): "Upon the Thief" and "The Thief"; "Upon Apparel" and "Against Pride in Clothes"; "Upon the Ten Commandments" and "The Ten Commandments"; "The Disobedient Child" and "Obedience to Parents"; "Of the Going Down of the Sun" and "A Summer Evening"; and "Upon the Pismire" and "The Ant or Emmet." Compare the lines of Bunyan's "Pismire":

> Must we unto the pismire go to school,
>   To learn of her in summer to provide
> For winter next ensuing? Man's a fool,
>   Or silly ants would not be made his guide.
> But sluggard is it not a shame for thee
>   To be outdone by pismires? . . .

with the following lines from Watts's "The Ant or Emmet":

> These Emmets, how little they are in our eyes!
> We tread them to dust, and a troop of them dies,
>   Without our regard or concern:
> Yet as wise as we are, if we went to their school,
> There's many a sluggard, and many a fool,
>   Some lessons of wisdom might learn.

All of the poems listed above show a similarity in ideas which is too marked to be accidental. It is highly probable that Watts, as he was constantly doing in his other works,[11] took these poems from Bunyan and "improved" them. *A Book for Boys and Girls* was the most popular children's work in the age; it would therefore be his most obvious model.

To the eighteenth century reader schooled in the neo-classic tradition the tortured rhymes and far-fetched comparisons of Bunyan probably seemed hopelessly amateurish beside the smooth verses of Watts, but many modern readers would be likely to prefer the rugged lines of the mechanick preacher. Watts and Bunyan represented two distinct social strata of dissent: one a sectarian mechanick preacher with considerable class antipathy and hatred of wealth, the other a typical rich man's minister. One cannot easily picture John Bunyan dawdling over a cup of tea with Lady Abney at Stoke Newington.

Some of the boorishness, i.e., measured by Stoke Newington standards, which Bunyan possessed is reflected in his work for children. In sophistication as well as in verse-technique, Watts's work marks a definite advance over the "country rhymes" of John Bunyan.

In *Divine Songs* Watts is tolerant, gentle and persuasive. In the Preface one finds no trace of the "fear" motivation which characterized the preface of most of the earlier godly books. Addressing "all that are interested in the Education of Children", Watts warns them that theirs is an "awful and important charge." He expresses the hope that his poems for children will teach truth and duty in an entertaining and delightful manner. He feels that, since they are written in language intelligible to the child, they will be easily remembered and will tend to displace the loose and dangerous sonnets of the age." They will also serve to give a "divine turn" and raise a "young meditation" in the thought of childhood. Watts tells the reader that the work is for *all* children; there is nothing in it that "savours of a party." In conclusion he confesses that he wrote the "Sonnets on Moral Subjects" with an "air of pleasantry" in an effort to "provoke some fitter pen" to write a complete book in the same vein with or without the "solemnities of religion" and "flowing with chearfulness."

The work contains twenty-eight divine songs, four rhymed commandments and rules, one "Hosanna" in three metres, one "Glory to God" in three metres, seven moral songs, and "A Cradle Hymn"—a total of forty-six pieces. The subject-matter of the poems is for the most part either frankly religious, as in "An Evening Song":

> And now another day is gone,
>   I'll sing my Maker's praise;

or practically moral as in "Against Quarrelling and Fighting":

> Let dogs delight to bark and bite
>   For God hath made them so, ...

> But children, you should never let
>   Such angry passions rise;
> Your little hands were never made
>   To tear each other's eyes.

But generously sprinkled among these two main types are songs taken from the Proverbs of Solomon, from the common occurrences of nature, and from everyday life in city and country. These songs teach patriotism:

> Tis to thy sov'reign grace I owe
> That I was born on British ground,
> Where streams of heav'nly mercy flow,
> And words of sweet salvation sound;

humaneness in the treatment of animals and of the poor and maimed:

> Should I e'er be rich or great,
>   Others shall partake my goodness,
> I'll supply the poor with meat,
>   Never shewing scorn nor rudeness.
>
> Where I see the blind or lame,
> Deaf or dumb, I'll kindly treat them; . . .

and love of nature:

> Lord, how thy wonders are display'd,
>   Where'er I turn mine eye, ...
>
> There's not a plant or flower below,
>   But makes thy glories known, ...

In general they are wholesome, pleasant, and charming little poems written with good understanding of a child's interest.

The best poem in *Divine Songs* is the dramatic lullaby, "A Cradle Hymn." [12] For some reason Watts apologizes for inserting the poem in the work: "Some copies of the following *Hymn* having got abroad already into several hands, the author has been persuaded to permit it to appear in public, . . ." [13]

Was Watts afraid that his poem on the "Virgin and Babe" was too similar to Catholic treatments of the subject? It does remind one of medieval Catholic verses on the same theme.

The poem opens on a tender note:

> Hush! my dear, lie still and slumber;
>   Holy angels guard thy bed!
> Heav'nly blessings without number
>   Gently falling on thy head.

But it rises to a dramatic climax. The mother becomes so angry with the "cursed sinners" who neglected and affronted the infant Jesus that her harsh and raised voice awakens the child:

> Soft, my child; I did not chide thee,
>   Though my song might sound too hard.

It ends on a note of evangelical hope:

> May'st thou live to know and fear him,
>   Trust and love him all thy days!

Eight of these poems, however, show in varying degrees the "fear" or "threat" tradition of the good godly books. These pieces [14] assure hell-fire for those children who do not read their Bibles, who forget to pray, and who disobey their parents. A good example of this type is "The Danger of Delay":

> 'Tis dang'rous to provoke a God;
> His power and vengeance none can tell;
> One stroke of his almighty rod
> Shall send young sinners quick to hell.

The age of Watts was used to such admonitions in children's books. The attitude was by no means confined to dissenters; witness Daniel Waterland's remarks on religious education:

Let them be informed how dreadful his Vengeance is towards those that offend him: How he drowned a whole World at once for sinning against him; how he rain'd down Fire and Brimstone out of Heaven upon Sinful Sodom; . . . how he ordered a Man to be stoned to Death for breaking the holy Sabbath, . . . Let but the Children have a list of these and the like Examples of Divine Vengeance lodged in their Memories, . . . as a kind of antidote against sin.[15]

The children of the eighteenth and early nineteenth centuries were probably harmed no more by brimstone poetry and sermons than modern children are by the horrors of gangster movies. But whatever the effect such poetry had, one must bear in mind that Watts was far gentler than any of his predecessors or contemporaries. The charm of classics like "An Evening Song," "A Morning Song," "The Summer Evening," "The Sluggard," and "The Busy Bee" goes far to compensate for the harshness of the "threat" poems listed above.

Judged by the number of its editions, *Divine Songs* has been the world's most popular children's classic. Wilbur Macey Stone has counted over six hundred American and English editions of the work, and he estimates that approximately seven million copies have been sold.[16] The influence of such a work has been far too great to treat in detail here, but I shall touch briefly on some of the significant indications of its popularity.

Among the first to imitate the work was Philip Doddridge, who published in 1743, *The Principles of the Christian Religion, Expressed in Plain and Easy Verse*. Mrs. Barbauld's *Hymns in Prose for Children* (1775) was inspired by *Divine Songs,* and though she questions his method in her Preface, she praises the pioneer work of Watts:

Among the number of books composed for the use of children, though there are many, and some on a very rational plan, . . . it would be difficult to find one calculated to assist them in the devotional part of it, except indeed Dr. Watts's Hymns for Children.[17]

And in 1789 Mrs. Trimmer's *A Comment on Dr. Watts's Divine Songs for Children with Questions* transformed the work into a text for Sunday School use. Her Preface informs us that of all the religious books ever written for children *Divine Songs* is the most delightful.

In 1802 there appeared *Moral Songs for the Instruction and Amusement of Children. Intended as a Companion to Dr. Watts's Divine Songs* by John Oakman and others. The work was a direct imitation of *Divine Songs* as the following example shows:

> How craftily the spider weaves,
>   And draws her slender threads!
> Yet sudden chance her hope deceives
>   And spoils the net she spreads.[18]

In the following year, the Taylor sisters—Jane and Ann—published their *Hymns for Infant Minds*. The preface of their famous work respectfully admits that:

The *Divine Songs* of Dr. Watts, so beautiful, and so universally admired, almost discourage, by their excellence, a similar attempt; and lead the way, where it appears temerity to follow. But as the narrow limits to which he confined himself, excluded a number of useful subjects, the following Hymns, though with much diffidence, are presented to the public.[19]

And so it goes through the first half of the nineteenth century, both in England and America. Practically every child's religious work of the century drew upon Watts. The same may almost be said of every primer. Sunday school texts explained the meaning of every word in *Divine Songs*. Primermakers searched for key-verses to use in their alphabet lessons. The Unitarians re-wrote the songs freeing them of their strong flavor of Calvinism.[20] The hymnody of the Evangelical Sunday School movement was influenced by the work.[21] The *Divine Songs* became all things to all publishers of children's works. Even standard works like Janeway's *Token* regularly included *Divine Songs,* either wholly or in part, between their covers.[22]

In his bibliographical studies of this little work, Mr. Stone came upon many curious facts which reveal just how intimately *Divine Songs* entered into the life of English-speaking childhood of an earlier day. One copy in his possession shows that three generations of one family had been taught from it. The copy which once belonged to Watts's niece, Betty Brackstone, contains the following quaintly spelled inscription:

> Betty Brackstone, Her Book, God give Grace therein to Look, but wen the bel be gins to tole, Lord Jesus Christ reseive her Sole. A Men.[23]

And an *English Primer,* printed in London in 1825, offers a very pleasing poetical compliment:

> What sweet-er book to me be-longs
> Than Dr. Watts's book of Songs?
> O! I would learn them all the day,
> I'm sure I love them more than play.
>
> When I'm grown up,—yes, quite in age,
> Still I shall love his plea-sing page;
> Still I shall love the songs I sung,
> That taught me good when I was young.[24]

Darton observes that Watts gave children enjoyment for over a century and then became suddenly obsolete and even ridiculous. The reason for this loss of prestige, he believes, was not any inherent fault in Watts's work, but was rather the use to which the book was put by parents and teachers. Watts was made a task, not a pleasure. Few poets can survive being recited constantly in public, and at least four of Watts's poems had that distinction for several generations. Watts's reputation was therefore seriously harmed by over-praise "as a theologian for the nursery." [25] Lewis Carroll took full advantage of the fact when he parodied so delightfully Watts's "Busy Bee":

> How doth the little crocodile
> Improve his shining tale, ...

and "Sluggard":

'Tis the voice of the Lobster: I heard him declare
"You have baked me too brown, I must sugar my hair."

In verse-technique and in understanding of the child's world, *Divine Songs* was unprecedented and unrivalled until the Taylor sisters and Newbery began to write and publish. Written by a dissenter, these verses "were yet the denial and, in a social sense, the end of the Puritan aggressive, persecuting, frightened love of children. . . . They must ever be a landmark, early but clear, in the intimate family history of the English child, ..."[26]

In poetic quality *Divine Songs* is Watts's most even and sustained performance, and yet he wrote handicapped, as it were, by the literary traditions of his age. First of all, he had to violate Neo-classic canons and write "condescendingly." He never quite finished apologizing for this breach; he knew the critics would laugh at his diction, but he had the courage to use it. Second, he had to write a book for all Christian children, not just for dissenters. This put an added handicap on diction and phraseology. And the greatest handicap of all was the purpose of the work, to make religious and moral truth beautiful, but maintain a *via media* between the triviality of the secular and the sombre seriousness of the religious. The popularity of the *Divine Songs* is ample proof that Watts surmounted all these obstacles and produced a book which ranks as a minor English classic.

Watts entered the text-book field in 1721 when he published *The Art of Reading and Writing English*.[27] The work, dedicated to the Abney girls for whom it was written, was produced because he could find no spelling-book to satisfy his designs. He further tells us that he had no intention of publishing it, but he was urged to print it for use in a charity-school sponsored by the Abneys at Cheshunt, Hertfordshire. These two circumstances are important: first, that he was teaching girls; and, second, that he printed it originally for a charity-school. Both circumstances tended to make the work simple and practical.

Watts could find no spelling-book to answer perfectly his design, which was to lead English readers into an easy acquaintance with their mother-tongue, without constraining them to acquire the knowledge of other languages. He placed this idea in a catchy motto on his title page:

> Let all the foreign tongues alone,
> Till you can spell and read your own.

Watts's stand in this matter was educationally unorthodox; Latin as the basis for all language instruction was firmly entrenched in the eighteenth century curriculum. As a matter of fact, many educators of the last generation felt that a Latin background was indispensable if English were to be profitably and correctly studied.

Feeling that a textbook should be practical, Watts presented his material in a simple, easy, and inviting fashion. He wasted no time in discussing controversial issues. He wished both children and adults who had been denied educational advantages to learn from his *Art of Reading and Writing English* at least how to read their Bibles. As for quibbling over spelling and the irregularities of the English language, Watts considered such an occupation a waste of time:

too curious and exquisite a nicety in these minute affairs, is not worth the tedious attendance of a reasonable mind, nor the labors of a short life.[28]

Watts's text is based on Thomas Dyche's[29] *A Guide to the English Tongue*.[30] The tables, comparisons, and lists all come in essence from Dyche, but Watts simplified and clarified them to suit his purposes. The main difference between the two works is that Watts is briefer and simpler. Dyche's method leans definitely towards the classic or Ciceronian type of pedagogy; he even presupposes a knowledge of Greek and Hebrew words as well as of Latin.

This tendency to borrow and improve is also evident in two unpublished manuscripts of Watts.[31] The first of these is "Mr. [undecipherable]'s Shorthand corrected and improved by J. Watts." The second is a "Geometry" to which Watts affixed the following note:

This book was written meerly for my own use when I taught Mr. A. Shallet[32] the Principles of Geometry by Father Pardies Elements, in order to facilitate & shorten my Labor & his Learning.[33]

Using Pardies as a base because he was "more short, more natural, more easy," Watts simplifies the work to the point where "anyone might learn the practical pt. of Geometry without studying all the theory." The problems and illustrations added both to the "Shorthand" and to the "Geometry" are so practical that they strike one as surprisingly modern. His prefaces as usual were both an apology and a justification of his unorthodox methods.

Watts's *Logic: or, the Right Use of Reason in the Enquiry after Truth* was published in 1724. Like most of his texts it was an improvement of another's original work. In this case Watts, according to Samuel Johnson, followed Le Clerc with added material from Locke and Aristotle.[34] The book was written to aid young Hartopp in his mastery of logic; but Watts's friend, John Eames, saw it and persuaded him to publish it.

The aim of the work as set forth by the author was a laudable one, the giving of a "Variety of Rules to guard against ERROR in the affairs of Religion and Human Life as well as in the Sciences." To Watts, logic enabled fallen man to repair in some measure the ruins of his original defection. True logic was a living practical science and not a mere quibbling over hard and technical words. Watts felt that most writers on the subject had reduced it to an unintelligible jargon fit only for the "mere use of the schools." He determined to give it back to the world of everyday living. Perhaps the best commentary on Watts's success in this attempt to simplify the language of logic is that literally hundreds of examples and definitions in Johnson's *Dictionary* are taken from Watts's *Logic*.[35] Students at both Oxford and Cambridge[36] used the text of this dissenter; it was a very popular work in the academies of both old and New England.[37] The *Logic* was a competent textbook, clearly written and adequate for its purpose.

The same may be said of the *Knowledge of the Heavens and the Earth made Easy; or, the First Principles of Astronomy and Geography* (1726). It too was written because Watts could find no "plain and easy" text on the subject. For its age and for its avowed purpose of introducing the study of astronomy to beginning students, it was an excellent text. The outstanding feature of the work is its clarity.[38]

Knowing the value of a good recommendation, Watts, before publishing, sent the work for revision to John Eames, F.R.S., associate of Isaac Newton, and the best known scientist and science teacher among the dissenters. Eames prefaced the text with the following note of commendation:

I think myself obliged in justice to the ingenious author as well as the public, to assure them that the alterations I have ventured to make in the revisal of this work, are but few and small. The same perspicuity of thought and ease of expression which distinguish his other works running thru the whole of this, I do not question but the world will meet with equal pleasure and satisfaction in the perusal.[39]

There was appended to the *Philosophical Essays* (1733) a *Brief Scheme of Ontology* which, printed separately, came to be used as a textbook. The Preface to the work tells the usual story: finding no simple scheme of ontology, Watts decided

to write one that would be free from "those barren and per-
plexing subtilities which have over-run this branch of learning." [40] He succeeded in his design, for the work is a handbook of lucid definitions. The *Ontology,* the *Logic* and the
Improvement of the Mind are related works, for in each of
them, Watts sought to simplify and popularize the study of
the various forms of philosophy.

*The Improvement of the Mind: or, A Supplement to the
Art of Logic, Part I* was published in 1741; Part II was published posthumously in 1751. It is the most popular work that
Watts produced in the secular field. The book is not a text
in the modern sense. It is really a student's guide to study,
containing a "Variety of Remarks and Rules for the attainment and Communication of Useful Knowledge, in Religion,
in the Sciences, and in Common Life." It was one of the best
known textbooks of the late eighteenth and early nineteenth
centuries.

Dr. Johnson's well-known praise of the work throws light
on the origin of Watts's inspiration:

Few books have been perused by me with greater pleasure than his
Improvement of the Mind, of which the radical principles may
indeed be found in Locke's *Conduct of the Understanding,* but
they are so expanded and ramified by Watts, as to confer upon
him the merit of a work in the highest degree useful and pleasing.
Whoever has the care of instructing others, may be charged with
deficience in his duty if this work is not recommended.[41]

The recommendation of an American teacher writing in
1831 makes an extravagant claim for the *Improvement:*

Probably no other work, upon the same subject has been so highly
and justly approved, ... Of all human compositions, then, this
is probably the most useful for the young, . . .[42]

This book was an attempt to bring logic definitely into
the work-a-day world of a student's activities. It makes reason

practical by transforming it into a working instrument. In *Logic,* Watts made reason understandable; in the *Improvement* he made it usable. He tells the reader how to outline books, how to read, how to debate, how to conduct a scholastic disputation, how to teach, how to write, and how to preach. His rules and admonitions, based as they were on experience, are simple and practical. Never attempting any heights of theory, he is nevertheless always comfortably reasonable and competent in all of his advice. The *Improvement* was a "human" text; many sections of it could still be used to advantage by modern students.

Turning now to the catechetical works of Watts, we find that they too came into existence as a protest against the practice of his age. Feeling that the *Assembly Shorter Catechism*[43] was still too advanced for younger children, he published in 1730 his book of *Catechisms.* This work contained "A Discourse of Catechisms;" the "First Set" (for children four or five years of age); the "Second Set" (for those eight or nine); The "Assembly's Catechism *with Notes*" (for those ten or twelve); "A Preservative from the Sins and Follies of Childhood and Youth," added to which was a "large Catalogue of Remarkable Scripture Names, collected for the use of Children."

Watts was by no means the first to feel that the *Shorter Catechism* was too difficult for younger children. John Owen, Thomas Gouge, Matthew Henry, Cotton Mather and many others in both old and New England had attempted simpler versions of this catechism; but it remained for Watts to introduce the graduated scale of age-levels, and to write so pleasingly and popularly that he revitalized the whole field.[44]

Watts felt that religious knowledge should be learned, like any other knowledge, in logical steps suitable to the capacity of the pupil. The length and phraseology of the catechism for the child of four could not be expected to be the same as that for a child of ten. *The Shorter Catechism* with its hundred and seven questions couched in stern theological phraseology was obviously too difficult for a child to understand. He could memorize it only, and to Watts, memory without understanding was undesirable. Children must be taught that they are "sinful creatures" who have offended the great God that made them, but they must be taught in a way so "natural and entertaining" that their "native curiosity" would be invited to aid in the learning process.

Watts's works in this field have been published in languages ranging from Armenian to Zulu. They became the common property of all Protestantism. Tract societies used them for missionary efforts, the Sunday School Movement found them handy textbooks, and eighteenth century New England found in them popular auxiliars to its own efforts in the field.[45] They took their place beside the *Divine Songs* and completed a system of worship for childhood almost as influential as the "System of Praise."

Watts's other works in the field of religious education, though not so well-known as *Divine Songs* and *Catechisms,* show nevertheless the same reforming spirit and the same faith in the efficacy of systematic instruction. Even prayer, Watts felt, could be improved by the right method of teaching, and to this end he wrote *A Guide to Prayer: or, A Free and Rational Account of the Gift, Grace and Spirit of Prayer; with plain Directions how every Christian may attain Them.*[46] He tells us in the Preface that:

The duty of prayer is so great and necessary a part of religion, that every degree of assistance toward the discharge of it will be always acceptable to pious minds. . . . The form, method, and expression, together with other attendants of it, such as voice and gesture, have been so little treated of, that few christians have any clear or distinct knowledge of them; . . . . Now while institutions of logic and rhetoric abound, that teach us to reason aright, and to speak well among men, why should the rules of speaking to God be so much untaught?[47]

In this work Watts was touching a very sensitive issue. Dissent became self-righteous when comparing its system of spontaneous prayer with the forms of the Establishment's *Book of Common Prayer*. Even Watts, as we have seen, ridiculed on one occasion the Church's forms of prayer.[48] But many dissenters were appalled by the enthusiastic nature of prayer as it was conducted in some of their pulpits and secretly longed for more correctness. Nonconformist irregularities on this score had long been amusing to the Church. Like other sensitive and intelligent Independents, Watts hated to have his group charged with singularity or enthusiasm. He therefore attempted to reform dissenting prayer.

It is interesting to note Watts's concern for decorum cropping up in the work. He divides the act of prayer into eight parts: invocation, adoration, confession, petition, pleading, profession, thanksgiving, and blessing; giving elaborate directions and rules for each phase. He tells how to compose prayers, how to time them, and how to deliver them. His admonitions on correct postures, on the use of uncommon and outworn words, on vulgarity, obscurity, and mystical expressions are all definitely Neo-classic in spirit. It is hard to reconcile this Watts with the Watts of the "inward witness" and "extraordinary visitation" sermons, but one must remember that Watts is not advocating "forms of prayer," but prayer according to the rules of reason and good taste. "The Spirit of God, when he [sic] is poured out as a spirit of prayer in the most glorious measures, doth not contradict the rules of a natural and reasonable method."[49] To Watts, God becomes a sort of divine Lord-Mayor who must be addressed in correct terms.

In 1728 Watts returned to the subject with his *Prayers Composed for the Use and Imitation of Children*. This was practically the *Guide to Prayer* put into catechetical form and scaled to the various age levels. His child's prayers for morning and evening are beautiful in their infant simplicity and soon found a place in the *New England Primer*.[50]

The last two works in this group of religious texts are not particularly important or distinctive although both ran to many editions.[51] They are a continuation of the catechetical method, a method which Watts, one must confess, overused. The first, *A Short View of the Whole Scripture History* (1732),[52] is merely an outline of the Bible plus additional material from Josephus and the *Apocrypha*. The work was planned as a "parlor-book" and was furnished with interesting drawings of the Ark, the Temple at Jerusalem, the dress of the priests, and other pictorial matter for the entertainment of the whole family. Watts advises in his preface that it be placed where the children and servants may amuse themselves with it.

The second work, *Questions Proper for Students in Divinity, Candidates of the Ministry, and Young Christians* (1740), is not in the usual question-and-answer catechetical form, but consists of questions on various religious problems which the reader addresses to his own conscience. It makes an excellent handbook for "Candidates of the Ministry," because it contains practically the same material found in the *Humble Attempt*.[53] The book is highly evangelical. It was in use at least until the third decade of the nineteenth century.[54]

Although he touches on the subject in the *Improvement of the Mind* and in prefaces to practically all of his educational works, Watts's theories of education were presented most adequately in two essays now to be considered. The first of these, *An Essay towards the Encouragement of Charity Schools* (1728), treats one of the most interesting experiments in eighteenth century pedagogy. At the same time it crosses swords in controversy with the age's best known iconoclast, Mandeville.

The era of the late Stuarts gave rise to a very important educational experiment—England's earliest attempt to provide through charity-schools education for the children of the poor.[55] The origin of this movement is connected with the activities of the religious societies during the reign of James II. The first charity-school in England was founded by the Jesuits in the Savoy in 1687. In an effort to counteract the influence of the Catholics, the Protestant religious societies began to teach the poor to read the Bible and the Church catechisms; and in 1688 Dr. Tenison, rector of St. Martin's Parish, London, established the first Anglican charity-school. The same year Arthur Shallet founded a dissenter school in Gravel Lane, Southwark, in opposition to another Jesuit venture in Pulteney.[56]

Starting as a proselyting agency in the reign of James II, the charity-school had become by the eighteenth century a very popular institution. It was one charitable enterprise which religious groups of all beliefs agreed was good. Bishops and clergy praised the idea, the *Spectator* gave it Godspeed,[57] and Queen Anne asked Archbishop Tenison "to encourage and promote so excellent a work and to countenance and assist the Persons principally concerned in it."[58] The schools grew apace. Churches and charitable individuals like the Abneys endowed schools. Pious persons made provision for these institutions in their wills. By 1735 there were 1329 charity-schools in England.[59]

The popularity of this form of charity was enhanced by the showmanship of those in charge of it. Each year the children in the schools dressed in white and marched to the annual service at St. Sepulcher's or St. Paul's, where they sang, quoted the church catechism, and in other ways impressed the audience with their Christian knowledge and good behavior. These annual services (the earliest of which was held at St. Andrew's, Holborn in 1704) were held on Whitsun Thursday at St. Sepulcher's until they became so important that they had to be removed to St. Paul's. The sermons for the occasion were usually delivered by the most important divines in the Church and were printed for distribution. The dissenters also used the methods employed by the Establishment, but their sermon was preached on January 1 at Gravel Lane in Southwark, the home of their first charity-school.

The charity-school sermons of the distinguished divines present an interesting study.[60] Almost every one contained the two following themes: the rich should store up treasures in heaven by giving to the poor; and the rich, in order to secure a peaceful citizenry for the future, should give a limited education to the children of the poor. Of course, every preacher warned against educating the children above their place in life. The sermons of the great dissenting divines differed from those of the Anglicans in two or three small details. The dissenters had to protest that they were not teaching schism and sedition in their schools. They were also more pointedly anti-papist, and they placed a larger emphasis on the soul-saving purpose of charity-schools. Otherwise they were at one with the Establishment.[61]

While the religious leaders could see only good in the flourishing of these schools, there were others who felt that schemes to elevate the poor must of necessity jeopardize the interests of the great. Education would make the poor forget their place, grow ambitious, and become a menace. The strongest expression of this attitude was given by Bernard Mandeville in *An Essay on Charity and Charity-Schools*.

Mandeville's essay opens with an attack on the age's most highly cherished argument for charity—namely, that one thereby stored up treasures in heaven that would stand one in good stead after death. After some rather pointed personal remarks on this type of next-world insurance, Mandeville attacks the whole theory of public charity. He feels that where it is too extensive it "seldom fails of promoting Sloth and Idleness" and is ruinous to the commonwealth. By emphasizing charity, as in the "Enthusiastick Passion for Charity-Schools," one merely encourages laziness and beggary.

Nobody, Mandeville argues, will do unpleasant work unless he is compelled to by necessity; but there is an "Abundance of hard and dirty Labour" to be done if the state is to prosper.

Poverty in the lower class is the only means of getting persons to do this work; hence it is absolutely necessary that this class be cultivated with care, for the surest wealth in a non-slave state consists in a "multitude of Laborious Poor." Therefore, since it would be ruinous to abolish poverty and impossible to do away with unpleasant labor, the only thing to do is to recognize these facts and try to adapt the poor to the part they have to play. Education in charity-schools gives the poor the notion that they are too good for menial labor. If they are taught trades, they will disturb the natural balance in that field which society ordinarily maintains. In either case discord would be created, for a "well-order'd society" demands in its make-up a "certain Portion of Ignorance." The teaching of the poor is therefore a menace to society at large.

F. B. Kaye observes that though Mandeville's remarks may sound unfeeling and brutal to us, they are not, if seen in their historical perspective, unusually harsh. Andrew Fletcher (*Political Works,* 1737) and J. F. Melon (*Essai Politique sur le Commerce,* 1761) both advocated that labourers be reduced to a condition of slavery for their own well-being. Mandeville's adversaries were as little desirous as he was to lessen labourers' hours and to increase their wages. Mandeville himself was conscious of his apparent harshness and apologized for it on the ground that it would be cruel to teach the poor to expect things that they could not possibly get. It would be a real kindness to inure them when young to the hardships they would have to meet when they grew up. Only in that manner could they find happiness. In short, Mandeville's views "rested on the current economic attitude," but he was criticized because he "omitted the flavoring of sentiment and moralizing with which his contemporaries sweetened their beliefs." [62]

Watts's answer[63] to Mandeville was an elaboration of a Charity-School Annual Sermon preached in November 1727 against the *Fable* and other attacks on charity-schools. The work, one of Watts's happiest efforts, is really more than a defense of these institutions; it is a plea for humaneness in education.

The preface to the work was addressed to the managers of dissenting charity-schools. Watts urged them to instruct the pupils in the Bible, the Protestant Succession, patriotism, and obedience; to teach useful trades; and to eschew all cruelty in their instructing. He asked these managers to investigate the families into which their graduates were to be placed as apprentices and to demand pay for the first year in order to encourage the children to make good. These last two suggestions were far too advanced for Watts's age. Even at the end of the century, the abuse of apprentices was widespread.[64]

Watts's essay opens with some concession to the opinions of Mandeville and his group. He admits that there are valid objections to the idea of educating the poor. These children were decreed to a position of poverty by God, and it would be unreasonable to attempt change. Moreover, he admits that poor children "should not be generally educated in such a manner, as may raise them above the services of a lower station." (He feels, however, that the children of parents who had come down in the world should be given preferential treatment in charity-schools.) But after these concessions, Watts characteristically lifts his argument to higher ground. Will you allow, he says in effect, the souls of any children to perish for want of knowledge of God's Word just because they are poor? The appeal was humanitarian and evangelical, not sociological.

Watts then considers the objections raised by Mandeville. To keep the poor ignorant in order to keep them in their place is a foolhardy procedure, he believes, because an ignorant common people "are the fittest tools for ambition and tyranny, for treason and public mischief." Knowledge is the best guarantee of morality and liberty that one can have. The knowledge of right and wrong which one obtains through reading the Bible and the catechisms will be the surest protection against insubordination, arrogance, and sedition among the poor.

In answer to the objection that it is enough to teach the poor to read the Bible without trying to include writing in the curriculum, Watts says, in effect, that he does not insist upon the latter art, but that it would be rather useful to take notes on sermons. Concerning the objection that possession of ability in the two arts would make for haughtiness, Watts asserts that if everyone could do both there would be no occasion for haughtiness: "I wish that there was not the meanest figure of mankind in Great Britain, . . . but knew how to read his Bible." [65]

Watts's scheme of charity-school education calls for a three-year program with the student beginning his work at the age of eight or nine. The plan is based upon a full day's program of school work. If, however, the boys are required to work one half of each day, the course will be proportionately longer. Watts also insists that boys who are brighter than their fellows should not be penalized for their superior ability but be allowed to remain the full time. The boys will of course be put "to trade" when they finish. Mandeville had asserted that charity-school products would flood and cheapen the apprentice market and thereby harm the prospects of taxpayers' sons. There are not enough to do that, argues Watts; moreover, the menial field is certainly over-crowded. The boys would have to become apprentices or starve.

Watts said nothing new in his essay. It was simply a compendium of existing arguments in favor of charity-schools to be found in the sermons of the advocates of the idea. [66] But his view was the most humane in the century. In preaching gentleness and kindness on the part of teacher and master, in advocating investigation of the homes in which girls and boys were to be placed, and, above all, in pleading for the right of all to gain access through reading to Christian salvation, Watts was far ahead of most of his contemporaries. His influence with respect to these schools may be seen best at the close of the century. Mrs. Trimmer was a disciple of Watts, and her two books, *The Economy of Charity* (1787) and *Reflections upon the Education of Children in Charity Schools* (1792), particularly the latter, are really résumés and elaborations of Watts's principles as presented in the *Essay*.

The educational theories of Watts are presented in *A Discourse on the Education of Children and Youth*, published for the first time in the authorized edition of his works (1753). The *Discourse* opens on the note already sounded in the essay on charity-schools: namely, that though the better people should have the more education, each child should have "so much as is necessary for its well being both in soul and body here and hereafter."

The four principles of instruction as presented by Watts are: first, teach religion; second, instill curiosity by instructing children to notice the world about them; third, train the memory; fourth, teach children to judge and to reason. Watts felt that the memory was important as a basis of learning, but he insisted that it be joined to understanding.

On the physical side, he urged occasional indulgence in sports, but insisted that children be taught to work. This he meant for all children, but he thought that those who were later to get their bread by manual labor should be especially conditioned by "toilsome and vigorous labours almost from their infancy." [67] Hard work for children, he believed, would decrease the age's terrible child mortality.

Watts was an early advocate of vocational guidance. Find out early, he advised, what a child is really capable of doing and cultivate those abilities which show most promise. Make education practical and not merely ornamental. He suggested that even children of the better class would do well to have instruction in business. Latin for the poor he considered utterly futile; their time could be much better spent in learn-

ing geography and astronomy. French, too, he considered unnecessary unless one had occasion to use it practically.

In the matter of recreation for the child, Watts was singularly broad. The teacher should alternate play and study, but
see to it that no jests on sacred things or cruelty to animals be
allowed. For the winter evenings, he suggested dice or cards,
and reminded us that the Bible says nothing against these
pastimes; therefore he left it to others to prove them "unlawful." Yet he thought that more useful and instructive games
could be played, and suggested card-games based on grammar,
astronomy, and other subjects, all of which seems quite modern. He insisted that ghost stories, amorous romances, and
books of martyrs be kept away from younger children. The
last, he believed, tended to produce superstition and melancholy in the child. In all instruction gentleness should rule and
the hope of reward should be used rather than the fear of
punishment.

Watts was not exactly a prude. He had lived too long among
the rich to cavil over gaming and dancing in the home. But
he was strongly opposed to balls, masquerades, gaming-
houses, and the theatre. The student could learn the ways of
the world safely through reading the *Spectator* instead of
attending the theatre.[68]

Like Defoe, Watts urged education in reading, writing, and
arithmetic for girls. The following rather pointed request
shows that he had no high opinion of eighteenth century
female spelling:

And I beg leave here to intreat the female youth, . . . to maintain
their skill in writing which they have already learnt, by taking
every occasion to exercise it: and I would fain persuade them to
take pains in acquainting themselves with true spelling, the want
of which is one reason why many of them are ashamed to write.[69]

Girls, he advised, should be taught more useful things and
fewer social niceties. Watts compared Antigone's daughters,

who "could manage the tea-table at ten years" but who could "scarce read a chapter in the new-testament," with those of Phronissa into whose hands the Bible and Collier[70] had been put early, and who had learned enough about house-work to manage the servants. The daughters of Antigone were married before they were sixteen to a "laced coat and a fashionable wig." He failed to tell us whether the model daughters of Phronissa ever got husbands at all.

Miss Gardiner, in her summation of Watts's stand on female education, feels that:

Such counsels, if not at all points acceptable to the convinced feminist, are the voice of sanity and kindness sounding in the midst of a troubled world.[71]

Summarizing the work of Watts as an educator, one finds that he was influential first in guiding the educational work of his own group. The academies after 1690 were largely supported by boards composed of outstanding ministers within each denomination. These organizations furnished scholarships and other financial support, picked tutors and students, recommended curricula, and in general supervised the work of the academies under their control. The two most important boards of this sort among the Independents were the Congregational Fund Board[72] and the Coward Trust.[73] Watts was an important member of both during his lifetime. Because of his position and because of his educational writings, he was commonly accepted by his colleagues as the principal adviser on matters educational. The Independents turned to him to pick and "pass on" tutors, as in the case of Doddridge; to recommend curricula for their schools;[74] to set up catechetical courses;[75] and to supply texts.[76]

One cannot point to any specific radical change in these schools brought about by Watts; he was not that kind of educator. His was a mild but definite influence upon the methods and attitudes of his day. Preaching gentleness and understanding, he was above all an advocate of the "plain and easy" in learning. Knowledge to him was a practical instrument to be used. It must therefore be secured in the easiest possible manner. Watts's textbook technique was the result of this theory, and the popularity of these works was testimony to the soundness of his position.

Watts, of course, is predominantly Lockean in his concept of education. It would be comparatively simple to show that most if not all of his theories came from Locke's educational works; but this is not so important as to note that through his popularization of Locke, Watts helped to prepare the ground for modern education.[77] The influence of John Locke played a large part in undermining the Ciceronian concept of education still in vogue in eighteenth century English schools.[78] Although Watts can by no means be placed beside his master as an educational influence, he did a good job in providing suitable texts for a more liberal curriculum. He helped to make Locke practicable. Because of this humble but necessary service, he deserves a small place among the influential secular educators of the century.

In the field of religious education, Watts's position is not so modest. His poetry for children and his renovation of catechetical procedures give him a supreme place. His influence extended far down into the last century; to nineteenth century English-speaking Protestants he was still

. . . one of those to whom we have been taught to look with a sort of filial confidence and attachment. We have been accustomed to breathe out our devotions in his words from our very childhood; as soon as we could speak we lisped praises to God in his Divine Songs; and his name has become associated with the holiest and dearest emotions of our souls. It is connected with those pure feelings of piety, which we remember to have first caught from the lips of our mothers, ...[79]

To another writer:

Watts is a 'household word.' Is there an individual born of Christian parents that has not in childhood lisped the 'Divine Songs for Children'? We scarcely think there can be one, speaking the English language, who has not.[80]

We can no longer make this claim for the educational materials and methods of Watts. He is no longer a "household word," but statements like those above attest the great influence both in secular and religious education that he exerted even as late as two generations ago.

In his catechisms and religious poetry, Watts brought over into the eighteenth century material which had been an integral part of earlier Puritan religious life. And in each case, under the benign influence of Augustan rationalism and incipient sentimentalism, he improved and humanized the subject-matter with which he worked. Giving it a new and fresh interpretation, Watts sent it down to the Trimmers, the Barbaulds, and the Taylors at the end of the century. Through him the spirit of the "good godly books" came to the Sunday School Movement.[81]

CHAPTER V

Controversies

When I am in doubt about any point, and set my thoughts at work in a search after truth, I think I ought to retire more than hitherto I have done, from the noisy and furious contests which the several factions and parties of christians are engaged in. I am unwilling to contend in a dispute, . . . upon the subject into which I am enquiring.[1]

IN CONDEMNING controversy, particularly "noisy and furious contests," Watts was following seventeenth century Puritan precedent. Many of the divines of that century professed to abhor debate even while they were engaged in it. John Goodwin in *Imputatio Fidei* (1642) had argued that intemperance in controversy prevented "rational inquiry and discussion";[2] John Howe in his Trinitarian argument with Sherlock stated that harm was done to the "common interest of religion" when the "club or faggot" argument took the place of the rational,[3] and John Bunyan, although he entered violently into innumerable pamphlet and oral debates, professed in *Grace Abounding* to deplore combats of this sort.[4]

But Watts was consistent in profession and practice. By nature charitable, he was intelligent enough to grow. His views changed as opponents convinced him, and he confessed his convictions and stated his doubts with equal honesty. With reason and scripture as his pilots, he was from his youth to his grave an open-minded and undogmatic searcher after religious truth.

Such a person could never be a great controversialist, and Watts certainly was not. But it was impossible for any eighteenth century minister to keep entirely aloof from controversy.

The mere statement of one's faith meant taking sides in several of the important doctrinal disputes of the age. Moreover, there was always the enemy, Deism, which each orthodox minister felt it his duty to attack. Although he did not seek controversy, Watts was perforce drawn into it several times.

The two major controversial questions of Watts's career were Deism and Trinitarianism, but even upon these questions he did not enter into personal and direct debate with those who held opposing views. His attacks were general, because he felt that wrangling over religious issues was detrimental to the cause of religion. And yet Watts was unwittingly the cause of several heated minor controversies, two of which may be cited in passing.

In his *Humble Attempt* (1731), Watts hinted that the dissenters led better lives than the Churchman. John White, B.D., "Sometime Fellow of St. John's College, Cambridge", wrote a pamphlet, *A Letter to a Gentleman Dissenting from the Church of England* (1743), attacking this position. Watts did not answer White, but Michaijah Towgood (1700–92) published in 1746 *The Dissenting Gentleman's Answer to the Reverend Mr. White's Three Letters*. Towgood was an able controversialist and in answering White produced one of the age's important works on the subject of disestablishment.

The doctrine of total depravity became the subject of a theological controversy in the first half of the eighteenth century; and there appeared, in 1740, two important works on the subject. The first, *The Scripture-Doctrine of Original Sin, Proposed to Free and Candid Examination,* written by John Taylor, a liberal dissenting divine of Norwich, was a brilliant attack on the doctrine. It was later instrumental in undermining the fundamental ideas of Calvinism both in England and America. The second work was Watts's *The Ruin and Recovery of Mankind*. In this treatise Watts attempted to prove the "universal degeneracy" of mankind. To a second edition of his work published in 1741 Taylor added a supplement in which he refutes the arguments presented in *Ruin and Recovery*. Watts mentions Taylor's supplement in the preface to the second edition of *Ruin and Recovery,* and adds new material to his essay to refute Taylor's arguments, but he refuses to enter into direct controversy. He does, however, refer the reader to a defense written by his friend, David Jennings. But strong support on Watts's side of the debate came from an unexpected source after his death. Jonathan Edwards wrote in 1758 *The Great Christian Doctrine of Original Sin Defended,* a spirited refutation of Taylor's argument.[5]

Watts hated Deism intensely; it stood for everything in religion that he detested. It was the antithesis of evangelicalism, and the cold spirit of logic upon which it was raised affronted the warm experimental religion which he preached so zealously. Watts helped to raise money to publish Leland's defense of Christianity;[6] he was perpetually attacking Deism in sermon, essay, and preface; yet nobody, so far as I know, answered Watts's attacks. His best attack on Deism was an unconscious one. His sermons on the "Inward Witness" and his evangelical "System of Praise" did far more than all of his set arguments to oppose the spirit of the movement.

Watts's first essay against Deism, *A Caveat against Infidelity, or the Danger of Apostasy from the Christian Faith: with an answer to various queries, Concerning the Salvation of the Heathen, and the hope of modern Deists, upon their pretences to Sincerity, etc.,* was published in 1729, although it was written in 1722. This is the year of Law's *Serious Call* and virtually the middle-point of the whole Deistic controversy.[7] Watts distinguishes in this work between those who have never been exposed to the light of God and who therefore do not believe, and persons like the Deists who have been so exposed, but who deny the Son of God. In treating the latter, Watts adopts the typical orthodox attitude of his age—the Gospel is surrounded with light and evidence enough to satisfy any one who wishes to be convinced. Those who are not convinced are simply stubborn. No man in England can be sincere in his beliefs and not be a Christian. The argument, of course, adds nothing to the settlement of the controversy. Its total want of logic is shocking, but it was one widely used by the orthodox group.[8]

In 1731 Watts returned to the issue with the *Strength and Weakness of Human Reason*. This work was in the form of a dialogue on the question of the "sufficiency of reason" between an "inquiring Deist" and a "Christian Divine." Logisto is merely an "inquiring" and not a convinced Deist; Pithander is the parish rector. Watts admi⁺ that he allows Logisto to be convinced too easily, and the whole debate resolves itself into the position that, though reason is theoretically common to all men, practically it is not, witness the immorality of savages and heathen.[9] Revelation is therefore necessary. Watts knew the literature of Deism, but his arguments and refutations again added nothing new to the controversy.

The Redeemer and the Sanctifier (1736) was another "conversation piece" among a few friends. Watts states that he "has been often grieved to see such a new sort of christianity published and propagated in the world, as leaves out the propitiatory sacrifices of our blessed saviour, and the sanctifying operations of the holy Spirit, which in his esteem are two of the chief glories of the gospel."[10] Christ was not sent to "restore the religion of nature"; his death on the cross was not merely a "noble testimony which he gave as a martyr to the doctrines which he preached." Christ was sent to do what the law of nature could never do, to save sinful man. In this essay Watts answered the Deists by an appeal to faith rather than to reason:

What is the advantage pretended or hoped for by all this force upon the scripture, . . . to make it appear more like the religion of nature, both to ourselves and our infidel acquaintance? But give me leave to ask in the name of God, why are we so much ashamed of these peculiar and supernatural glories of the Gospel, . . . ?

Must all the revealed doctrines of God and his Son be brought down to the relish and the gust of infidels, before we who call ourselves christians dare to believe them? [11]

In the next anti-Deistic work, *Self-love and Virtue Reconciled only by Religion* (1739), Watts attacks Shaftesbury:

There have also been some deists who have reproached christianity as a mere selfish and mercenary thing, because of the rewards and punishments it proposes; and have maintained that true virtue should be practiced for the sole motive of it's own rational excellency and loveliness, that is, the fitness of things. [12]

Watts's answer to the "virtuoso theory" is that God's will is necessary to reconcile the conflicting actions in which the doctrine of the "fitness of things" may cause us to indulge. God's word rather than "inward harmony" would act as a final judge of "fitness." The emphasis is here lifted from reason and placed upon revelation. It was safer there.

The Ruin and Recovery of Mankind (1740) is the last of Watts's anti-Deist treatises. As its principal argument is one which has been used in all of the other anti-Deist works, we must consider that argument. The fundamental question in these essays is that of the relation of reason to revelation. This question was the "essential issue" between early seventeenth century Puritan and Anglican;[13] for Watts's age, it was the crucial issue between orthodoxy and Deism. In spite of the highly controversial nature of the period, practically all thinkers, both orthodox and Deist, were agreed that there are only a few simple, self-evident and immutable truths easily knowable by even the humblest intellects. But there was obviously a sad discrepancy between fact and theory, for most men did not know and did not follow the dictates of reason or of divine truth. In order to explain this paradox the thinkers of the age resorted to the following compromise: man, they said, was originally created capable of following the light of reason

within him, but he had so degenerated as to require, according
to the Deists, intellectual regeneration; or, according to the
orthodox, the special help of revelation.[14]

Watts of course used the latter argument. To him as to his
Puritan forbears, man was a fallen and totally depraved creature. Not only reason but revelation as well was insufficient to
save him unless it were aided by the power of grace. The
"heavenly influence" was necessary to make revelation effica-
cious, for only the regenerate man could receive God's message from His word. The evidences of man's inability to
help himself, Watts felt, were obvious; all things showed his
"ruin." But Watts was not willing to throw reason overboard
altogether. Reason showed the necessity for revelation; it also
corroborated and compared the several evidences presented by
revelation. Although reason had become somewhat dim because of man's fall from original rectitude, it was still a God-
given light to be used to the fullest extent within its limits. In
Ruin and Recovery Watts therefore endeavors to demonstrate
rationally that reason is insufficient for man's salvation.

But *Ruin and Recovery* is an interesting treatise in other
respects. When Watts discusses the "recovery" of mankind,
he falls into some peculiar beliefs. In explaining some of the
Calvinistic dogmas through the light of reason, he succeeds in
explaining them away. Take, for example, his explication of
the doctrine of election. It is logical, he feels, that God should
guarantee through election that a certain number be saved to
partake of His grace; but on the other hand, there is no reason
"why the strictest Calvinist should be angry, that the all sufficient merit of Christ should overflow so far in its influence, as
to provide a conditional salvation for all mankind, since the
elect of God have that certain and absolute salvation which
they contend for, secured to them by the same merit; . . . ."[15]

Watts quotes Calvin's *Commentaries* on several texts of
scripture as authority for this view and adds in a footnote that
the *Institutes* written when Calvin was younger possess most

of the "rigid and narrow limitations of grace." His *Commentaries,* on the other hand, were the "labours of his riper years and maturer judgment." [16]

We see Watts in this work clinging to the forms of Calvinistic dogmas but explaining away their harshness. There *are* elect, he says, but there is also a conditional salvation for all; the infants of the unregenerate cannot expect to be saved, but they will not suffer eternally, for God will mercifully annihilate them; the virtuous heathen will be treated gently; and though man is a fallen creature, corrupt and totally depraved, his very rottenness but enhances the beauty of Christ's supreme sacrifice. Watts could not conceive of God as being cruel, unfair, or unreasonable. When first considered, some of the tenets of Calvinism seemed to make Him so. But, Watts asserts, if one examines these tenets in the light of reason, one will find that the true meaning need not necessarily be the commonly accepted meaning of such dogmas. Watts was a product of the rationalistic spirit of the eighteenth century as well as of the believing spirit of the seventeenth. In *Ruin and Recovery* he tries to reconcile the two. He sincerely felt that his compromise ought to win any Deist over to the camp of orthodoxy.

Though broad even to the point of admitting Arianism and Socinianism to the family of accepted sects, Watts could not accept Deism. It ranked with Catholicism and atheism in his esteem, and in his essay, *Orthdoxy and Charity United,* he stated emphatically that it was impossible to "comprehend" those who "oppose, renounce, or deny the doctrines of the atoning sacrifices of Christ." The Bible, he felt, gave no encouragement to such charity.[17]

The Trinitarian controversy worried Watts even more than the Deistic, because it touched a vital spot in his own beliefs. From 1696 (when he wrote to his friend, Pocyon, "sometimes I seem to have carried reason with me even to the camp of Socinus"[18]) down to his death, he was concerned with and disturbed by the various interpretations of the "person" and position of Christ in Christian theology. His "Songs of Solomon" present one aspect of this conflict; his Trinitarian tracts another—the effort to find conviction and peace.

Anti-Trinitarian doctrine had been preached surreptitiously in England since the days of Elizabeth.[19] Exponents of Socinianism, Sabellianism, and Arianism had been persecuted by the Cromwell government, and after the Restoration the Church was just as intolerant. It ranked Anti-Trinitarianism with papistry, atheism, and Mohammedanism. But the thread of Anti-Trinitarianism had carried on through men like Firmin, Biddle, Penn, Nye, and, *sub rosa,* Milton and Locke. By the end of the century the leaven of the doctrine began its work in the Establishment. In 1690 two books were published which brought the question of the Trinity into open debate: *Naked Gospel* by Arthur Bury, an Anglican divine, and *The Doctrine of the Blessed Trinity Briefly Explained* by John Wallis, Savilian Professor of Mathematics at Oxford. The publication of these works started a furious triangular debate among Dr. Sherlock, Dr. South, and John Howe. The Socinians intensified the discord with several anonymous publications. The controversy was stopped temporarily by the Blasphemy Act of 1698,[20] but the members of the Establishment returned to it in the years 1710–12.[21]

In the ranks of dissent the controversy was reflected in the disputes that broke up the "happy union" of the Independents and Presbyterians.[22] It also appeared among the Baptists, for in 1693 Matthew Caffyn of Horsham, Sussex, was accused by the Baptist General Assembly of denying the divinity of Christ. When the Assembly refused to expel him, a secession took place and a rival Baptist General Association was organized.[23] The controversy, however, was primarily a church affair; only one dissenter, John Howe, took an active part in its early stages.

In 1710 William Whiston, Professor of Mathematics at Cam-

bridge, published the *Historical Preface,* and in the following
year *Primitive Christianity.* These two works asserted that the
primitive doctrine of the church was "Eusebian, commonly
called Arian." He was expelled from his chair at Cambridge,
and the Trinitarian controversy was again opened. Samuel
Clarke came to the defense of his friend Whiston with the
publication of the *Scripture Doctrine of the Trinity* (1712).
This latter work exerted a powerful influence among the dissenters, and the first fruit of its unorthodox planting came in
Exeter in 1717, when James Peirce and Joseph Hallet were
accused of Arianism. The Exeter dispute was carried to London and became the famous Salters' Hall Controversy of
1719,[24] in which a few orthodox ministers of nonconformity
tried to impose subscription to the Athanasian Creed upon all
dissent. This dispute started Watts on his public discussions of
the Trinity.[25]

Watts published in 1722 (three years after Salters' Hall)
The Christian Doctrine of the Trinity. The preface to the
work stated that the author wished to avoid all controversy
and give the "plain, naked doctrine of scripture, in plain, easy
language" for the practical use of Christians. Salters' Hall was
still fresh in his mind, and he felt that a review of the "Scriptural" account of the Trinity without the aid or encumbrance
of "Human Schemes" would act as oil upon the troubled
waters of dissent.[26]

The Christian Doctrine is not radically unorthodox. Watts
merely suggests that the Bible need not be taken in a literal
sense when it refers to the persons of the Trinity. In one sense
of the word, the Spirit may be an attribute of the Godhead
personified in order to convey its functioning to the Christian
reader. It need not be an individual apart from the Godhead.
Concerning the Son, Watts is even more cautious. He hints an
interest in the "indwelling scheme," [27] and warns us that the
scheme is not one to be "rashly rejected." The whole essay
seems to be a straw-in-the-wind venture as well as an attempt

to reconcile by means of redefinition the views of orthodox Trinitarians and those of Arians, Socinians, and Sabellians.

Like most compromises, the essay provoked attacks from both sides, the orthodox and the unorthodox. Thomas Bradbury, defending orthodoxy, accused Watts of making "the divinity of Christ to evaporate into meer attribute" and acidly reproached him:

. . . it is a pity, after you have been more than thirty years a teacher of others, you are yet to learn the first principles of the oracles of God . . . . Was Dr. Owen's church to be taught another Jesus, that the Son and Holy Spirit are only two powers in the divine nature? [28]

Watts's reply to this charge was that though the doctrine of the Trinity was a first principle, the particular mode of explaining it was not. But he added that he could accept practically any explanation which did not insist on "three distinct conscious minds." [29] This was contrary to reason and therefore could not be the explanation.

From the unorthodox side, Watts was answered by Martin Tomkins, a dissenting minister who had been dismissed by his congregation at Stoke Newington for his "Arian or Unitarian principles." Tomkins' answer, *A Sober Appeal to a Turk or an Indian, Concerning the Plain Sense of Scripture, relating to the Trinity. Being an answer to Mr. J. Watts's late Book*,[30] came out in 1722. The work is a 155-page refutation, in the typical controversial manner of the age, of Watts's quotations from the Bible with others from the same source carrying contrary meanings. Tomkins was an able scholar and controversialist. In so far as jockeying of Bible texts can prove anything, he convinces the reader that the Bible states that there is one God only. Moreover, he was a frank and open fighter and, like so many of Watts's opponents, had a genuine respect for the aims of the latter.

In 1724 Watts published *Three Dissertations relating to the*

Christian Doctrine of the Trinity. In the preface to the work, he complained because his original treatise on the subject (*Christian Doctrine,* 1722) had brought attacks from both the Arian and the orthodox sides. He suggested that his opponents pick some "author of superior" rank with whom to debate, and he accused the unknown author of *A Sober Appeal* (it was an anonymous publication) of distorting his statements by removing them from their context.

But Watts was generous enough to admit the superiority of his opponent's treatise and to profit by the latter's arguments:

I own the light I have received from this author in the different turn he hath given to some few of those scriptures which I had brought as proofs of my doctrine, which I must acknowledge carries such a degree of probability, as to weaken the force of my arguments derived from thence, . . . for I would not willingly pervert one text of scripture . . . to support any article of my faith.[31]

The first of the three dissertations, *The Arian Invited to the Orthodox Faith,* was an attempt to show that the Arian belief concerning the "proper deity of Christ" was not actually irreconcilable with that of the orthodox. The two were not so far apart as the average Christian supposed. In his proof of this contention, Watts made certain concessions to the Arian point of view which outraged some of his ultra-orthodox friends. In a letter to Thomas Prince, Cotton Mather expressed in no uncertain terms the attitude of this group:

Sir,—Having first Expressed my Satisfaction on what you have written to Mr. Watts, I will freely, and in the most open-hearted Manner, offer you a Little of my Opinion, about the *Disquisitions,* which that Man has Lately published.

I take him, to be a very Disqualified person, for the Managing of the vast Subject he has undertaken; . . . He is not only too shallow for it; but also led away with a Spurious and Criminal Charity, for those Abominable Idolaters, the Arians, . . . whom to treat as a great part of the Dissenters are Wickedly come to do, is an High-Treason of a greater and blacker consequence than ever an Atterbury was charged withal.

His complements to that execrable crew of Traitors (I mean, the Arians) are unchristian, and scandalous, and have a Tendency to destroy the Religion of God. . . .

Could his predecessor [Isaac Chauncy] once again take his pen into his hand, he would charge him with nothing Less than grievous Haeresies.[32]

In 1725 appeared the second group of Trinity essays, *Four Dissertations relating to the Christian Doctrine of the Trinity*. In the preface Watts admits that his sentiments have changed concerning certain beliefs which he once held and which some of his earlier works expressed:

I thank God, that I have learned to retrace my former sentiments, and change them, when upon stricter search and review, they appear less agreeable to the divine standard of faith.[33]

In these essays, Watts goes deeply into Biblical scholarship to prove the preëxistence of the soul of Christ. He makes the Spirit a literal divinity but a figurative personality. In short, by 1725 Watts had practically arrived at the position concerning the Trinity which he was to hold the rest of his life, but he was unwilling to assert it too definitely. He was not quite convinced himself.

These essays, it should be noted in passing, were alienating friends. Bradbury had come out forcefully against them; Cotton Mather, as noted above, was acidly condemnatory although Watts probably never saw his comment. Even his best friend in America, Colman, felt that "My dear Watts has looked so long at the sun as to weaken his sight."[34] Watts realized the gravity of his position and was aware of the criticism. He wrote to Colman in 1726:

I am sorry if I have been so unhappy as to offend any of my brethren . . . . My sincere design has been to introduce ideas as far as possible into the room of meer words and phrases, and to vindicate the true and proper deity of Christ and the Holy Spirit against the later Arian oppositions. But I must confess that I have endeavored to do it in such a way as might make the great doctrine appear consistent with reason, ...[35]

The next step in the growth of Watts's thinking on the question was taken in 1729 when he published the sixth edition of his 1721 volume of *Sermons*. To one of the sermons on the Trinity, Watts added the following footnote:

This discourse was delivered about twenty years ago, and the reader will observe some warmer efforts of imagination than riper years would indulge on a theme as sublime and abstruse. Since I have searched more studiously into this mystery of late, I have learned more of my own ignorance; So that when I speak of these unsearchables, I abate much of my younger assurance; nor do my later thoughts venture so far into the particular modes of explaining this sacred distinction in the Godhead . . . . Reason and Scripture join to teach me, that there can be but one God, and this God is a Spirit! What distinctions may be in this one Spirit, I know not: Yet, since I am fully established in the belief of the deity of the blessed Three, though I know not the manner of explication, I dare let this discourse appear now in the world, as being agreeable so far to my present sentiments on this subject.[36]

The next stage in Watts's Anti-Trinitarian development took the form of a minor debate with Martin Tomkins over the matter of Doxologies.[37] Tomkins, after leaving Stoke Newington, had gone to Hackney and there worshipped with one Mr. Barker, who happened to be a zealous Trinitarian. Tomkins remonstrated with Barker for using Doxologies after prayer, especially "those which were often sung from Dr. Watts's Psalms and Hymns." Barker refused to heed the protests; consequently, Tomkins published his objections to the use of Doxologies in a pamphlet, *A Letter to the Rev. Mr. Barker, A Calm Inquiry whether we have any Warrant from Scripture, for Addressing Ourselves in a Way of Prayer, or Praise to the Holy Spirit, etc.*[38]

9

Barker took no notice of the work, but Watts, whose hymns were freely quoted, wrote a defense of himself in the margins of Tomkins' book, and read these remarks to the latter although he refused to give him the copy. Remembering as much of Watts's comment as he could, Tomkins replied in a letter, dated April 21, 1738. Watts again answered Tomkins, this time in shorthand and again in the margin of Tomkins' letter. Through some means the latter also received this answer. It is not necessary to go further into this *sub rosa* controversy carried on in an "amiable Christian spirit" between the two. Tomkins' stand on the matter is this: there is no mention of any one worshipping the Holy Spirit in Scripture; consequently, though it may not be unlawful to do so, it is unnecessary, and since it is offensive to some it ought to be stopped. Watts answers that the silence of the Scriptures is not necessarily prohibition, and since the majority of people want to worship the Spirit as an integral part of the Godhead, the wishes of that majority should be satisfied.

Tomkins thereupon asked Watts whether he still considered the Doxologies among the noblest parts of Christian worship, as he had stated in the *Hymns and Spiritual Songs*. The marginal answer of the latter was frank: "I freely answer—I wish some things were corrected." But he added that since he meant them at the time, it would be better to let them remain unchanged, because corrections would "bring further and false suspicions on my present opinions." Moreover, Watts admitted that he had sold the copyright to the book "for a trifle," over thirty years before.

The exchange between Watts and Tomkins showed clearly that Watts had changed his opinions on the Trinity since 1707. He was still proceeding carefully, unwilling to offend needlessly. His opinion on the nature and importance of the Spirit was similar to that of Tomkins, but Watts had a public to consider, and he could not afford the iconoclasm of the radical Anti-Trinitarian.

The next Trinitarian work, *A Faithful Enquiry after the Ancient and Original Doctrine of the Trinity Taught by Christ and His Apostles*,[39] was published supposedly in 1745 and immediately suppressed, but there is some question concerning the matter. In 1802 the work, edited by Gabriel Watts (no relative of Isaac), appeared with the following note:

In a blank leaf of the original work was written, in a fair hand, the following sentence verbatim:—The Doctor printed off only fifty copies of this work, and shewed them to some friends, who all persuaded him that it would ruin his character in his old age, for publishing such dotages, and at length he was prevailed to burn them; so that the whole impression of fifty was destroyed without publication, except this single copy of it, which by an accident escaped the flames.[40]

If this work were published by Watts in 1745, there was no reason for suppressing it. All that it said concerning the Son of God and the Holy Spirit had either appeared already in the 1725 Trinity essays or was to appear at greater length in the two 1746 treatises. Why burn this tract and preserve the others in which the same material was presented in greater detail? *A Faithful Enquiry* was evidently merely the beginning of an abridgment of Watts's writings on the Trinity. The editor of the 1810 edition of Watts's works, George Burder, felt that "some officious disciple of the Doctor's procured a copy and printed it, either without his consent, or subsequent to his death." [41] In any case it added nothing new to Watts opinions on the Trinity.

In 1746 Watts published his last two treatises on the Trinity, and in them he sought to summarize the arguments in favor of the "indwelling scheme" which he had been advancing since 1722. The first, *Useful and Important Questions concerning Jesus the Son of God Freely Proposed,* was a strong but elaborate plea for the scheme; but the essay affixed to the work showed that Watts was still not wholly satisfied with his own explication of the abstruse doctrine. He warned the reader that belief in a particular explanation of the Trinity was not necessary to salvation so long as one believed in the divineness of the Trinity itself. There were many excellent Christians who had conflicting views on the matter; and since the scriptures do not give anywhere a definite explication of this mystery, no one Christian should be too insistent upon forcing his own scheme upon the world.[42]

In *Useful and Important Questions* Watts proposed certain queries to bring out Christ's relation to the Father. In the second essay, *The Glory of Christ as God-Man,* he stated the doctrine of the "indwelling scheme" in positive terms. In order to avoid Socinianism (i.e., making Christ a mere creature) on the one hand and orthodoxy (in which Deity would be degraded in crucifixion) on the other, Watts submitted the theory that Christ possessed his human soul before coming into the world. In Watts's scheme, Christ became a two-fold person dwelling in God and of God and yet containing a human soul. He justified his position on pragmatic grounds:

I easily persuade myself that most christians will agree with me thus far, that if this doctrine be true, it gives a natural and easy solution of a great number of difficulties in the word of God, it adds beauty as well as clearness to many expressions . . . and it enables us to answer many inconveniences and appearing absurdities which the arians fling upon the common explications of the trinity. But if there be any sufficient argument to refute this doctrine and to prove it false, I am not so fond of it as to persist obstinately in the defense, nor make all things truckle and yield to this supposition.[43]

Again Watts tried to compromise through a reasonable reinterpretation of the terms found in the Bible. And of course such a compromise was acceptable neither to the orthodox nor to Socinians.

Caleb Fleming,[44] in *A Letter to a Friend, Containing select*

Remarks upon the Rev. Dr. Isaac Watts's Treatise, entitled, The Glory of Christ, as God-Man (1746), using the same texts which Watts offered in proof of his scheme, strongly assailed the latter's conclusions. Attacking Watts from the unorthodox point of view, he flatly advised the Doctor to accept the union between God and the Son as an "intelligent moral created Being" and let the rest of his scheme go.

It should be noted that Watts appended to *The Glory of Christ* "a Short Abridgment of that excellent discourse of the late Thomas Goodwin, on the glories and royalties that belong to Jesus Christ as God-Man, ..." He added the following statement by way of introduction: "Hereby the pious reader will easily perceive, that the manner in which I have expounded many scriptures, is nobly patronized and supported by this great author, whose name and memory are honoured among evangelical writers, ..." [45]

Thomas Goodwin (1600–80), one of the most influential of the seventeenth century Puritans, was a spiritual father of independency.[46] In the work mentioned above, Goodwin, like Watts, was seeking an interpretation of the scriptures that would answer logically all of the questions raised by the many and conflicting references to Christ in the Bible. At the same time he wanted an interpretation that would glorify rather than debase Christ's position in the Trinity.

In *Useful and Important Questions* (Question III), Watts also leaned heavily upon "The Fountain of Life Opened, or a Display of Christ," a sermon by John Flavel (1630?–90), another seventeenth century Puritan divine. Flavel's works were very popular in the early eighteenth century. Written in the plain style of the Puritans, they express strong evangelical sentiments. Flavel was an enthusiastic writer, and, like Watts, he felt that the acceptance of Christ as God-man allowed for a more passionate and mystical expression of that immense love which caused the Saviour to leave the bosom of God for sinful man:

What an astonishing act of love was this, for the Father to give the delight, the darling of his soul out of his very bosom for poor sinners? . . . O matchless love! a love past finding out! if the Father had not loved thee, he had never parted with such a son for thee.[47]

As *The Glory of Christ* was Watts's last Trinitarian treatise, it is time to summarize his belief. There is but one God, and the "Deity itself personally distinguished as the Father, was united to the man Christ Jesus, in consequence of which union, or indwelling of the Godhead, he became properly God." [48] The human soul of Christ existed with the Father from before the foundation of the world; it was united of course with that of the Father before the Saviour's appearance in the flesh. As for the Spirit, it is God in being the active energy or power of the Deity; but it has no actual personal existence. Though Watts's explication of the Trinity was not radically unorthodox, it was surely not that of the Athanasian Creed.

But Watts was never wholly convinced on this irking mystery. His final doubts are preserved in the most passionate bit of writing that he ever produced, *The Author's Solemn Address to the Great and ever-blessed God on a Review of what he had written in the Trinitarian controversy, prefixed by him to some pieces on that Subject which it was not judged necessary to publish*.[49] This essay was published posthumously in the authorized works, but it had been prefixed to the 1745 suppressed edition of *A Faithful Enquiry*. All of the agony of ignorance and doubt is expressed in this fervent appeal to God for light:

How shall a poor weak creature be able to adjust and reconcile these clashing ideas, and to understand this mystery? Or must I believe and act blindfold, without understanding? . . . I want to have this wonderful doctrine of the all-sufficience of thy Son and thy Spirit for these divine works, made a little plainer.[50]

Watts then gently chides God for leaving him so blind and helpless in this quest for truth:

Hadst thou informed me, Gracious Father, in any place in thy word, that this divine doctrine is not to be understood by men, and yet they were required to believe it, I would have subdued all my curiosity to faith, . . . But I cannot find thou hast any where forbid me to understand it or to make these enquiries. . . . I have, therefore, been long searching . . . . Surely I ought to know the God whom I worship, whether he be one pure and simple being or whether thou art a threefold deity, ...[51]

The doctrine, continues Watts, is too abstruse for simple understandings; it leads to disputes and to the temptation "to give up thy word and thy gospel as an unintelligible book, and betake myself to the light of nature and reason." His conclusion is a soul-stirring plea for light:

Help me, heavenly Father, for I am quite tired and weary of these human explainings, so various and uncertain. . . .

I entreat, O most Merciful Father, that thou wilt not suffer the remnant of my short life to be wasted in such endless wanderings, in quest of thee and thy Son Jesus, as a great part of my past days have been; . . . .[52]

Theophilus Lindsey's[53] comment on the *Solemn Address* is a good analysis of Watts's dilemma:

Thus this eminent Divine, . . . after all his labour and researches, appears to have gone out of the world, unsatisfied with respect to the God he was to worship. He could not divest himself of his early prejudices in favour of the received interpretation of certain texts, relating to Christ and the holy Spirit; still thinking something of divinity or true Godhead, as he speaks, belonging to the Son and Spirit, and yet not able to reconcile it to that strong conviction of the Divine Unity, . . . with which he seems deeply penetrated throughout the whole of his prayer.[54]

The real controversy over Watts's beliefs, however, did not begin until after his death. The irony of the whole situation was that the saintly Watts, the Christian oracle for millions of pious souls, should be claimed after death by the Unitarians and become the source of a fierce polemic and propagandist battle between that group and the forces of Trinitarian orthodoxy in the English-speaking Protestant world. The latter half of the century saw many of the best Presbyterian ministers going over to the Unitarian side. Because of his importance and influence in the Christian world, Watts was an ideal person to be claimed for the Unitarian cause. On the other hand, the forces of orthodoxy which had venerated the name of Watts for so long were unwilling to give him up without a struggle. They were determined to keep him untainted. From shortly after his death until about 1860, the pages of literary and religious magazines were filled with letters and essays concerning Watts's Unitarian beliefs or the lack of them. The Unitarians, on the basis of his confessions to Tomkins, seized his *Hymns* and freed them of Calvinism. His *Divine Songs* and his *Catechisms* were "doctored" by Mrs. Barbauld, Priestley,[55] and others. The Unitarian stand was that Watts, if he had lived longer, would have become a Unitarian.

Moreover, the fact that some of his papers were destroyed by his literary executors lent fuel to the fire.[56] Some of Watts's orthodox friends tried to exonerate him by saying that he went crazy near the end of his life and became Unitarian, but that before he died he regained his sanity and died orthodox. The Unitarians, on the other hand, claimed that his last thoughts were strictly Unitarian. According to Southey, Dr. Johnson is supposed to have commented on the question:

I know not on what authority the story rests, that an Unitarian lady, once in conversation with Johnson, claimed Dr. Watts as a convert to her sect, and said, that although he had defended the Trinitarian doctrine in his works, he opened his eyes at his death.

"Did he, Madam?" Johnson is said to have replied; "then the first thing he saw was the devil." [57]

The controversy concerning Watts's Unitarianism was possibly started in 1764 by Dr. Nathaniel Lardner,[58] when he informed his friend, John Wiche that

. . . that great and excellent man, Dr. Isaac Watts, who never was an Arian, was in the latter part of his life an Unitarian, and would gladly have promoted that doctrine, if able. Somewhat of this, I suppose, appeared in public; insomuch that at his interment, . . . an ignorant preacher, who stood near the grave, was heard to say, *And pity his works were not buried with him.*[59]

On January 18, 1768, Lardner wrote to one Mr. Merivale concerning Watts's beliefs:

But in the latter part of his life, for several years before his death, and before he was seized with an imbecility of his faculties, he was an Unitarian. . . . He was very desirous to promote that opinion, and wrote a great deal upon the subject. But his papers fell into good hands, and they did not think them fit for publication. I also saw some of them.[60]

One notes that Lardner reverses the formula and makes Watts insane while holding orthodox views on the Trinity.

In a second letter to Merivale, dated March 8, 1766, Lardner asserted: "I question whether you have any where in print Dr. Watts's last thoughts upon what we call the Trinity." [61] And in a third, dated June 24, the same year, he told Merivale the following anecdote:

My nephew Neal, . . . was very intimate with Dr. Watts, and often with the family where he lived. And sometimes in an evening, . . . he would talk to his friends in the family, of his new thoughts concerning the person of Christ, *and their great importance, and that if he should be able to recommend them to the world, it would be the most considerable thing that ever he per-*

formed. My nephew came to me, and told me of it, and that the family were greatly concerned to hear him talk so much of the *importance* of those sentiments.[62]

Lardner felt that Watts's inability to recommend these new sentiments was caused by his lack of a "proper way of reasoning." Neal as executor had in his charge the papers left by Watts. Lardner admitted that they were not "fit to be published," but insisted that Watts's last thoughts were Unitarian.

In 1782, the *Monthly Review* (Vol. 66, p. 170) printed a résumé of Lardner's letters given above and emphasized an issue raised by the latter, namely, that the literary editors of Watts's estate had destroyed valuable Anti-Trinitarian papers left in their hands:

Dr. Watts's papers (many of which contained the most explicit renunciation of some of his former sentiments with respect to the doctrine of the Trinity) were mutilated, and published in a very imperfect manner. Some were wholly suppressed, and it was with difficulty that Dr. Doddridge could rescue from destruction a certain curious paper . . . entitled *A Solemn Address to the Deity etc.*[63]

Samuel Palmer (1741-1813) entered the controversy at this point with a well-written defense of Watts, *An Authentic Account of Dr. Watts's last avowed Sentiments concerning the Doctrine of the Trinity, etc.*[64] Palmer took a sane position in his defense:

But though it is undeniable that Dr. Watts did not continue in the same views of the subject which he entertained in the early part of his life, there is no decisive evidence that he materially altered his sentiments concerning the Trinitarian doctrine within any short space of his death, and it is highly improbable that he should.[65]

Palmer then reviewed all of Watts's later writings and gave a list of the works (including those destroyed)[66] left by Watts to be published at the discretion of the executors. The titles of these essays, Palmer stated, showed that Watts added nothing new to his Trinitarian stand. Palmer felt that though Watts was unorthodox in his views, his unorthodoxy was really deviation from the "common manner of explaining" these doctrines rather than from basal ideas. This point, was well taken, because Watts believed that his way made for genuine orthodoxy.

But all this does not prove that Watts was not Unitarian. The controversy, as inevitably it would, turned next to the matter of the definition of "Unitarian," and we find Palmer and the editor of the *"Monthly Repository"* [67] engaged in a heated controversy over the terms "Socinian" and "Unitarian" as applied to Watts. The source of the controversy was the publication of *Belsham's Memoirs of Lindsey* (1812) in which Belsham had given his version of Watts's change in later life. Palmer had answered this attack with a work, *Dr. Watts no Socinian* (1813). Both versions were reviewed in the volume, and of course the magazine being a Unitarian organ, the testimony of Lardner and Lindsey was given more prominence than that of Palmer. On the matter of definition, the reviewer made one important distinction. To Lardner, the word "Unitarian" probably meant only Anti-Trinitarian. In this light, Watts could with some justice be called Unitarian, but such quibbling would be cheap.

Each new publication or republication of any work on or by Watts raised the issue and provoked Unitarian and orthodox verbal conflicts. *The Christian Disciple and Theological Review*[68] rehashed the whole controversy in a review of the 1816 edition of Watts's *A Faithful Enquiry*. The reviewer frankly stated that the Unitarians wanted Watts because his name had become "associated with the holiest and dearest emotions of our souls." *The Christian Register* (Boston, Jan. 29, 1825) quoted a letter from Watts to Thomas Prince to prove the former a Unitarian. An undated pamphlet, *Was Dr. Watts a Believer in the Supreme Divinity of Jesus?*, published by the Massachusetts Evangelical Book and Pamphlet Society, argued just as strongly and at much greater length to prove that Watts was not a Unitarian.

Even Milner,[69] whose life of Watts came out in 1834, aroused the Unitarians when he denied Watts's connection with that group and added some disparaging remarks concerning the sect. *The Christian Reformer: or Unitarian Magazine and Review*[70] attacked not only the theology of Milner's biography but his scholarship as well. The reviewer was unfair to the biographer, but Milner's orthodox smugness had irritated the Unitarian beyond critical endurance. The reviewer, of course, presented the whole case for Watts's Unitarianism.[71]

Was Watts really a Unitarian? The answer is now largely a matter of definition, but of this we may feel certain: Watts never considered himself one. The question is now seldom raised, for we are far more concerned with Watts's general religious influence than with his particular sectarian bias. His writings on the question of the Trinity interest us primarily as the efforts of a candid and pious soul honestly but hesitantly groping for the truth.

CHAPTER VI

Sermon and Essay[1]

WATTS'S period of literary activity covered forty-two years (1705-1747) of one of England's most important literary eras. During this interval the modern novel was born, the familiar essay under Addison and Steele developed into full maturity, and prose satire under Swift reached a height never equalled before or since. But these phenomenal activities seem to have passed over Watts as though he were in another age, and in one sense his prose works belonged to another age. Even though his style is largely typical of the eighteenth century, even though he imitates in an unconvincing way the essays of the *Spectator,* Watts is nevertheless a belated seventeenth century prose writer. His sermons and treatises of the popular religious type are eighteenth century continuations of the work of Dod, Greenham, Rogers, Perkins, Goodwin, Baxter and other seventeenth century Puritan divines. Like his poetry, they too were written for that religious element which lived and moved beyond the pale of the ordinary Neo-classic tendencies of the day.

Watts's sermons are contained in the following publications: *A Sermon Preach'd at Salters' Hall, to the Societies for Reformation of Manners* (1707); *Sermons on Various Subjects, Divine and Moral, Vol. I* (1720-1); *Vol. II* (1723); *Vol. III* (1729); *Death and Heaven* (1722); *The Religious Improvement of Public Events* (1727); *A Collection of Sermons Preached at Berry Street by Several Ministers* (1735);[2] *The*

World to Come, Part I (1739), *Part II,* (1745); and *Evangelical Discourses* (1747).[3]

Two of the sermons listed above are topical and for that reason deserve separate mention. The first was the Reformation Sermon delivered at Salters' Hall on October 6, 1707 to the Societies of London and Westminster. Watts's address was an earnest exhortation to the "informers" and other officers of these unpopular organizations to ignore adverse criticism and persist in their work. Conscious of his severity, Watts admitted that he had "meditated a gentler subject." Some members of the Societies, however, had assured him that the looseness of the times demanded strict censure of those opposing their efforts. In his defense of the Reformation Societies, Watts was decidedly out of character. He did not know enough about the world to write this type of sermon.

The second topical sermon, *The Religious Improvement of Public Events,* was occasioned by the death of George I and the "peaceful succession of George II." In the preface, Watts stated that, after thirty years in the ministry, this was the first political sermon that he had published. Feeling that several of his brethren were better qualified to write such sermons, he had not planned to publish *The Religious Improvement,* but had been persuaded to do so by his congregation. As a matter of fact, Watts was not a good political preacher. He was too mild and too unworldly to do the kind of politico-religious rabble-rousing usually found in such works. And though a loyal Whig, he was never particularly enthusiastic in his personal allegiance to the House of Hanover. As a consequence, the sermon is a conventional consideration of the blessings bestowed upon England by God through the first George.

The remaining publications contain the sermons which are typical of Watts and which deal with the evangelical subjects so congenial to his particular talent. I cannot discuss in detail all of the sermons contained in these publications; nor is it really necessary, for they are almost monotonously similar in form and content. Watts was a good but not a great sermon-writer. His sermons are clearly and logically written; they contain only the necessary dogma and practically no controversy; but they are neither profound nor highly imaginative. They deal for the most part adequately and sincerely but not brilliantly with the usual subjects found in seventeenth century pulpit literature.

Watts's reputation as a sermon-writer rests primarily upon the following publications: *Sermons on Various Subjects, Death and Heaven,* and *The World to Come.* In these works, as we shall see later, Watts is characteristically evangelical, and it is this quality with which we shall be most concerned. But for the present it is necessary to discuss Watts as a preacher and to show his indebtedness in the field to his Puritan background and heritage.

It is difficult to conceive of Watts as a great preacher in the oratorical sense, for he was weak physically, had a thin voice, and possessed neither the pulpit-energy of a Whitefield nor the rough humor of a Bradbury. His appearance was not prepossessing. Only about five feet tall, with grey eyes, pale complexion, low forehead and prominent cheek bones, he was by no means a handsome man, and yet he was not ugly. His friends commented on the "spiritual mobility" of his countenance. But he *was* a popular preacher; all contemporary opinion attested this. And David Jennings felt that this popularity could be attributed only to the inherent spirituality of Watts's pulpit manner:

It is no Wonder, that a Man thus richly furnished with Gifts and Graces, was an admired Preacher. Though his Stature was low, and his bodily Presence but weak, yet his Preaching was weighty and Powerful. There was a certain Dignity and Spirit in his very Aspect, when he appeared in the Pulpit, that commanded Attention and Awe; and when he Spoke such strains of truly Christian Eloquence flowed from his Lips, and these so apparently animated with Zeal for God, and the most tender Concern for your

Souls, and their everlasting Salvation; as one would think, could not be easily slighted or resisted.[4]

Gibbons also comments on the "respectable and serious auditory" that Watts always commanded, "the ease and beauty in his language," and the "unaffected solemnity in the delivery of the most sacred and momentous truths." Watts's diction, Johnson tells us, was purer than that of the celebrated Dr. Foster.[5] The church was always crowded, Gibbons adds, whenever Watts preached.[6]

Watts preached with a restrained fervor that impressed and won listeners by the sheer force of sincerity. But his fervor was always under control. "I hate the thought," he once said, "of making anything in religion heavy or tiresome." Long and intricate sermons, he felt, drove the young away from the church. For this reason he was opposed to the "branching sermon" which cut the sense of the message into numerous minor ideas. He hated involved explications of obscure texts and felt that all of his remarks should be understood by the meanest capacity in his congregation. He tried to speak out of his own heart directly to the hearts of his auditory.

Watts was very seriously concerned about the so-called moralistic preaching fashionable in his day, particularly in the Establishment. The aims of such preaching were set forth in Burnet's funeral sermon upon Tillotson:

It was judged by the members of the Establishment the best way . . . first to establish the principles of natural religion, and from that to advance to the proof of the Christian Religion and of the Scriptures: not to enter much into the discussion of the mysteries of those sublime truths contained in the Scriptures concerning God the Father, the Son, and the Holy Ghost, and concerning the persons of Christ; and to consider the whole Christian doctrine as a system of principles all tending to the reforming men's natures, and governing their actions, the restraining their appetites and passions, the softning their tempers, and sweetening their humours, the composing their affections, and the raising their minds above the interests and follies of this present world.[7]

This type of preaching, Watts believed, accounted in large part for the infidelity of the age. Several of his letters to Edmund Gibson, Bishop of London, stated very strongly his convictions on the matter, and Gibson was inclined to agree with Watts.[8] Both believed that the age required a reformation in its preaching in order to stop the decay of religion which was evident in all denominations. Gibson sought to stir the Church by means of his "Charges." [9] Watts prepared a special message for the preachers of dissent, *An Exhortation to Ministers*.[10]

He tells them that they must first of all possess an active experimental religion of their own before they can hope to save a single soul. They should also be learned men, with a knowledge of oratory, rhetoric, the arts and sciences, the ancient writers, and the Fathers; but they should conceal this knowledge as they use it. They must speak to be understood by the ignorant but in such a manner as to convince the most learned. Controversy and disputes ought to be avoided as far as possible; natural religion should be used as a groundwork for revelation. The minister must not read a prepared paper like a schoolboy but should have a few notes from which he could speak convincingly out of his own experience. He must search the souls of his auditory by varying his approaches to suit the differing states and degrees of sin possessed by his hearers.[11] He should lead an exemplary life in the world but avoid being "stiff or haughty," "gloomy or sullen." He must never forget the importance of his position as a minister of God, but must be pleasing and cheerful, and seek always to win people through his kindness, gentleness, and meekness. And above all the minister must always be warm and affectionate in his efforts to save sinners from their headlong plunge into hell:

10

Awaken your spirit, therefore, in your composures, contrive all lively, forcible, and penetrating forms of speech, to make your words powerful and impressive on the hearts of your hearers, . . . Practice all the awful and solemn ways of address to the conscience, . . . Try all methods to rouze [sic] and awaken the cold, the stupid, the sleepy race of sinners; . . . endeavour to kindle the soul to zeal in the holy warfare, and to make it bravely victorious over all the enemies of its salvation.[12]

The admonitions, the advice, the ideas, and on occasion the imagery of Watts's remarks on preaching could have been taken from any one of numerous Puritan sermons or treatises on the same subject; for Watts in this work is definitely carrying on the tradition of "spiritual" preaching which began at Cambridge about the time of Cartwright's expulsion in 1570. It was encouraged by the founding of two new "Puritan" colleges, Emmanuel in 1584 and Sidney Sussex in 1596. From Cambridge after this period came a steady stream of spiritual preachers to occupy the pulpits of the land and to win greater and greater support for the Puritan cause.[13]

Just as the experimental preaching of Watts was opposed to the moralistic type of the eighteenth century Establishment, the spiritual preaching of the Puritans was a reaction against the so-called "witty" preaching of the more conservative Churchmen.[14] According to Professor Haller:

The themes of Anglican preaching were the divinely established authority of church and crown, the classic loci of the sacred epic hallowed by catholic Christian tradition, and the virtues and vices defined by the historic dialectic of medieval moral science. . . . They [the Anglicans] drew upon sixteenth-century humanism as well as upon the Christian fathers. They carried into the pulpit the stylistic methods of contemporary literary fashion. They delighted particularly, . . . in conceit and word play. They too exploited that arresting combination of dramatic emotionalism with flashing intellectuality—of poetic with realistic imagination—which was the distinguishing characteristic of metaphysical wit. Their sermons were elaborately tessellated with allusions to classical, patristic and medieval writers, punctuated by sudden descents into the familiar and the bizarre. Too often they merely coruscated laboriously with recondite erudition and verbal ingenuity.[15]

The Puritans opposed the so-called Anglican "Wisdom of Words" with "Words of Wisdom." They put aside most of the stylistic tricks and the literary allusions of the Churchman and made use of more homely and natural similies, tropes, and proverbs. Their main emphasis was not placed on pleasing the learned and the fashionable but on winning souls to God and to the Puritan cause. Their preaching was "practical and affectionate"; practical in that it taught men what to believe and how to act; affectionate in that it appealed in the final analysis to a man's emotions. The aim of such preaching was to make every man ask himself the all-important question: What must I do to be saved?[16] Every person was made to see himself, as Professor Haller observes, under the eternal image of the pilgrim and the warrior.

Puritan preaching was also "plain and perspicuous" and "English." That is, the preachers used simple and lucid sentences without too much display of erudition; they analyzed clearly the marks and indications of pride and humility in the sinner's soul, and in so doing they often made use of realistic image or easily understood types or characters. They were "English" in that the preachers used and adapted to Puritan themes traditional medieval pulpit conventions. They also used the style of the newly popular English Bible which was, as they expressed it, dictated by the Holy Ghost and which was therefore the perfect model for discourse. Above all, Puritan preaching was experimental, that is, it tended to probe the individual conscience through the preacher's experimental knowledge of his own doubts, fears, and hopes.

Preachers usually came to the pulpit with only the heads of their discourses written out. To these preachers the "uses" or practical "applications" to be drawn from the texts were of paramount importance. John Dod's method was to ascend the pulpit with nothing but the "Analisis of Text, the proofs of Scripture for the Doctrine, with the Reasons and Uses." He began by opening one or two verses, giving the sense of them so briefly and so plainly that the most ignorant could follow him. Next he cleared the doctrines by reference to the Scriptures themselves. Finally he spoke "most largely" in application, probing men's hearts in such a manner as to leave them "nothing to object against it." [17] William Perkins' method as given in the *Art of Prophecying* was not essentially different from that of Dod.[18]

The fathers of the Puritan style of preaching were Richard Greenham, John Dod, Arthur Hildersam, Richard Rogers, and Henry Smith. But the teacher from whom above all others the method was learned was the great and influential William Perkins of Cambridge. His *Art of Prophecying* and his *Of the Calling of the Ministerie* are classic expositions of this type of preaching. Both were influential throughout the seventeenth century. Perkins' work on the art of preaching and on the duties and position of the minister was continued by Richard Bernard (*The Faithful Shepherd*, 1621), William Chappell (*The Preacher, or the Art and Method of Preaching*, 1656), and others.[19] Baxter in sections of *The Christian Directory* and *The Reformed Pastor* brought the tradition down to the close of the seventeenth century, and Watts's *An Exhortation to Ministers* is an eighteenth century continuation of the tradition. Watts's work, combining the purposes of the two treatises by Perkins mentioned above, transmitted to the eighteenth century practically unchanged the methods and aims of Puritan preaching.

Watts not only preached in the Puritan manner; he also preached Puritan subject-matter. "The Christian Sabbath," "The Knowledge of God by the Light of Nature," "God's Election," "Death a Blessing to the Saints," "Faith the Way to Salvation," "The Difference between the Law and the Gospel"—all typical seventeenth century subjects—were often touched on at Bury Street. And the evangelicalism inherent in the Puritan "applications" and "uses" assumed an even larger significance in Watts's sermons, for he showed to a great degree the tendency of Puritanism to soften in the eighteenth century into an emotional Protestantism which luxuriated in feeling.

Watts's evangelicalism tends to appear in the treatment of two recurring subjects: the world to come and the insufficiency of human reason. In the first the evangelical appeal is made through a vivid and moving description of the glories of heaven for the saved and the horrors of hell for the damned. *Death and Heaven; or, the Last Enemy Conquered, and Separate Spirits made perfect; with an Account of the Rich Variety of their Employments and Pleasures* is, as the title adequately describes it, an elaborate and quaintly imaginative picture of the glories of heaven. The theme was suggested by an anonymous work, *The Future State* (1683), and an essay by Sir Richard Blackmore, *Letters of Religion between Theophilus and Eugenia* (London, 1720).

Watts believes that immediately after death a man's soul is given a new "vehicle" which is kept until the Day of Judgment when the original body will be returned. With this new vehicle the soul receives immediate reward or punishment. For the saints the pleasures of heaven are varied because every man takes his peculiar genius there. One's knowledge is heightened and magnified beyond any earthly perfection. There are classes for the young saints in which men like Sir Isaac Newton teach mathematics and the "presidents," Paul and Moses, lecture on Jewish law. It is amusing to note that Watts is unwilling to give up learning even in heaven and cannot conceive of a future world of bliss in which one does not improve oneself mentally and spiritually. Heaven therefore becomes for him a sort of celestial academy with God as headmaster and all the archangels and prophets as tutors.

Heaven to Watts is an actual physical place to be reached through saintly living. It is a promised land in which one finds rest and peace. It is that "holy world" in which dwells "God himself, who is original love; there resides our Lord Jesus Christ, who is love incarnate; and from that sacred head flows an eternal stream of love" blessing all the "inhabitants of that land." [20] And Watts, when he writes on the "full assurance of the love of God," speaks with almost antinomian fervor and zeal. His belief in a future world is exceptionally strong, and the sincerity of his emotion touches the reader. The sermon has therefore been extremely popular. [21]

The World to Come; or, Discourses on the Joys and Sorrows of Departed Souls at Death, and the Glory or Terror of the Resurrection [22] is, as we can see by the title, similar in theme to *Death and Heaven*. In this work, Watts depicts even more lavishly the heavenly scene; but his final emphasis here is on the soul preparing for heaven; consequently, he emphasizes the theme of the Last Day when sinners shall meet the wrath of God. [23] Highly experimental and enthusiastic, the work becomes on occasion definitely mystical. [24] The mood here is the prose counterpart of that found in his mystical poems on the Song of Solomon theme. [25]

On the question of the sufficiency of human reason, Watts was not always consistent. At times he seemed almost rationalistic, [26] but his characteristic position was that reason, though important, was not the whole of mind. "The quibbles of logic, against the sense and experience of a true christian," he once wrote, "are but as darts of straw and stubble against the scales of a leviathan." [27] And in a letter to his friend Samuel Say, he frankly expressed doubts concerning the efficacy of reason:

Never since the Apostles days were equall Arguments for Christianity produced as this Age has produced . . . . these Sons of Wit and Unbelief have been solidly refuted by dint of Reasoning. And what is the effect of all this. Few are convinced. Deism prevails still. [28]

This attitude appears again and again in his works, but it is seen at its best in a sermon on the "Inward Witness of Christianity." [29] The definition of the term shows clearly Watts's stand:

It is a witness that dwells more in the heart than in the head. It is a testimony known by being felt and practiced, and not by mere reasoning; the greatest reasoners may miss of it, for it is a testimony written in the heart; and upon this account it has some prerogative above all the external arguments for the truth of christianity.[30]

Watts here shifts the ground of credibility from reason to feeling, but he is too typical of his age to risk the charge of enthusiasm. He therefore hastily adds a compromising appeal to reason:

Though this inward evidence of the truth of christianity be a spiritual nature, and spring from pious experience, yet it is a very rational evidence also, and may be made out and justified to the strictest reason. It is no vain, fanciful, and enthusiastic business, ...[31]

This warning does not detract from the power of his original statement, for he later buttresses his position with the claim that the inward witness is superior to the Bible as an evidence of Christianity. Deists and skeptics can attack and twist the meanings of Holy Writ, but the Christian who has this inward witness can solve all difficulties by simply saying: "I am well assured that the doctrines of this book are sacred, and the authority of them divine: For when I heard and received them, they changed my nature, ...[32]

Watts here relies on the "Inner Light" or witness of the Spirit. Such reliance was a prominent feature of seventeenth century Puritanism, particularly among the Quakers and other sectarians, with whom it often assumed an enthusiastic character. In *De Doctrina Christiana* Milton has expressed the usual Puritan stand on the theory:

Under the gospel we possess, as it were, a two-fold Scripture; one external, which is the written word, and the other internal, which is the Holy Ghost, written in the hearts of believers, ... Hence, although the external ground which we possess for our belief at the present day in the written word is highly important, and, in most cases at least, prior in point of reception, that which is internal, and the peculiar possession of each believer, is far superior to all, namely, the Spirit itself.[33]

Watts's position is essentially that of Milton.

A further extension of the Inner Light theory is found in Watts's sermons touching the question of the "extraordinary visitation of the Spirit." A belief in the extraordinary visitation (that is, God appealing directly to the individual heart for some particular purpose), as opposed to the ordinary (which all men would receive through grace), laid one open to the accusation of enthusiasm. The question figured largely in sixteenth and seventeenth century religious literature, but most of the best minds tended to deny belief in the extraordinary visitation because of the enthusiastic implications attendant upon acceptance of the doctrine.[34]

In the *Guide to Prayer* (1715), Watts, while not denying the extraordinary visitation, wrote as one convinced that such an experience was not likely to come to his rational age:

In our day, when we have no reason to expect extraordinary inspirations, the Spirit of God usually leads us in so soft and silent a manner, agreeable to the temper of our own Spirits, and concurrent circumstances of life, that his workings are not to be easily distinguished by our selves or others, from the rational motions of our own hearts, influenced by moral arguments; . . . .[35]

But in the *Evangelical Discourses* (1747), he spoke as an old man and his attitude had changed:

I am very sensible, that in our present age, the Spirit of God is so much withdrawn from the christian church . . . that a man exposes himself to the censure of wild enthusiasm, . . . if he ventures to discourse at all on a theme like this [the Extraordinary

Witness]: But as I am persuaded these things were frequent matter of christian experience in the primitive days of the gospel, and in scenes of sharp persecution, so I am satisfied that God has not utterly with-held his divine favours of this kind from his churches and his children, for sixteen hundred years together; . . . .[36]

Watts gave a list of saintly persons, all seventeenth century divines, who, according to their own testimony, had been visited with extraordinary manifestations of the Spirit. John Howe left a note in his Bible stating that on December 26, 1689 and on October 22, 1704 he had received a "signal pledge of divine favour." The evangelical John Flavel received while on horseback tokens of God's love "that greatly surpassed all the rational and inferential pledges that ever he had." Joseph Caryl, Dr. Thomas Goodwin, and the great Dr. Owen all attested the immediate intercession or visitation of the Holy Ghost. And, as Watts pointed out, these men were no rattle-brained enthusiasts.[37] Watts accepted their testimony, because he too felt that God had visited New England in the same manner during the Revival. He was convinced that there were some honest and sincere souls whose knowledge, reason, and faith were so feeble that they derived almost all evidence of the love of God from holy raptures, visions, and other enthusiastic phenomena. These divine manifestations must not be despised, he felt, because they were sent "to confirm our faith, to exalt our joy to a heavenly degree, to be a bright and shining evidence of our interest in the Father's love, and to establish all of our other characters of adoption and put them beyond the power of doubt." [38] The effect of the extraordinary visitation of the Spirit, like the "white stone of absolution" could not be explained adequately to some one else. "None knows but he that receives it." [39] The fruits of such a witness were love, joy, peace, faith, meekness, gentleness, temperance, and goodness, whereas the "warm presumptions of fancy, or the delusions of the devil" left different fruits, for Satan could not "counterfeit the works" of God.[40]

In his sermons Watts was rebelling against the coldness of Neo-classic religion. Leslie Stephen observes that, unlike most of his contemporaries, Watts "addresses the heart rather than the intellect; and in his hands Christianity is not emasculated Deism, but a declaration to man of the means by which God pleases to work a supernatural change in human nature." [41]

Watts's sermons formed another portion of that bridge between the religious consciousness of the seventeenth century and that rekindling of religious consciousness which resulted in the evangelical movements of the eighteenth. The rhapsodic description of the world to come, the appeal to the heart rather than to the head, the probing of the individual conscience—all of these Puritan patterns and practices found a new interpretation and a new vitality in the Evangelical and Methodist revivals. Watts of course was not alone in these efforts, but the popularity of his works made him a significant figure in the transition from the old to the new Puritanism.

It is difficult to make the essays of Watts interesting to the modern reader. They deal largely with issues of importance only to the student of Puritan and Augustan theology. In most of these works, Watts is merely restating simply and clearly some abstruse theological problem that had troubled the previous generation and which was of interest only to the more conservative and orthodox of his own. But the essays are of significance to the student seeking to understand the mind of Watts. They show again that peculiar mixture of seventeenth century theology and eighteenth century philosophy referred to earlier. They also help to throw light on bypaths of Augustan thought which are often overlooked. Since, however, they have primarily only an esoteric importance, I have tried to discuss them as briefly as possible. Whenever it was practicable, I have showed their relation to better known works and authors.

The *Essay Against Uncharitableness* (1707), deals with a subject which appears in practically every other treatise that

Watts wrote. He feels that the differences over which Christians fight are usually inconsequential. The exercise of a little charity would prevent most of the dissension in the religious world.

The year 1725-6 brought to England a wave of suicides, probably caused by the financial distress attendant upon the crash of the South Sea Bubble.[42] In *A Defence against the Temptation to Self-Murther* (1726), Watts attributes these suicides to "skeptical humour," "growing atheism," and "disbelief of a future state." There is nothing particularly new in the treatise. It contains the typical religious clichés against self-murder. Part of its content was borrowed from a sermon on suicide by Increase Mather.

J. H. Harder believes that the increase in the number of suicides in the first decades of the eighteenth century was symptomatic of the growth of sentimentalism in that century. There was much literature on the subject. Many of the writers who defended suicide used the examples of ancients such as Brutus and Cato to justify the act. When Eustace Budgell drowned himself in 1734 he left a note stating: "What Cato did, and Addison approved, cannot be wrong." Pope's "Elegy to the Memory of an Unfortunate Lady" (1717) was also considered an approval of suicide, and John Donne was frequently called in to testify in defense of the act. The Reverend Mr. J. Adams, rector of St. Albans and Chaplain-in-ordinary to the King, wrote in 1700 *An Essay concerning Self-Murther* to refute the principles of *Biathanatos*. All of this concern with suicide, Harder asserts, was but a part of the "morbid tendency of the cult of melancholy."[43] Watts felt the same, and he was about to add an essay on melancholy to the tract when he discovered that a recent book on the subject had been issued, made up of extracts from Baxter's works.

In 1729 Watts published *The Doctrine of the Passions Explained and Improved* and *Discourses of the Love of God, and its Influence on all the Passions*. The two essays are really one, the first an introduction to the second. Watts's aim here is a curious one. He wishes to evolve a system whereby the passions may be used to promote religious discipline. In short, he is attacking openly and philosophically the coldness of eighteenth century religion, but he wishes at the same time to avoid the opprobrious epithet "enthusiast". Religion, he asserts, may be both passionate and reasonable if one will but use the passions as they should be used, without abuse—a typical Neoclassical compromise.[44]

The essay should be compared with the *Humble Attempt* in which Watts urges the ministers to throw off their "cold and languid style" and preach movingly, for here he is asking his readers to approach Christianity not as a thing to be argued about but as one to be felt. The question of the use of the passions in matters religious was a disturbing one for Watts's age. Watts, however, did not face the issue as squarely as did Jonathan Edwards in his treatise, *The Distinguishing Marks of the Spirit of God* (1741). Edwards admitted without hesitancy the use of passion, even violent passion, in the religious experience, but tried always to find out whether its origin was divine or satanic. Watts was too much the compromiser to go as far as Edwards, but their fundamental attitudes were similar. Both attitudes have a common origin—disgust with the frigidity of Neo-classic theological practices.[45]

In an effort to rehabilitate the dissenting cause, Watts published in 1731 *An Humble Attempt towards the Revival of Practical Religion among Christians*. This work, which has been mentioned earlier in the present chapter, was an answer to Strickland Gough's *An Enquiry into the Causes of the Decay of the Dissenting Interest* (1730).[46] Watts's stand was that religion had "decayed" not only among the dissenters, but in the age as a whole. In the light of this fact he felt that dissent had a special mission:

What is that we mean by asserting the right and freedom of conscience in our separation from the established church, but more effectually to promote the kingdom of God amongst men, . . . and better to carry on the blessed work of the salvation of souls? [47]

Watts tells the dissenters that if they are not better spiritually than the members of the Establishment they are foolish, for they are losing in two worlds—material advantages here and spiritual ones in the world to come. A hypocrite is bad anywhere, but to be a hypocrite among dissenters is, he feels, "a degree of folly that wants a name." Dissenters should not only lead better lives but should be more tolerant than others, for dissent has failed when it begins to persecute those who differ in some of the "lesser points of religion."

The essay as a whole was a strong plea for a revival of experimental preaching and of the "practical religion" of the seventeenth century Puritans. The work was not only the best answer to Gough's attack; it was also one of the best statements of the spiritual function of dissent that the age produced.

In 1737 Watts published *Humility Represented in the Character of St. Paul.* The work makes a good Sunday school lecture on the subject of humility, and that is about all that one can say. There is, however, a very interesting sidelight given in it on Watts's class-philosophy. Humility is a lesson to be learned by servants and by the poor in order that they may enjoy the position in which God has placed them. [48]

The Holiness of Times, Places, and People, under the Jewish and Christian Dispensations, Considered and Compared in Several Discourses (1738) is Watts's attempt to clear up several of the irritating theological problems of his age. The essay deals with the questions of the "perpetuity of a Sabbath," that is, whether to celebrate the first or the seventh day as the Sabbath;[49] the administration of the Lord's Supper, whether at noon or night;[50] the holiness and consecration of places of worship; forms of worship; and the difference between the visible and invisible church, the Jewish and the Christian church. It was a nice problem for Watts and his contemporaries to decide just how far the Jewish discipline in the Old Testament

was to govern Christians. Watts believed that each new dispen-
sation was all-sufficient and that it practically nullified the
commands of the one which it succeeded if those commands
were not implied in the new.[51] He therefore emphasized the
New Testament at the expense of the Old, and it was in this
light that he attacked the issues presented in the essay. Watts
made no new contribution to the settlement of these long dead
controversies. He was merely rehashing arguments used by
Puritans for over a century, but his work was at least tolerant
and readable.

In 1739 Watts published *A New Essay on Civil Power in
Things Sacred,* an excellent treatise on disestablishment from
the dissenter point of view. Since the time of Henry VIII, the
question of toleration had been a battle-ground for English
religious and political debate.[52] The seventeenth century saw a
practical culmination of the argument in the 1689 Act of Toleration, but the issue flared up again during the reign of Anne
and was alive during the whole eighteenth century. The dissenters wanted equality; toleration was only half-victory. They
knew that even this sort of compromise was a patronizing condescension on the part of the Church. The Establishment said
in effect: we are right; you are wrong, but if you behave yourselves we will not bother you. Walpole and other political
leaders took this position when dealing with dissent.

From 1732 until 1739 the dissenters under the leadership
of Dr. Chandler had worked to effect the repeal of the Test
and Corporation Acts, but in March of the latter year the bill
to bring about this reform was defeated in the Commons.[53]
A New Essay, written in the same month, tried to give a dis-
passionate view of the dissenter position on the matter of
"penal laws and tests in civil and religious affairs." Watts defined his aims in the preface:

The author was very much desirous to try 'how far his reason
could establish a national religion', and adjust and limit the com-

mon rights of mankind, both sacred and civil, under this establishment, in any country whatsoever, wherein religion may be professed in various forms; and at the same time to maintain a perfect consistence with all due liberty of conscience, and support the just authority of supreme rulers.[54]

Watts's arguments in this essay are based upon a variant of the "Inner Light" theory which was accepted by seventeenth century thinkers. God "by the light of reason hath led mankind into civil government." [55] But Watts hastens to add: "Though civil government is an ordinance of God, and appointed by him according to the light of reason, . . . yet in it's proper aims and designs it hath no direct reach or authority beyond the benefit of men in this world, ..." [56] With civil government dictated by the "candle of the Lord" within us and yet restricted to matters of this world, what type of established church could one derive?

Watts's answer is a national church based solely upon natural religion. The minimum requirements of worshipping God publicly, praying for the welfare of the nation, and attending lectures on morality are practically the only restrictions imposed by his scheme. There should be no persecution of any sort no matter what beliefs were held by the inhabitants of his hypothetical country; but Watts felt that Catholics because of their "persecuting principles" and because they were subjects of a foreign potentate who could absolve them from oaths, should be barred from holding office. Under such a scheme dissent and the Church of England would be on the same footing—separate but equal sects under one comprehending national establishment.

Like many an earlier Puritan, Watts was seeking to show that the only "natural" establishment was one in which all true Protestants could seek unmolestedly and unrestrictedly the truth of religion. As an Independent statement of tolerance and liberty, *A New Essay* follows in the tradition begun by John Goodwin's *Theomachia* (1644); Watts's stand, however, was broader than that of Goodwin. He was more closely related in spirit to Roger Williams, for Watts was pleading for absolute liberty and tolerance in things religious. He concluded his essay with a thought from Bayle: namely, that in the final analysis "heretics have as much right to persecute the orthodox, as the orthodox have to persecute them." [57]

We note in this essay a dependence upon reason which is not always characteristic of Watts. The "Inner Light" here is not that of the enthusiast; it is rather that "candle" which Watts's age insisted that all men had. As Professor Miller observes, "The Puritans did not really believe that the law of nature was extinct or useless, whatever harsh things they said in their more pious moods." [58] Watts usually wrote in a "pious mood," but in this essay he writes almost like a Deist. There was a distinct conflict between the Watts of the "extraordinary witness" and the Watts of the *Essay on Civil Power,* but Watts probably never saw it. This inconsistency I shall discuss in the last chapter, for it was an integral part of Watts's character.

The Harmony of all the Religions which God ever Prescribed: containing a brief Survey of the several Public Dispensations of God toward Man, or his appointment of different forms of Religion in Successive Ages (1742) was designed by Watts to show how God by degrees and in a way of emblem or figure reconciles a sinful world to Himself. Avoiding controverted points, he gives a résumé or "compendious arrangement" of the discoveries of God's grace as effected through Adam, Noah, Abraham, Moses, and finally through Christ and his apostles. Feeling that every Christian should know and understand the grounds of his belief, Watts in this work simplified for popular consumption some essential theological data.

In 1745 Watts returned to the theme of charitableness with his *Orthodoxy and Charity United: In Several Reconciling Essays on the Law and Gospel, Faith and Works.* The 1707 essay was included in this new work as "Essay VII". Watts was still trying to compromise differences of opinion on theological stands by new interpretations. Such interpretations simply angered the orthodox and had no effect on the unorthodox. Laudable as they were, Watts's efforts were futile. He tried too often to reconcile those holding radically opposed religious viewpoints by means of reasonable explanation. He never seemed to understand fully the insufficiency of mere logic in settling religious differences.

The Rational Foundation of a Christian Church (1747) was among the last works of Watts. The aim of the essay was still that of the reformer, to remove superficial differences and unite all Protestants through the use of reason and charity. Watts sought to show that the principles upon which the Christian church rested were not only natural and reasonable, but were also so similar to those which supported all other societies, that there should be no debate about them.

In church polity, Watts was a disciple of John Owen; and *The Rational Foundation* was written in the tradition of the latter's *An Enquiry into the Original, Nature, Institution, Power, Order, and Communion of Evangelical Churches* (1681)[59] and *The True Nature of a Gospel Church and its Government* (1689). By reason and revelation, Watts defends the dissenter type of worship. One of the discourses appended to the work, *A Pattern for a Dissenting Preacher,* draws an excellent analogy between the preaching of dissent and that of Christ and his apostles. It is a fine defense of experimental preaching and religion as contrasted with the legalistic and moralistic types of the Establishment.

Watts's two philosophical works come from the years 1732 and 1733 respectively. The first publication, *An Essay on the Freedom of the Will,* is more important as the inspiration for Jonathan Edwards' famous work on the same subject than it is in its own right. In the essay Watts attempts to prove freedom of the will by means of the so-called "argument from indifference."[60] It is not a very impressive argument, and we

11

are far more interested in Watts's ultimate purpose in asserting the freedom of the human will than we are in his dialectics. Watts feels that if man has no will to choose, then rewards and punishments are senseless. If there is no free will, God and not Adam brought sin into the world; and if all the things in the world are as they are from necessity, even God is not free.

These arguments may not be logically watertight, but their practical import is clear. Watts believed that man fettered by the "doctrine of necessity" was really not a credit to God. Moreover, in the face of such a stern decree, all gospel-acceptance, all preaching, and all religions were meaningless and futile. He could not justify his position with the logic with which Edwards later presented the other side, but he was certain that his approach placed both God and man on a higher spiritual plane. Watts was unconsciously a Christian pragmatist in his thinking.

The second publication, *Philosophical Essays on Various Subjects,* is a marvel of inclusiveness, dealing with "Space, Substance, Body, Spirit, the Operations of the Soul in union with the Body, Innate Ideas, Perpetual Consciousness, Place and Motion of Spirits, the Departing Soul, Resurrection of the Body, the Productions and Operations of Plants and Animals: with some Remarks on Mr. Locke's Essay on the Human Understanding. To which is subjoined a Brief Scheme of Ontology."

The preface to this work gives an account of Watts's philosophical development. In his youth he studied Descartes. Descartes prepared the way for Newton, and from the latter Watts learned the experimental approach to philosophy. After Newton he studied Locke,[61] from whom he learned the great lesson of tolerance:

These leaves [Locke's] triumphed over all the remnant of my prejudices on the side of bigotry, and taught me to allow all men the same freedom to choose their religion, as I claim to choose my own.[62]

This lesson, by and large, was the most important in Watts's whole career; it was the seed-bed of his usefulness in an age of controversy and theological strife.[63]

Philosophical Essays, written for the "leisured upper class," was designed to be a popular and not a technical work. Its purpose was, of course, to display God's wisdom in the animal and vegetable worlds. Watts could scarcely conceive of philosophy having any other purpose.

Leslie Stephen deals summarily with Watts's philosophical beliefs:

His philosophy was the expression of a desire to preserve part of Descartes' theory about the soul, whilst accepting Newton's physical philosophy, and a good deal of Locke's metaphysics. Such a crude amalgam could have no great value in itself, and occasionally he descends to mere childishness, as in some remarks upon the awkwardness of a complete resurrection of the body of a dropsical patient.[64]

Watts's philosophical speculations were colored too much by his piety to be of much value. Certain ideas which were repulsive to that "sacred veneration of soul" due to the majesty of God were, he felt, in their very nature untrue and to be rejected. This is the attitude he took in his strictures on Locke's theory of the *tabula rasa.* For Watts the theory was untenable because it denied that man instinctively knew right from wrong, thereby erasing all moral responsibility. Man has a moral sense which is innate, he contended, "a sort of pathetick instinct or disposition towards goodness." Any theory which asserted the contrary was unchristian and therefore false.[65]

The doctrine of the "moral sense" immediately brings Shaftesbury's *Characteristics* to mind, and we have already seen that Watts disapproved of Shaftesbury.[66] But this doctrine in the eighteenth century need not necessarily come from the

latter's work. It was given popular expression long before the
publication of *Characteristics* (1711). Isaac Barrow's sermons,
written before 1677, and John Hartcliffe's *A Treatise of Moral
and Intellectual Virtues* (1691)[67] are explicit on the point, as
are also the works of John Preston.[68]

Watts's metaphysical fancy sometimes led him into quaint
surmises. For instance, he was concerned with the state of
Methuselah's body in the next world: "because all the atoms
that ever belonged to the animal body of Methuselah in nine
hundred and sixty-nine years would make a most bulky and
disproportionate figure at the resurrection." [69] And when he
philosophized on his pet theme, the world to come, there was
no limit to his metaphysical fancy. One gem on this theme concerned itself with the following problem:

They are yet further puzzled to conceive whether a soul departing
from any place, for example, from London at noon, would find
out its friend who died there the foregoing midnight, since a direct
ascent would increase their distance and separation, far as the
Zenith is from the *Nadir;* . . . .[70]

It surprises us that such an approach to philosophy should
be taken seriously, but many of these views were common
enough among certain classes in Watts's age.[71] At least one
person felt that Watts's attacks on Locke were worthy of refutation. This was Vincent Perronet, A.M., Methodist vicar of
Shoreham in Kent, "chaplain to Right Hon. Earl Stanhope"
and friend and intimate of the Wesleys. Perronet's work, *A
Second Vindication of Mr. Locke* (1738), was aimed primarily
at Bishop Butler, but he added "Reflections on some Passages
of Dr. Watts's Philosophical Essays." Perronet is no better
logician than Watts, and his quibbles over the disagreements
between Locke and Watts need not concern us here.

Another work, however, has recently been found which
throws light on the place which the *Philosophical Essays* occupied in the minds of certain eighteenth century readers.[72] It is

an edition of the essays annotated by Mrs. Piozzi, the friend of Johnson.[73] Mrs. Piozzi's first raptures in her annotations are elicited by the style of Watts's preface:

This is a singularly beautiful Piece of Writing—I mean the Preface for the Work itself—Like every Metaphysical Enquiry it leaves Men where it found them, only impress'd with honest Veneration for so much Candour joined to so much learning.[74]

At the end of the "Table of the Essays," Mrs. Piozzi writes:

If one is to read Metaphysical Disquisitions in hope of that Truth which perpetually escapes the search of Man; it is best to read Watts or Beattie; for all other Metaphysicians seek rather to confound their opponents, than instruct their Readers: Watts and Beattie to great Strength of Mind add a religious Moderation not to be found in other Philosophers.[75]

But in a note following the preface to the essay on ontology, Mrs. Piozzi throws out Beattie:

I can bear to read no author but himself [Watts] upon the subject —No, not Beattie—The Irony and Sarcasm of a Scotsman is always offensive, ...[76]

Throughout the annotations, Mrs. Piozzi makes conventionally sententious remarks of agreement or disagreement with Watts's sentiments. Her views on the world to come are as fantastic as those of Watts. She is carried away with the latter's prose and at one point inscribes the following surprising comparison:

This is like Ajax's prayer in the Iliad. Scarce inferior to Homer in Poetical Expression. O admirable Isaac Watts![77]

A later comparison is just as startling:

Sweet Modest Watts! he is a writer by no means *meaner* than Locke. He is greater, because his Mind took in more sciences; he had a larger capacity.[78]

The literary essays of Watts are to be found in two works: *Reliquiae Juveniles: Miscellaneous Thoughts in Prose and Verse, on Natural, Moral and Divine Subjects* (1734),[79] and *Remnants of Time Employed in Prose and Verse*. The second work, although completed by 1740, was left in manuscript and published by the literary executors in the authorized edition of 1753. I shall treat the two together since both were supposedly written in younger years, and Watts originally intended that the material of the second work be included in the first.

I have used the word "literary" to distinguish these essays; perhaps "miscellaneous" would be a better term. They are short prose compositions on religious, moral, and critical themes, the shortest a paragraph in length, the longest seven pages (in the 1753 edition). Like the philosophical essays mentioned above, they were not written for individual publication but primarily for diversion. The essays as a whole are not particularly good, but they furnish another index to the mind of Watts. He is thinking aloud in these little pieces, and they show even better than his more formal essays the real Watts with all of his little weaknesses and prejudices as well as his many fine qualities.

The *Spectator* influence is very strong in these essays, but Watts lacked the sophistication of Addison and Steele; consequently, his efforts at imitation of the periodical tend to become a bit too heavy. One essay, however, "One Devil Casting out Another," [80] does achieve some of the lightness of the *Spectator* satires. Latrissa is sick unto death; nothing can help her, and all hope is gone. But her friends come in and inadvertently mention a pet enemy of Latrissa. She rallies immediately, proceeds to berate her enemy, and soon forgets that she is ill.

A more solemn influence of the *Spectator* is to be found in "The Churchyard" which echoes Addison's Westminster essay. "The Rake Reformed in the House of Mourning" has the same melancholy theme and is a sort of prose counterpart of Young's *Night Thoughts* (Book I). The "Retirement", the "Vanity of

Life", and the "Last Day" themes are all here, for Watts had the interesting habit of rewriting in prose many of his finer poetic pieces.[81]

We find also in these essays a certain attitude towards nature common in the age. It is a Newtonic approach to nature which foreshadows both Hervey and the romanticists. In his "Meditation for the First of May" and "Divine Goodness in the Creation," the author looks through the wonders of nature to the glory of God. The beauties of nature are to Watts not sufficient in themselves, but they are highly important in that they carry the mind of the observer irrevocably to the contemplation of the Grand Artificer of earth and sky.

Several other characteristic subjects appear in these brief essays. The first is not pleasant. It is Watts's hatred of Catholicism. In "Roman Idolatry", "The Table Blessed", "Purgatory", "Formality and Superstition", and several other pieces, he shows a relentless hatred of papistry. This was the one chink in his armour of charitableness, but one must remember that most Englishmen of his day shared his feeling. One must also note that this hatred extended not necessarily to individual Catholics but to the idea and institution of Catholicism. It is ironical that he could not apply the admonition against blind allegiance to sects in "Souls in Fetters" to his own attitude towards Catholics.

There are also essays of the patriotic sort like "The Thankful Philosopher" in which the character thanks God that he was born in England in the eighteenth century and not in a savage land. There is no sympathy with the "noble savage" in Watts. Other essays like "Entrance upon the World", which were lay-sermons of evangelical advice to the young and which were written for persons of "meaner understandings", were taken by the Religious Tract Society and sold in the penny chapbooks far up into the nineteenth century.[82]

These essays show Watts trying to be entertaining and light, but he is not successful in his efforts. He is far too moral and religious for this sort of thing; moreover, having no sense of plot, he often bungles a good idea. His invention of names was faulty enough to bring forth Johnson's denunciation,[83] and the pieces as a whole are amateurish. But his style in these essays is the clear limpid prose of the eighteenth century with no sign of affectation or singularity. Watts here is often quaint, but that quaintness is not one of expression.

In the *Improvement of the Mind,* Watts takes the lines from Horace's *De Arte Poetica* beginning:

> . . . . Ut sibi quivis
> Speret idem; sudet multum, frustraque laboret
> Ausus idem.

and "Englishes" them thus:

> Smooth be your style, and plain and natural,
> To strike the sons of Wapping or Whitehall.
> While others think this easy to attain,
> Let them but try, and with their utmost pain
> They'll sweat and strive to imitate in vain.[84]

This is the style of Watts's personified "Pellucido" whose writings are so simple and plain that many, until they attempt to write in the same manner, consider them commonplace. We achieve Pellucido's style by avoiding unnaturalized foreign words, fantastic, affected, vulgar, and obscure words, cloudy language, and undue length of sentence. We must also read and imitate clear authors, acquire a large vocabulary, know our subject thoroughly, and "talk frequently to young and ignorant persons upon subjects which are new and unknown to them" and make them understand what we are saying.[85]

These are excellent rules for acquiring a style capable of pleasing both the "sons of Wapping or Whitehall," and Watts generally wrote as he advised others to write. In essay and in textbook, Watts's style is eminently clear, plain and unaffected. The only serious fault he has is a tendency to prolixity. But

Watts's sermon style is on occasion quite different. The editor of the *Monthly Review* felt that it was too florid and pathetic. He thought that

The doctor's early relish for poetry, and long acquaintance with the muses, may probably have occasioned such a florid diction, such a diffusive and pathetic style, as some critics of a severer turn of thought may be ready to object to, as not so properly adapted to theological discourses, whether popular or polemical.[86]

The editor had in mind the style of writing found in thousands of passages of the following sort in Watts's sermons:

Awake, O my soul, and bless the Lord with all thy powers, and give thanks with holy joy for the gospel of his son Jesus. It is Jesus by his rising from the dead has left a divine light upon the gates of the grave, and scattered much of the darkness that surrounded it. It is the gospel of Christ which casts a glory even upon the bed of death, and spreads a brightness upon the graves of the saints in the lively views of a great rising-day. O blessed and surprising prospect of faith! O illustrious scenes of future vision and transport![87]

This is Watts's pulpit style. In it he is putting into practice his advice to ministers to be experimental, warm, and affectionate. Purposely pathetic, he was trying to save souls and not to please Neo-classic critics. Any consideration of Watts's prose style must take into account the practical aims of these sermons, for with Watts the evangelical mission always came first. Literary decorum had to be sacrificed to the larger purpose. In the words of Palgrave, he was "one of those whose sacrifice of art to direct usefulness have probably lost them those honors in literature to which they were entitled." [88]

CHAPTER VII

The Adventurous Muse

IT HAS been customary among certain critics to smile at the poetry of "Mother Watts". Pope, it is said, originally included Watts along with Brome and Samuel Wesley in a line of the *Dunciad* (1728).[1] With his parodies of *Divine Songs,* Lewis Carroll did much to make the name of Watts amusing to the late nineteenth century. And as late as 1920, one finds an author still poking fun at the quaintness of "The Little Busy Watts." [2]

But in every age since that of Watts, there have been scholars who have found that Watts's poetry, far from being quaint, is in the main well-written and on occasion very good. Samuel Johnson thought Watts's judgment exact, his imagination "vigorous and active", his ear well-tuned and his diction "elegant and copious". Though opposed on principle to devotional poetry, Johnson felt that Watts had "done better than others" what no man can do well.[3] To Cowper Watts, though often careless, was yet a "man of fine poetical ability", "frequently sublime in his conceptions and masterly in his execution." [4] In the romantic period Southey credited Watts with having a "skillful ear", an "active fancy", and a "mind well-stored with knowledge". He has, concluded Southey, that "rare merit of being seldom dull".[5] And Saintsbury, writing in the early twentieth century was fascinated by Watts's prosodic versatility. He found Watts "really worth reading".[6]

In recent years there has been something of a renascence of

Watts. From the *Nation* for March 16, 1927 came this word of praise, mingled, of course, with the usual depreciation:

Watts may be mawkish and twaddling; but his poetry will not die; it is too well written. It has an uncanny felicity, for it is the product of an ingenious and poetically sophisticated mind.[7]

In 1933, the late A. E. Housman compared Watts with Pope (a name not usually mentioned in the same breath with that of Watts):

Nuns fret not at their convent's narrow room, and the eighteenth century, except for a few malcontents, was satisfied with what its leading poets provided. 'It is surely superfluous' says Johnson, 'to answer the question that has once been asked, whether Pope was a poet, otherwise than by asking in return, if Pope be not a poet, where is poetry to be found?' It is to be found, Dr. Johnson, in Dr. Watts.

> Soft and easy is thy cradle,
>   Coarse and hard thy Saviour lay;
> When his birthplace was a stable,
>   And his softest bed was hay.

That simple verse, bad rhyme and all is poetry beyond Pope.[8]

Writing in 1935 from the college in Watts's home-city of Southampton, Professor V. de Sola Pinto asked for a new evaluation of Watts's work:

It is time that his [Watts's] poems were rated at their true worth, and no longer dismissed with the productions of Yalden, Pomfret, Blackmore and other small fry of Dr. Johnson's and Chalmer's collections or lost in a rosy mist of conventional piety.[9]

And in his recent work, *Religious Trends in English Poetry* (1939), Professor Fairchild has given Watts an important place among the eighteenth century divine poets:

Although he [Watts] was in several respects a typical Independent minister of his age, he was one of a very few men who, . . . preserved the old spiritual ardor of Dissent; and he was literally the only man who gave that ardor anything like a significant poetic expression. His ministry and his writings form a link between the zeal of the seventeenth and the revived zeal of the later eighteenth century.[10]

To Cazamian, writing in a similar vein, Watts was a "link between the spiritual fervour of a still active though latent religious life, and the possible renovation of poetry." [11] He was the poet of that deep current of imaginative and religious emotion which, flowing beneath the surface of Neo-classic religion and art, brought to the eighteenth century the ardor of the seventeenth. The following pages of this chapter will attempt to treat Watts in that light.

In order to study him as the poet of the "latent religious life" of the age, we must keep in mind the political and philosophical compromise which, after a hundred years of struggle, the Revolution of 1688 brought to English life. There was compromise between Crown and Parliament, between Church and State, and between Whig and Tory. In the sphere of taste and criticism there was an analogous compromise which nourished two great streams of influence flowing side by side.[12] One was the highly articulate upper-class stream of intellectual and rationalistic tendencies which may be grouped under the term Neo-classic. The other was that deep, more or less inarticulate religious and emotional stream which may be termed the evangelical.[13] The two tendencies, though converging at times, were by nature opposed. The second stream had been strengthened by the rise of middle-class morality; it saw the nucleus of even greater strength in the rise of Religious Societies. In prose literature it had Bunyan, Baxter, and a host of lesser men; it was soon to express itself more emotionally in the rise of a hymnology. Finally it produced an eighteenth century poet in Isaac Watts, who, with his poetry and his "System of

Praise," became a leading exponent of the evangelical tendencies of the age.

The poetry of Watts is a result of the conflict between the growing rationality and the strong religious passion of the age. Schooled in Neo-classic thought, Watts spoke the language of the initiate, but he had a religious mind that openly rebelled against the coldness and formality of the Compromise's religion and art. From this clash came his efforts to reform the poetry of his day, to add new forms, to revitalize its content. Seeing the spiritual poverty of the Neo-classic poetry, he tried to renovate it with an infusion of the evangelical strain.

Watts's scheme for the renovation of poetry is set forth in the Preface to the second edition of *Horae Lyricae* (1709). He opens with a complaint against the wretched state into which poetry has fallen:

It has been a long complaint of the virtuous and refined world, that poesy, whose original is divine, should be inslaved to vice and profaneness; that an art inspired from heaven, should have so far lost the memory of its birth-place as to be engaged in the interests of hell! How unhappily is it perverted from its most glorious design.[14]

The profanation and debasement of the divine art of poetry have gone so far that some "weaker christians" imagine that poetry and vice are naturally akin. "They will venture to sing a dull hymn or two at church, in tunes of equal dulness; but they still persuade themselves, . . . that the beauties of poetry are vain and dangerous." It is strange that persons with the Bible in their hands should have "so wild and rash an opinion."[15] Have they forgotten, asks Watts, that many parts of the Old Testament are Hebrew verse?

After this attack on the Puritan attitude towards poetry, Watts comes to the main issue of the Preface. Boileau had questioned in *L'Art Poétique* whether the doctrines of the

Christian religion would "indulge or endure a delightful dress." To refute Boileau, Watts cites the example of Racine and Corneille. Cowley's *Davideis* and the two *Arthurs* of Blackmore, he also feels, "experimentally confuted" the French critic. The Christian mysteries, Watts admits, do not need the gay trappings necessary to beautify "heathen superstition." They have a "native grandeur, a dignity, and a beauty" in them, which though not utterly denying ornament, make easier the work of the poet who uses them. Like Milton, Sprat, Cowley, and other seventeenth century writers, Watts believed that the fables of antiquity were becoming exhausted and outworn. They were but the "tinsel trappings" of pagan error, whereas the Bible is God-inspired truth.[16] Moreover, the language of the Bible has stronger figures, bolder metaphors, and images "more surprising and strange" than are to be found in any profane writer. If the modern poet will but model his style upon the Hebrews, he will surpass even the writers of classic antiquity. Go then, advises Watts, to the Bible for both the subject-matter and the form of modern poetry. Make poetry the handmaid of religion. Let its one great purpose be to allure souls to God.

Watts then discusses the means of bringing about this reformation in poetry. First, as to the mechanics, the poet may use couplets, but couplets that are written like blank-verse, because the "tedious uniformity" of Neo-classic couplets with their perpetual chime of even cadences "charms to sleep with their unmanly softness." Or the poet may use blank verse, but not necessarily Miltonic, because Milton is sometimes "harsh and uneasy." Or he may use the "free and unconfined numbers of Pindar."

As for the themes to be used in this reformed poetry, the passage in which Watts describes the subject-matter rivals and recalls that describing similar aims in Giles Fletcher's *Christ's Death and Victory*:[17]

The affairs of this life, with their reference to a life to come, would shine bright in a dramatic description; nor is there any need or any reason why we should always borrow the plan or history from the ancient Jews or primitive martyrs; . . . But modern scenes would be better understood by most readers, and the application would be much more easy. The anguish of inward guilt, the secret stings, and racks, and scourges of conscience; the sweet retiring hours, and seraphical joys of devotion; the victory of a resolved soul over a thousand temptations; the inimitable love and passion of a dying God; the awful glories of the last tribunal; the grand decisive sentence, from which there is no appeal; and the consequent transports or horrors of the two eternal worlds; these things may be variously disposed, and form many poems.[18]

And the poet who deals with these themes must have a divine inspiration:

If the heart were first inflamed from heaven, and the muse were not left alone to form the devotion, and pursue a cold scent, but only called in as an assistant to the worship, then the song would end where the inspiration ceases; the whole composure would be of a piece, *all meridian light and meridian fervour;* and the same pious flame would be propagated, and kept glowing in the heart of him that reads.[19]

The Preface ends on a high note; it is the same stand taken earlier by Milton:

He that deals in the mysteries of heaven, or of the muses, should be a genius of no vulgar mold: And as the name *Vates* belongs to both; so the furniture of both is comprised in that line of Horace,

> 'cui mens divinior, atque os
> Magna sonaturum'.[20]

When Watts implies that poetry should have a moral function, he is expressing a view common enough in his age.[21] The theory in Watts, however, goes deeper than usual. Poetry has fallen from grace; in order to regain its former glory, it needs to become reconciled with religion. The poet must become an original genius, divinely inspired to lead and to influence men in the way of truth. This Platonic concept of the poet's function was exemplified in Milton's life;[22] it found expression in the preface to Cowley's collected poems (published in 1656), and in Edward Phillips' *Theatrum Poetarum*. It was also given critical justification in the works of Richard Blackmore and John Dennis, both of whom Watts mentions favorably in his Preface.[23]

Watts may have been directly influenced by Dennis and Blackmore. Both figure largely in the Preface to *Horae Lyricae*. But Watts knew thoroughly the critical writings of the seventeenth century, and it would be safer to say that the three writers made use at approximately the same time of a theory which was generally known in the preceding century. Watts, Dennis, and Blackmore therefore jointly brought over into the eighteenth century this Platonic-Renaissance view of the divinely inspired poet. From this point we can trace it through works like Aaron Hill's "The Creation", Thomson's "Winter", Collins' "Ode on the Poetical Character", Joseph Warton's "Ode to Fancy", Akenside's "The Pleasures of the Imagination", Isaac Hawkins Browne's "On Design and Beauty", and James Beattie's "The Minstrel" to the romantic movement at the end of the century.[24]

Watts was not only asking that poetry become the handmaid of religion. He was protesting with all of the power at his command against the sterility of Neo-classic poetry. With the Bible and Christian experience as a background, the poet must replace the cold rhetoric of Augustan satire and imitation with religious truth carried alive into the heart. Poetry in short must regain its lost essential ingredient of religious enthusiasm. Watts's attempted reformation of poetry was of course a futile gesture, but it foretokened a later and successful effort. The Preface to *Horae Lyricae* remains as a record of Watts's attempt.

The poetry of Watts is contained in the following publications: *Horae Lyricae* (1706), *Divine Songs* (1715), *Reliquiae Juveniles* (1734), *Remnants of Time* (published posthumously, 1753), and *The Posthumous Works* (published by a "Gentleman of the University of Cambridge" in 1779). This last work presents some problems and will be discussed in "Appendix B." These volumes will not be considered separately but simply as the poetry of Watts. And though treated elsewhere, the hymns will be used whenever necessary for purposes of illustration.

Before discussing this poetry, I must refer once more to Watts's religious beliefs. He was a Calvinist, and the doctrines of that faith permeate his poetry. But at least he was not one of the more rigid Calvinists. As we have seen, he explained away predestination, the most important doctrine of Calvinism.[25] And though there is much so-called Calvinistic gloom in his poetry, there is also much more evangelical hope. Watts laid far more emphasis on regeneration than on reprobation. In him Calvinism has softened into incipient sentimentalism.

Calvinistic influence expresses itself in two ways in Watts's verse. It is found, first, in poetic renditions of the main tenets of the sect, for example, the doctrine of God's unknowableness ("God only known to himself"):

> Stand and adore! how glorious he
> That dwells in bright eternity!
> We gaze, and we confound our sight
> Plung'd in th' abyss of dazzling light;

or the doctrine of election ("Condescending Grace"):

> Mortals, be dumb; what creature dares
>   Dispute his awful will;
> Ask no account of his affairs,
>   But tremble, and be still;

or the doctrine of the division of the world into saints and non-elect ("The Atheist's Mistake"):

> Hence, ye profane, I hate your ways,
> I walk with pious souls;
> There's a wide diff'rence in our race,
> And distant are our goals.

Second, Calvinism, with its strict morality, its emphasis on the saints' worldly asceticism, its despising of all things here below, carries over into the general atmosphere of Watts's poetry and gives it an unhappy quality. The themes of eighteenth century melancholy poetry are therefore ever present in Watts's work.

In her recent work, Miss Sickels observes that the reader of the eighteenth century was familiar with the following themes and moods of melancholy: "pensive joys of solitude and retirement", "death and ruins", "death and corruption", "the generally unsatisfactory nature of human life", "the illusiveness of worldly pride and ambition", "white melancholy and black", "melancholy neo-classic and religious", "melancholy sincere and assumed", "melancholy praised as the muse of virtue and reviled as the enemy of society", belief in hell, and the "spleen" and "vapors".[26]

These themes (the product of the combined influences of Milton and the Latin classics at work upon the background of early seventeenth century Burtonian melancholy) existed at the turn of the century as common elements in both the classical and the Biblical literary tradition, and they offered to any poet giving them a new turn and a fresh impulse the possibility of appealing to a large audience.[27] In *Horae Lyricae* (1706) one finds most of the themes and moods listed above. To a limited extent, Watts does give a new turn and a fresh impulse to these melancholy themes, sending them down to the poets of the mid-century.

The retirement theme as presented by Watts expresses often the idea of withdrawal from a blind following of the inbred custom of the world:

> Wisdom retires; she hates the crowd,
>   And with a decent scorn
> Aloof she climbs her steepy seat,
> Where not the grave nor giddy feet,
> Of the learn'd vulgar or the rude,
>   Have e'er a passage worn!

Or it takes the more spiritual attitude of retirement within oneself:

> When I view my spacious soul,
> And survey myself awhole,
> And enjoy myself alone,
> I'm a kingdom of my own.

Or it may take even the extreme attitude of "sanctified affliction" in which the Christian welcomes sickness because it foretokens withdrawal from the world of flesh:

> My cheerful soul now all the day
>   Sits waiting here and sings;
> Looks thro' the ruins of her clay,
>   And practices her wings.[28]

The "generally unsatisfactory nature of human life" and the "illusiveness of worldly pride and ambition" are themes which are either stated or implied in most of Watts's poems. To him

> Bright and lasting bliss below
> Is all romance and dream;

he finds that

> —the whole round of mortal joys
> With short possession tries and cloys;
> 'Tis a dull circle that we tread; . . .

and Watts feels that

Life's a long tragedy: This Globe the stage,
. . . .
. . . . The Actors many;
The Plot immense: A flight of daemons sit
On every sailing cloud with fatal purpose;
And shoot across the scenes ten thousand arrows
Perpetual and unseen, headed with pain,
With sorrow, infamy, disease and death.[29]

In "The Hero's School of Morality", he advises the contemplation of a "ruined monument" as a cure for all earthly ambition:

He guessed, and spelled out, Sci-pi-o.
. . . . He
That living could not bear to see
An equal, now lies torn and dead;
Here his pale trunk, and there his head;
Great Pompey! . . . .
Thy carcase, scattered on the shore
Without a name, instructs me more
Than my whole library before.[30]

But Watts's *taedium vitae* is always motivated as in "Felicity Above" by the assurance of future bliss:

Why move my years in slow delay?
    O God of ages! why?
Let the spheres cleave, and mark my way
    To the superior sky.

The death-hell theme is represented best in the well-known "Day of Judgment":

I

When the fierce North wind with his airy forces
Rears up the Baltic to a foaming fury;
And the red lightning, with a storm of hail comes
        Rushing amain down,

IV

Tears the strong pillars of the vault of heav'n,
Breaks up old marble, the repose of princes;
See the graves open, and the bones arising,
    Flames all around 'em!

V

Hark, the shrill outcries of the guilty wretches!
Lively bright horror, and amazing anguish,
Stare thro' their eyelids, while the living worm lies
    Gnawing within them.

The imagery of this poem is forceful and impressive; the sweep of the metre adds to the effect of tumult on the Last Day. The piece is a striking example of the intensity and vividness of Watts's best work. Miss Reed feels that the "Day of Judgment" links Young's "The Last Day" and Aaron Hill's "The Judgment Day" with seventeenth century works like Flatman's "A Dooms-Day Thought," Roscommon's "The Day of Judgment," Wigglesworth's "The Day of Doom" and Pomfret's "On the General Conflagration, and Ensuing Judgment." "The enormous popularity of . . . the 'Day of Judgment,'" she observes, "is sufficient evidence of the continuance into the eighteenth century of the seventeenth century emphasis on the vanity of life and the horrors of death and judgment. While Watts consistently offset these ideas by the thought of the saving power of Jesus and the bliss of the good in heaven, popular imagination seized most readily upon the gruesome parts of his poetry, and fed therewith that religious melancholy which Burton described in the Anatomy." [31] "The Day of Judgment" is a significant eighteenth century poem.

A special group of poems in this melancholy vein may be found in Book III of *Horae Lyricae*, containing poems "Sacred to the Memory of the Dead." There are seven funeral elegies in this book, and three more, plus many epitaphs, in both English and Latin, in *Reliquiae Juveniles* and *Remnants of*

Time. Watts was morbidly concerned with the theme of death. With him it was not a mere poetic convention, for most of his letters and practically all of his sermons stress the "four last things."

Moreover, the funeral elegy was one type of poetry which the Puritan tradition readily condoned. Draper feels that there was a "distinctive elegiac literature" during the period that could be definitely associated with the Puritan and dissenting tradition, and that this elegiac literature presents in theme and imagery an interesting contrast to the poetry, even the elegiac poetry, produced for "aristocratic consumption." [32] The poetic model in this field for the seventeenth century Puritans, Draper asserts, was Francis Quarles. Though he was an avowed Royalist, his works, particularly his *Emblems* and *A Feast for Worms,* found high favor with the Puritans. These works contained a "magazine of elegiac ammunition" from which Puritan writers all through the century borrowed at will. Almost every theme found in the funeral elegy of later years was anticipated in Quarles's work.[33]

Although Watts's funeral elegies do not often possess the poetic lavishness found in those written by his Puritan predecessors, they do contain on occasion the phrases, the funeral machinery, and the macabre imagery of the earlier elegies. This material however was so generally diffused throughout the works of the century that it would be difficult to point to any one author as Watts's model.

Watts's most notorious funeral poem was "An Elegy on Mr. Thomas Gouge." This piece has probably done more to harm Watts's reputation than any other that he wrote. When he made a world cataclysm out of the death of a dissenting minister:

> Sion grows weak, and England poor
> Nature herself with all her store
> Can furnish such a pomp for death no more,

the critics justly lashed the poem. Watts's Pindaric Pegasus
runs away with him on this occasion, and the elegy is a monument to "Pindarick folly."

In "An Elegiac Ode on the Death of Sir Thomas Abney"
Watts shows none of the bathos and bombast found in the
above poem. This restrained and dignified elegy is formally
divided into two parts: "Private Life" and "His Public Character and Death." Watts's concern is not with the gloom or
horror of the grave but with the assured placed of Abney in
the world to come:

> We mourn; but not as wretches do,
> Where vicious lives all hope in death destroy:
>   A falling tear is nature's due;
> But hope climbs high, and borders on celestial joy.

Watts's best funeral ode is the elegy "To the Memory of my
honoured Friend, Thomas Gunston, Esq." Gunston was the
brother of Lady Abney and one of the poet's closest friends.
Watts tells us that in writing the poem he transcribed "nature
without rule and with a negligence becoming woe un-
feigned." [34] Based on "Lycidas," the elegy is one of the earliest
imitations of that poem in the century. [35] Watts, however, was
never a slavish imitator; he takes from Milton only the general plan and occasional phraseology. Using as a theme the
unfinished hall which Gunston was building, the elegy describes in typical, melancholy elegiac style the funeral proces-
sion to the "cold lodging in a bed of clay." It paints the midnight scene and the graveyard where the "lowing herds should
come." "Moaning turtles" murmur over the grave. Nature
mourns in general grief and drops her leaves as in "Adonais".
The poem ends with a description of the hall bathed in moon-
lit splendor, and Urania ceases her "doleful strain" to assure
us that:

> Gunston has mov'd his dwelling to the realms of day;
> Gunston the friend lives still.

One finds in this poem much of the "mortuary landscape" and other stock properties of the graveyard school. It is a forerunner of similar poems by Blair, Young, and Gray. It brings from the seventeenth century funeral poetry the "midnight scene," the "pensive thought," the Gothic landscape, the "stately elms," the "lonesome vault" and other funereal detail to be used by the Youngs and Grays of the mid-century. These are common ideas and images, and we cannot claim any direct influence except in the case of Blair,[36] but a poet as popular as Watts would have some share in planting these ideas and images in the poetic and popular mind of generations immediately following him.

To Watts poetic and religious inspiration are closely related:

> Change me, O God; my flesh shall be
> An instrument of song to thee
> And thou the notes inspire.

In "Asking Leave to Sing" Watts boasts concerning his muse:

> But when she tastes her Saviour's love,
> And feels the rapture strong,
> Scarce the divinest harp above
> Aims at a sweeter song.

His concern with "original genius" leads him to protest against the confining powers of

> Custom, that tyranness of fools,
> That leads the learned round the schools,
> In magic chains of forms and rules!
> My genius storms her throne:

Watts prefers the

> . . . . muse whose generous force
> Impatient of the reins,
> Pursues an unattempted course,
> Breaks all the critics iron chains,
> And bears to paradise the raptur'd mind.

Such an attitude looks forward to the romantic idea that genius is superior to rules. In Watts it is found highly developed, and is critically justified in the Preface to *Horae Lyricae*.

There is more nature poetry in Watts's works than one would expect. He was a keen observer, but his attitude is not romantic. We cannot know God through nature; we can only see proofs of the greatness and the majesty of the incomprehensible deity:

> Thy hand unseen sustains the poles
> On which the huge creation rolls:
> The starry arch proclaims thy pow'r,
> Thy pencil glows in every flow'r:
> . . . The meanest pin in nature's frame,
> Marks out some letters of thy name.
> . . . There's not a spot or deep or high,
> Where the Creator has not trod,
> And left the footstep of a God.[37]

"We espy some faint beams, some glimmerings of his glory breaking through the works of his hands, but he himself stands behind the veil, ..."[38] Nevertheless, Watts felt as did Bacon that the upper link of nature's chain was fastened to the throne of God.

Courthope believed that the Whig principles which gained ascendancy in 1688 were not as conducive to the production of poetry as the Tory principle of personal loyalty. The former were too intellectual and abstract to lend themselves readily to poetic expression.[39] As a consequence, Whig panegyric tended to exemplify that "faintness of thinking" which Johnson found in Addison's "Campaign". In this and in other respects the panegyrics of Watts are typical.

His first attempt at Whig panegyric comes from the year 1694, and the subject is Queen Mary rather than William ("On the Sight of Queen Mary, in the year 1694"):

> I saw th' illustrious form, I saw
> Beauty that gave the nations law:

> Her eyes, like mercy on a throne,
> In condescending grandeur shone.

William, however, is the central figure in the rest of these pieces. The first poem on him was written in 1695, a "Hymn of Praise for Three great Salvations, viz. From the Spanish Invasion, From the Gun-powder Plot, From Popery and Slavery by King William of Glorious Memory, who landed, Nov. 5, 1688." The poem shows Watts's hatred for James II and his acts of persecution.

In 1698, Watts wrote to his friend, David Polhill,[40] "An answer to an infamous Satire, called *Advice to a Painter;* written by a nameless Author, against King William III, of glorious memory, 1698." [41] To Watts, William is the "brave, the pious, and the just, who is abroad a hero, and at home a saint." He is:

> Sweet, with no fondness; cheerful but not vain:
> Bright, without terror; great, without disdain.
> His soul inspires us what his lips command,
> And spreads his brave example thro' the land.

Watts's third attempt in this vein is happier than the first two. It is "An Epitaph on King William III of glorious Memory," written in 1702. In this the poet's restraint is far more effective than the bombast of the earlier pieces. The epitaph begins in the manner of Jonson's poem on "Elizabeth, L. H.":

> Beneath these honours of a tomb,
> Greatness in humble ruin lies:
> (How earth confines in narrow room
> What heroes leave beneath the skies!)

Religion, Liberty, and Peace are mourners, and in the last stanza:

> Glory with all her lamps shall burn,
> And watch the warrior's sleeping clay,

> Till the last trumpet rouse his urn
> To aid the triumphs of the day.

In 1705 Watts wrote a poem "To her Majesty", Queen Anne,

> Queen of the northern world, whose gentle sway
> Commands our love, and charms our hearts t' obey;

but he printed a retraction of the piece in 1721, because the last part of Anne's reign was of a "different colour" from the first. The retraction is not only presented in the appended note, but also in an inserted poem, "Palinodia," in which he asks:

> Britons, forgive the forward muse
> That dar'd prophetic seals to loose.

George is the sovereign, not Anne, who will give the "dying nations day" and "crown the work that Anne forsook."

"On the Coronation of Their Majesties King George II and Queen Caroline," written in 1727, was the last of Watts's Whig panegyrics. The "faintness of thinking" referred to above is evident in this poem. William came bringing deliverance to Watts's group after a trying period. George II, other than being a member of the House of Hanover, had no special claim on Watts's affections. The poem is therefore a conventional panegyric with the usual parade of personified abstractions, and Watts is forced to end on his old note of loyalty:

> Great William shall rejoice to know
> That George the second reigns below.

Watts was not a great Whig panegyrist. His loyalty to Whig principles prompted him to efforts which seem forced. But he did have a deep love for William of Orange and just as deep a hatred for the Stuarts. When writing on either theme, he managed to produce at least representative Whig panegyric.

Watts's translations concern us next. In his poetical works there are twenty-four acknowledged translations and imitations—four from the French, seven from classical Latin (principally Horace), thirteen from modern Latin, ten of which come from Matthew Casimir Sarbiewski.[42] Except for the translations from the latter poet and from Horace, these works are not important. Usually mere snatches of verse, they were evidently done in odd moments. In the Latin poem "To the Reverend Mr. John Pinhorne," [43] written in 1694, Watts, pledging himself to the service of the Christian muse, decided to put aside the "romance" and "fictitious Panoply" of the classic poets.[44] He felt, however, that some of the heathen poets, if sufficiently purified, could be used to diffuse virtue. Horace was especially useful for this purpose:

> Horace shall with the choir be join'd,
> When virtue has his sense refin'd,
>   And purg'd his tainted page.[45]

To illustrate his theory he takes Horace's Ode 29 in Book III and translates it into "The British Fisherman." Like all of his short translations from the Latin, the experiment has no unusual merit, but it may be used to illustrate Watts's type of translating:

> Non meum est, si mugiat Africis
> Malus procellis, ad miseras preces
>   Decurrere, et votis pacisci,
>   Ne Cypriae Tyriaeque Merces
> Addant avaro divitias mari.
> Tunc me biremis praesidio scaphae,
>   Tutum per AEgeos tumultus
>   Aura feret, geminusque Pollux.

This is rendered in English by Watts:

> Let Spain's proud traders, when the mast
> Bends groning to the stormy blast,
> Run to their beads with wretched plaints,
> And vow and bargain with their saints,
> Lest Turkish silks or Tyrian wares
>   Sink in the drowning ship,

> Or the rich dust Peru prepares,
> Defraud their long projecting cares,
> And add new treasures to the greedy deep.[46]

The second stanza ends on the religious note, but the first is enough to show that Watts's method here is similar to that followed in his imitations of the Psalms. He not only translates, he modernizes as well.[47]

The most successful translations of Watts are those from Casimir. Similar in spirit, the two men wrote poetry that tended toward imaginative lavishness. In the Preface to *Horae Lyricae*, Watts calls Casimir "that noblest Latin poet of modern ages" and admits that in a few places "I borrowed some hints . . . without mention of his name in the title." In the *Improvement of the Mind* the praise is even stronger: "I will readily acknowledge the odes of Casimir to have more spirit and force, more magnificence and fire in them, and . . . arise to more dignity and beauty than I could ever meet with in any of our modern poets." Watts made his first acquaintance with Casimir under Pinhorne in Latin school and used him in both *Horae Lyricae* (1706) and *Reliquiae Juveniles* (1734). He translated Casimir into all kinds of stanzaic forms and for all purposes—religious lyrics, epigrams, and friendship poems. The finest of these translations, and the poem which Samuel Johnson liked best, is "The Celebrated Victory of the Poles over Osman the Turkish Emperor in the Dacian Battle." This is a long, well-sustained narrative poem in blank verse. There are two vivid descriptions, one of the battle, the other of the death of the two young princes; and the whole poem moves with such ease and spirit that one wishes that Watts had tried the type more often.

In Book I of *Horae Lyricae* Watts has several poems showing a "consciousness wider and deeper than normal."[48] These mystical poems record his attempts to ally himself with and to lose himself in contemplation of the eternal principles of the Godhead. In these pieces the evangelical principle is carried to its ultimate degree. The religious soul suffused with divine influence abandons all perceptions of sense and intellect and loses itself in mystical love.

The "tremendous lover" of these poems is sometimes the Calvinistic God ("The Incomprehensible"):

> Far in the heav'ns my God retires,
>   My God, the mark of my desires,
>   And hides his lovely face;
> When he descends within my view,
> He charms my reason to pursue,
>   But leaves it tir'd and fainting in th' unequal chase.

More often, however, the mystical lover is Christ, and following the seventeenth century tradition, Watts turns to the *Songs of Solomon* for the content of his "Divine Love" poems. One of the best and most restrained of these Canticles is found in the hymn:

> We are a garden wall'd around,
> Chosen and made peculiar ground;
> A little spot, inclosed by grace,
> Out of the world's wide wilderness.[49]

But Watts tells us in one of his sermons on the "foretaste of heaven" that there are some persons who love Christ with such "intense and ardent zeal" that their "transcendent affections" carry them away "captive above all earthly things." [50] In some of the "Divine Love" poems he shows this type of transcendent affection for Christ the "tremendous lover." His imagery becomes startlingly sensual:

> Once I beheld his face, when beams divine
> Broke from his eye-lids, and unusual light
> Wrapt me at once in glory and surprise.
> My joyful heart, high leaping in my breast,
> With transport cried, "This is the Christ of God;"
> Then threw my arms around in sweet embrace,

> And clasped and bowed adoring low
> till I was lost in him.

He seeks Christ "panting with extreme desire," he carves Christ's name in the bark of a lover's tree, he meets his loved one in "some lofty shade where turtles moan their loves." The passion in these poems is so shockingly detailed that without exception every biographer of Watts has stated or hinted dislike of the poems, even though each was aware that Watts was following the usual seventeenth century symbolical interpretation of the *Songs of Solomon*.

Watts became conscious of the changing taste in such matters; he apologized for the poems in the 1736 edition of *Horae Lyricae* and again in the Preface to Mrs. Rowe's *Devout Exercises* (1737). In the latter work he wrote like a Freudian: "I know it hath been said that this language of rapture addressed to Deity, is but a new track given to the flow of the softer powers, after the disappointment of some meaner love; or, at least, it is owing to the want of a proper object and opportunity to fix those tender passions." [51] Watts explained that this was not so either in his own case or in that of Mrs. Rowe. He confessed, however, that the "sense of mature age" had persuaded him that this language was not the happiest in which to disclose "warm sentiments of religion;" but he insisted that there were some souls "favored with such beautifying visits from heaven, and raptured with such a flame of divine affection" that they were constrained to use the language of divine love.[52]

A. Hamilton Thompson believes that Watts's best work on this theme "has nobility of thought and style," and that the language of the *Song of Songs* has seldom been used with "such faultless taste and beauty" as in the hymn quoted above, "We are a garden wall'd around." [53] In a few of these poems Watts approaches his ideal of devotional poetry, "all meridian light and meridian fervour." They glow with religious passion and intensity, and though such intimacy with divine persons as depicted in them is objectionable to many, the poetry is intrinsically of a high order. If Watts could have written all of his verse with the power and passion found in the "Divine Love" poems, his proposed renovation of poetry would not have seemed so visionary an objective. With these poems we arrive at the high water mark of Watts's evangelical verse.

In prosody Watts rebelled against the Neo-classic tradition. Even before Pope reached his maturity as a poet, Watts had written against the dominance of the all-powerful rhymed-couplet:

In the poems of heroic measure I have attempted in rhyme the same variety of cadence, comma and period, which blank verse glories in as its peculiar elegance and ornament. It degrades the excellency of the best versification when the lines run on by couplets, twenty together, just in the same pace, and with the same pauses. It spoils the noblest pleasure of the sound: The reader is tired with the tedious uniformity, or charmed to sleep with the unmanly softness of the numbers, and the perpetual chime of even cadences.[54]

In his *Reliquiae Juveniles*[55] Watts gave rules for avoiding this "too constant regularity." He suggested the use of a happy intermixture of spondees and trochees and double-rhymes, though he advised against the latter for serious poetry.[56]

With the "sweet Cowley" as master, Watts had been taken as a school-boy with the "Pindarick folly", and he never relinquished the form. He seemed to think that Pindarics were especially suited to express sublimity of thought, and in most of his poems dealing with the theory of divine poetry he used the measure.[57] "Two Happy Rivals, Devotion and the Muse" is intended to describe Watts's own Pindaric song:

> Wild as the lightning, various as the moon,
>   Roves my *Pindaric* song:
> Here she glows like burning noon
>   In fiercest flames, and here she plays

> Gentle as star-beams on the midnight seas:
>> Now in a smiling angel's form,
>> Anon she rides upon the storm,
> Loud as the noisy thunder, as a deluge strong,
>> Are my thoughts and wishes free,
> And know no number nor degree?
>> Such is the muse: Lo, she disdains
>> The links and chains,
>> Measures and rules of vulgar strains,
> And o'er the laws of harmony, a sov'reign
>> queen she reigns.[58]

Even in the use of Pindarics, Watts is unconventional, for he tells us that he has imitated the short line of the ancients rather than the long line, especially in the concluding verse, of modern imitators. He then adds:

In these the ear is the truest judge; nor was it made to be inslaved to any precise model of elder or later times.

In his study of the English ode Dr. Shuster finds Watts a disciple not only of Cowley but of Dryden as well, and he points out that Watts's remarks concerning the shortened last line come from the preface of Dryden's *Sylvae*. To Shuster, however, Watts is the only significant religious Pindarist in the early eighteenth century.[59]

One of the most interesting metrical experiments in the Augustan Age was Watts's "Day of Judgment" (quoted above). Showing a healthy reaction against the chilling uniformity of the couplet, the poem is also of importance in the history of classical metres in English. It is one of very few links (the Alcaics of Milton and Marvell may be considered as such) between Sidney's efforts in the Sapphic metre and those of the nineteenth century poets. According to Enid Hamer, Watts, by substituting stress feet for the quantitative used by Campion and Sidney, ushered in the second phase in the history of classical metres in English.[60] Cowper's poem, "Lines Written During a Period of Insanity", was inspired by the piece. The Sapphic rhythms of Southey, Lamb, and the *Anti-Jacobin* were in all probability influenced by Watts's experiment.

Milton occupied an important place in Watts's mind. Watts was one of the early imitators not only of *Paradise Lost,* but also of the "Minor Poems". Havens believes Watts to be the first in the eighteenth century to give reasons for the use of Miltonic blank-verse; unfortunately the age was not ready to listen.[61] It is interesting to note that to James Ralph, writing in 1729, Milton, John Philips, Thomson, and Watts were the only writers who, in his estimation, successfully employed blank verse in narrative poems. Ralph included Watts primarily because of the "Dacian Battle" in which he felt that the latter had "performed extreamly well, and in every line deserves the character of an artist." [62] The *Horae Lyricae* contains eight poems in "easy flowing blank verse." Although all of them do not show Miltonic influence, that influence crops up so often in Watts's poems that it would be tedious to list the evidences of it. Watts had a profound respect for Milton, but he never slavishly followed him. In the Preface, he gives us his frank opinion of Milton's faults:

In the Essays without rhyme, I have not set up Milton for a perfect pattern; though he shall be for ever honoured as our deliverer from the bondage [of couplets] . . . . The length of his periods, and sometimes of his parentheses, runs me out of breath: Some of his numbers seem too harsh and uneasy. I could never believe that roughness and obscurity added anything to the true grandeur of a poem: Nor will I ever affect archaisms, exoticisms, and a quaint uncouthness of speech, in order to become perfectly Miltonian. It is my opinion that blank verse may be written with all due elevation of thought in a modern style, without borrowing any thing from Chaucer's tales, or running back so far as the days of Colin the Shepard, and the reign of the Fairy Queen.

In his *Reliquiae Juveniles* he has also an essay, "Of the Different stops and Cadences in Blank-verse," in which he acknowledges again the supremacy of Milton but gives rules whereby Milton may be improved. One notes that Watts considers Milton "the parent and author of blank-verse among us." Milton is Watts's "Adventurous Muse" who

> Pursues an unattempted course,
> Breaks all critics' iron chains,
> And bears to paradise the raptur'd mind.

Watts's own blank verse is felt by some scholars to be a new departure:

This is a sort of blank verse hitherto unknown in England. It is not epic like Milton's or dramatic like that of Shakespeare and that of his successors. It is lyrical and meditative blank verse of the kind that was to be developed so brilliantly by Cowper and Wordsworth.[63]

It is at its best in short reflective poems like the "Epistle to Sarissa":

> Farewell, ye waxing, and ye waning moons,
> That we have watch'd behind the flying clouds
> On night's dark hill, or setting or ascending,
> Or in meridian height: Then silence reign'd
> O'er half the world; then ye beheld our tears,
> Ye witness'd our complaints, our kindred grones,
> (Sad harmony!) while with your beamy horns,
> Or richer orb ye silver'd o'er the green
> Where trod our feet, and lent a feeble light
> To mourners.

In the *Divine Songs* (1715) we find a treasure-house of all the metres not expected in the eighteenth century. There are anapaests, trochees, and feminine rhymes. There are mixtures of feminine and masculine endings, as in "A Cradle Hymn," and an impressive mixture of stanzaic forms. In Watts's poetry one finds blank verse, Pindarics, Sapphics, run-on couplets; ten, eight, and seven syllable couplets; triplets; and all the various typical quatrains: the eight and six and eight and eight, and double eight and six. Saintsbury's estimate of Watts's prosodic experiments is a terse but favorable summation: "In short, he has variety, and he has craftsmanship." [64]

The imagery of Watts reflects his peculiar mission in the field of poetry. As one would expect from his advice in the Preface to *Horae Lyricae,* the Bible was an important influence. Watts's work with metrical Psalms and scriptural hymns created in his poetic consciousness a reservoir of Biblical imagery and phraseology upon which he drew spontaneously. He was also particularly adept at changing Bible verses into metre. For instance the famous "Sluggard:"

> Tis the voice of the Sluggard; I heard him complain,
> "You have wak'd me too soon, I must slumber again."
> As the door on its hinges, so he on his bed,
> Turns his sides, and his shoulders, and his heavy head.

was made up of the following verses from the *Proverbs* of Solomon: xxvi:14, "As the door turneth . . ."; vi:10, "A little more sleep . . ."; xxiv:30, "I went by the field . . ."; and xxc:33, "Yet a little sleep, a little slumber, a little folding of the hands to sleep."

Miltonic imagery occurs usually in the blank verse and Pindaric poems of Watts. Phrases like "of brightness inexpressible," "the tangles of Amira's hair," and "hasty fate thrust her dread shears" abound. Watts tended to associate Miltonic imagery, like the Pindaric form, with the sublime in poetry.

Watts was well-read in seventeenth century literature; and though I cannot trace images to any one poet other than Milton, the following lines do show a belated metaphysical tendency:

> On the thin air, without a prop,
>   Hang fruitful showers around:
> At thy command they sink and drop
>   Their fatness on the ground;

and these:

> Our eyes the radiant saint pursue
> Through liquid telescopes of tears;

and these:

> When I within myself retreat,
> I shut my doors against the great;
> My busy eye-balls inward roll,
> And there with wide survey I see
> All the wide theatre of me.

But the characteristic imagery of Watts's poetry comes from that body of pious discourse which was the common property and language of the churchgoer, the popular preacher, the emblem-writer, and the popular tract-writer. Made up of Biblical phraseology mingled with evangelical theological commentary, it was a discourse that dealt concretely and emotionally with the vanity of life, death, judgment, the machinery of salvation, and the world to come. It spoke to the pious in images that had become highly conventionalized through generations of use.

Watts's evangelical poetry contains too many of these familiar images. The soul is forever taking an "awful chariot" or making "a daring flight" to a "mansion in the sky." Heaven is "my home," and "my native land," and a "celestial seat." The flesh is a "weak cottage," "a cage," or "prison walls." The world is a "mole-hill," "a stage of clay," a "bubble or a dust." Men are "mortal worms," "degenerate worms," and "despicable worms." And the gospel is a "golden chain" which saves man from the "unfathomable sea" of death. There are many variants of these and similar images. Watts seldom startles us with new and unexpected analogies. His practice reminds one of Johnson's dictum concerning the "perpetual repetition" which tended to occur in devotional poetry because of the "paucity of its topics."

Before attempting a final evaluation of Watts as a poet, we must reverse the medal and see him in his bad moments. He is an uneven poet and can sink, not often to be sure, but occasionally, to frightful depths of bathos. For example, it is hard to surpass in poetic bad taste the following lines:

> In limbs of clay tho' she [the soul] appears,
> Array'd in rosy skin, and decked with eyes and ears.

It is difficult to believe that the same person wrote the following charming verses:

> I've a mighty part within
> That the world hath never seen,
> Rich as Eden's happy ground,
> And with choicer plenty crown'd:
> Here on all the shining boughs
> Knowledge fair and useful grows;
> On the same young flow'ry tree
> All the seasons you may see;
> Notions in the bloom of light,
> Just disclosing to the sight;
> Here are thoughts of larger growth,
> Rip'ning into solid truth; . . .

It has been customary to accuse Watts of carelessness in his rhymes. Noting that he rhymed divine—sin, steal—will, cradle—stable, feed—bed, scenes—pen, dumb—room, suns—once, bestows—lose, stand—man, sport—dirt, boughs—grows, and growth—truth, some critics, classifying them all simply as false rhymes, have dismissed them as a part of Watts's indifference to such niceties. Others with more discrimination have pointed out that many of these so-called bad rhymes were admitted in Watts's day and are to be found in Pope as well as in Watts. But no one, to my knowledge, has suggested that Watts was deliberately using imperfect rhyme, assonance, and suspended rhyme for a wider range of effect. I cannot believe that he was indifferent to niceties of rhyme and metre. He knew too much about them and wrote too discriminatingly on them to be careless in such matters. And these "slips" occur too often to be mere carelessness. In the twelve-line passage quoted above there are three suspended rhymes. This seems too frequent to be accidental.

Though one finds a considerable number of assonant and imperfect rhymes in his works, Watts seems particularly fond of suspended rhyme. Usually considered a modern departure, suspended rhyme is found in Shakespeare, Marlowe and other Elizabethans as well as in the contemporary work of Spender, Elinor Wylie, and MacLeish. The latter poets, like Watts, vary effectively the suspended with the perfect rhyme. The technique of Auden, though exaggerated almost beyond recognition, is essentially akin to that of Watts. And the same may also be said of Emily Dickinson, in whom some critics find echoes of Watts.

But to return to the blemishes—perhaps Watts's most glaring fault is the poetic frowsiness into which he allows the Pindaric stanza to carry him on two or three occasions. The poem on Gouge is the best known example. The forced enthusiasm in these instances results in turgidity. His striving leaves the reader cold, and his heightened style becomes the false sublime. This is by no means the rule with his Pindarics, but a few bombastic examples have been weapons for derisive critics.

Watts's range was limited, but he was good within these limits. His diction was simple, pure, and singularly free of eighteenth century conventional phraseology. He possessed unusual metrical skill. He had fervor, but it was usually held within the bounds of good taste. On three great themes—God's Majesty, the heart of a Christian touched by the love of Christ, and the world to come—he sang in graceful verse sometimes with the religious emotion of a George Herbert, sometimes with the amorous imagination of a Crashaw, and always with the sincerity of a devout believer. He was at his best in short lyrics in which a single emotion of the Christian's heart is portrayed.

Watts's efforts to renovate poetry made little impression

upon the polite writers of the age; and in the Preface to *Reliquiae Juveniles* (1734), we find a pathetic admission of his failure as a poet:

> I make no pretences to the name of a poet, or a polite writer, in an age wherein so many superior souls shine in their works through this nation. Could I display the excellencies of virtue and christian piety . . . with all the beauty and glory in which Mr. Pope has set the kingdom of the Messiah . . . . Could I paint nature . . . in such strong and lively colors as Dr. Young has done; . . . I should have a better ground for a pretence to appear among the writers of verse, and do more service to the world . . . . But since I can boast of little more than an inclination and a wish that way, I must commit the provision of these amusements to such celebrated authors as I have mentioned, and to the rising genius's of the age: . . . .[65]

This statement compared with the confident 1709 Preface to *Horae Lyricae* sounds like the complaint of a disillusioned old man whose youthful plans failed to mature.

Watts's position in the field of English poetry, however, is not so modest as the above Preface claims. Perdeck,[66] Draper,[67] Schöffler,[68] and Fairchild[69] have shown in their respective works that pre-romantic tendencies were kept alive during the early eighteenth century by the religiously-inclined poets. Watts was a very important member of this company who in an age of versified rhetoric wrote feelingly of inspired truth. Through him the Sapphic experiments of Sidney, the Pindarics of Cowley, and the blank verse of Milton were given fresh treatment. Through Watts the melancholy, retirement, and graveyard themes of seventeenth century poetry were transmitted to the Youngs, Blairs and Grays of the mid-eighteenth century. Through him the Platonic-Renaissance theory of "original genius" was given a new turn and a critical justification. Watts is therefore a pre-romantic figure of some little significance.

But he is above all else the poet of the still active though latent religious life which carried over from the seventeenth century to blossom in eighteenth century Methodism and Evangelicalism. He was the poet from whom

> Each heav'n-born heart shall choose a favorite ode
> To bear their morning homage to their God,
> And pay their nightly vows. These sacred themes
> Inspire the pillow with ethereal dreams:
> And oft amidst the burdens of the day
> Some devout couplet wings the soul away,
> Forgetful of this globe: . . .[70]

He put into verse the thoughts, emotions, hopes, and fears of the thousands of everyday Englishmen left outside by the religion of the Compromise. Watts was the poet of that vast army of religious persons who read poetry not as a literary exercise but for spiritual food. Colonel Gardiner expressed the attitude of this group when he wrote to Doddridge:

. . . I have been in pain these several years, lest that excellent person should be called to heaven before I had an opportunity to let him know how much his works have been blessed in me, . . . well am I acquainted with his works, especially with his psalms, hymns, and lyricks. How often, by singing some of them when by myself, on horseback and elsewhere, has the evil spirit been made to flee away, ...[71]

The poetry of Isaac Watts deserves a place in the history of English literature not only because of its intrinsic worth, but also because it is the best lyrical expression of eighteenth century evangelicalism.[72]

CHAPTER VIII

System of Praise[1]

IN 1707 Isaac Watts published *Hymns and Spiritual Songs,* the first part of his "System of Praise." The second part, *Psalms of David Imitated,* appeared in 1719. These two works inaugurated a new era in English church praise.

In this chapter I shall attempt to trace the course of Protestant church song from its beginning down to Watts, evaluate Watts's contribution to and position in the field, and show his subsequent influence. It is hardly necessary to say that my treatment will be sketchy, for it is impossible to present adequately so vast a subject in a single chapter.

The hymnody of the Protestant English church may be said to have its origin in three sources: metrical Psalms and the practice of singing them; devotional poetry; and the genius and efforts of Isaac Watts. Although not the child of Luther as is commonly supposed,[2] congregational song was born of the forces making for the Reformation. Luther, however, because of his love for music, gave great impetus to the movement and there soon sprang up in Germany a tradition of hymn-singing.[3] On the other hand, Calvin, disliking the music of the old church because the "composures" were too human in origin, inclined to favor scriptural songs. Consequently, there started with Calvin a tradition of church Psalmody based upon the Latin Psalter. The Protestant churches of England and Scotland became Psalm-singing churches, and the practice, becoming fixed through the years, prevented the introduction of hymns into the service. For two and one half centuries these two divergent streams—the German hymn-singing and the English-Scotch Psalm-singing—went side by side. It was Watts who finally won the English over to the German practice.

Let us trace briefly the development of English hymnody from the first source. Working under the strict influence of Calvin, the early English-Scotch translators of the Psalms apparently strove to achieve "purity" above all else. Their insistence upon an almost literal transcription of the language of the Bible resulted in works like Sternhold and Hopkins' *The Whole Booke of Psalmes* (1562) in England, *The Bay Psalm Book* (1640) in America, and *Rous's Version* (1642) in Scotland.[4] It would be difficult to find poetry more uninspired than that written by some of the early Psalm translators, but their versions were officially adopted and remained in use for over two hundred years.

Almost from the beginning, however, polite churchgoers were repelled by the ungainliness of the official versions. Many efforts were made by late sixteenth and early seventeenth century poets to replace Sternhold and Hopkins with a version that was esthetically more satisfactory. George Sandys, James I, and George Wither were among those who produced improved versions of the Psalms, but their works did not obtain popular acceptance. George Wither even secured a letter-patent from the king ordering his *Psalms of David Translated in Lyrick Verse* (1632) to be bound with every Bible issued in England, but the people were not ready for such a version and simply refused it. It was almost a century and a half after Sternhold and Hopkins' first edition that any replacement of their version was accepted.

In 1696 Tate and Brady published *A New Version of the Psalms of David*. With the official recommendation of William III, this work became popular in London and in the metropolitan area, but it was still not accepted by the country at large. William Beveridge, Lord Bishop of St. Asaph, voiced the protest of the average churchgoer that the work was too poetic. But Tate and Brady had taken in their version the first step towards hymn-making. Breaking with the tradition of purity, they established the use of the Psalm-paraphrase.

The next step—the accommodation of the scriptural text of the Psalms to the worshippers in the translator's own age— was taken by John Patrick, "Preacher to the Charter-House, London." Patrick's work, *A Century of Select Psalms and Portions of Psalms of David, especially those of Praise* (1679), was the first to evangelize the Royal Psalmist. Patrick made free use of the language and ideas of Christianity in his paraphrases. He also selected Psalms and portions of Psalms to suit the purposes of Christian worship. In these innovations Patrick was definitely a forerunner of Watts, but the latter went much further in the evangelization of David. In the preface to the *Psalms of David Imitated,* Watts freely admitted his indebtedness to the Charter-House preacher.[5] He also borrowed lines and complete stanzas from the latter's works. In our survey, Patrick occupies the middle ground between metrical Psalm translation and hymn-writing.

The third and final step in the development that we are tracing is the making of scriptural songs, that is, songs which are not paraphrases or accommodations of the Psalms only, but of any part of the Bible. Nineteen such songs ("Veni Creator," "Nunc Dimittis," etc.) were appended to the 1562 edition of Sternhold and Hopkins, but as they were not used, they were dropped from later editions. Coming from the old church, these hymns, though translated into English, were considered too papist to use. The practice of making such songs for devotional use had been discarded entirely by the translators of Psalms. In 1659, however, William Barton, vicar of St. Martins, Leicester, published *A Century of Select Hymns,*[6] which was largely influential in re-establishing the practice of making scriptural songs. Barton's method was interesting; he selected passages from all parts of the Bible, joining two or more together to make a hymn. Beside each verse he put the "proof text" to show that the work was scriptural in origin. From this practice to the making of free hymns is but a short step. Barton helped to "fix the type and character of the English hymn as based upon Scripture and saturated with it." [7]

Summarizing briefly, we find that the poets in revolt against the literary ineptness of the pure Psalm-translations turned to paraphrasing. Paraphrase led to accommodation and evangelization. The making of scriptural songs followed naturally. We have also noted that two of these important advances in hymnody originated not with Watts but with Patrick and Barton.

The second source of the English hymn, its evolution from devotional poetry, is not so well-defined in its progress as the first. The writers who contributed to this development were in many cases unaware that they were helping to create a new type of devotional poem. The custom and tradition of Psalm-singing so dominated the minds of the Elizabethan writers that any verses made for the purposes of worship automatically took the form of Psalm-paraphrase. To writers like Spenser and Milton, the hymn was a religious ode, often very elaborate in its verse form. They did not think of the hymn in terms of public praise.

Many poets of the late sixteenth and first quarter of the seventeenth centuries—Jonson, Campion, Donne, Davies, Gascoigne, and the Fletchers—wrote devotional verse. But their works were usually personal and meditative, and though often set to music were not designed to be sung in public worship. In spite of their intention, however, some of their poems were simple enough in structure and in idea to be regarded as true hymns. For instance, Jonson's "Hymn on the Nativity of my Saviour" and Phineas Fletcher's "Drop, drop, slow tears" are still to be found in hymnals. Such devotional verse thus unintentionally helped to establish the hymn-type. One of these writers, Dr. Thomas Campion, had some concept of the function of the hymn. His *Two Bookes of Ayres* (c. 1612) may, with some extension of the term, be called an early hymn book.

The same comment may be made concerning the devotional poets of the second quarter of the seventeenth century—Quarles, Herbert, Crashaw, Traherne, and Vaughan. Practically all wrote devotional verse which is now included in the various hymnals, but they were unable to conceive of the hymn as poetry for public worship. The Psalm-singing tradition was still too deeply ingrained.

George Wither was the first Pre-Restoration devotional poet to show a definite consciousness of the function and purpose of the hymn.[8] His *Hymns and Songs of the Church* (1623) comprised two parts, the first consisting of scriptural paraphrases, the second of hymns for festivals, holidays, and special church occasions. These hymns of Wither "show a remarkable appreciation of the office and character of the Hymn, in their tone of simple piety, their method and structure." [9]

Wither secured a patent from James I which allowed his work to be bound with each copy of the *Psalter* issued. The Stationers Company, resenting this privilege, soon caused its withdrawal, but aside from this, the work was not accepted. It was too far in advance of the age. The hymns were read, however, as devotional poetry and had considerable influence upon later writers in this field. In 1707 Watts borrowed from at least two of Wither's hymns, deriving "Thee we adore eternal name" from the latter's "Behold the sun," and "A Cradle Hymn" *(Divine Songs)* from Wither's "Lullaby." [10]

After the Restoration a reaction against the metrical Psalm set in because of its Puritan association. As a consequence the Catholic element in the High Church was able to revive some interest in the breviaries, primers, and Latin hymns of the Roman Church and to encourage the writing of devotional poetry. Among the first influential devotional poets of the age was Samuel Crossman, Dean of Bristol, who produced in 1664

The Young Man's Monitor to which was added *The Young Man's Meditation, or some sacred Poems upon select Subjects and Scriptures.* Although Crossman felt that they would be read rather than sung, these poems are in Psalm metres and are definitely hymns.[11] John Austin, an Anglican who turned Catholic, was another important devotional poet. He published in Paris *Devotions, in the Ancient way of Offices: with Psalms, Hymns and Prayers: for every day in the week, and every holiday in the year* (1668). Original save for two or three hymns by Crashaw, this work was later instrumental in the fight to introduce hymns into the Church of England. It was reprinted as late as 1856.

Thomas Ken,[12] nonjuring bishop and author of the well-known doxology, "Praise God from whom all blessings flow," had been educated at Winchester College under the Puritan regime and returned there as an official in 1665. Ken published in 1694[13] *A Manual of Prayers for the Use of the Scholars of Winchester College* in which he inserted hymns to be sung mornings and evenings in the students' chambers. These hymns were not based upon Puritan precedents but were suggested by the models of the breviary. Though Ken's influence in the field of hymnody was not outstanding, the *Manual* was popular, and its hymns, which showed a marked tendency towards simplicity, helped in some measure to prepare the way for Watts.

Richard Baxter also played a minor part in this movement. He left an unfinished version of the Psalms, and his *Poetical Fragments* (1681) contain several original hymns intended for public singing. Though insignificant as a hymn-writer, Baxter was of importance in influencing men like Barton and Mason to write hymns. His name also lent prestige to the movement.

John Mason, rector of Water-Stratford, was probably better known and more influential than his fellow-Churchman Ken. In 1683 he published *Spiritual Songs, or Songs of Praise to Almighty God upon several Occasions. Together with the*

Song of Songs . . . paraphrased in English Verse. Mason's songs of praise were "free composures", written in common metre, and numbered as in a hymn book. The work, which was in its eighth edition when Watts's *Hymns* appeared, had a considerable influence on the latter; and Mason must be given some credit for helping to mold and to popularize the English hymn.[14]

These poets and others[15] of lesser importance in the field must be considered the predecessors of Isaac Watts and not his rivals. Their work in hymnody was tentative. Although they were moving in the right direction, their objective was not sufficiently visualized. Hymns are liturgical in essence and not literary; these writers placed too much emphasis upon the latter quality. It was not until the appearance of *Hymns and Spiritual Songs* (1707) that the type of the English hymn was definitely fixed. But the work of the devotional poets not only furnished Watts with themes and lines; it also helped to prepare the public mind for his later conquest.

Before considering Isaac Watts, I must comment on another movement which helped to make his success possible—the effort to introduce into the various churches the practice of hymn-singing. The years from 1662 to 1707 saw several important figures engaged in this endeavor. John Playford, prominent London music publisher and clerk of the Temple Church, and his son, Henry Playford, both tried, though with little success, to place hymn-singing in the Anglican service. Their books were never used regularly, but they are interesting examples of early hymnal publishing.[16] The *Supplement to the New Version of Psalms* by Dr. Brady and Mr. Tate, published in 1700, contained sixteen hymns. Authorized by the Queen in 1703, the *Supplement* became popular, but there is no evidence that the inserted hymns were frequently used. Benson, however, feels that they helped to "establish the principle that hymns were allowable as supplementary to the Psalms."[17] Among the Presbyterians Richard Baxter and Matthew Henry (a friend of Watts) tried to foster the practice of hymn-singing; they also were too far advanced for the masses of their denomination.

The Baptists, especially the Particular Baptists,[18] played an interesting part in the movement to introduce hymn-singing. In an epistle which he sent to his churches in Wales, Vavasor Powell advocated public singing even before the Restoration.[19] Professor Tindall asserts that Bunyan, like Powell and Keach, campaigned for years in the cause of hymn-singing. He touched on the issue in several pamphlets, but *Pilgrim's Progress* "afforded Bunyan an opportunity, which he embraced with enthusiasm, of enlightening the conservative by the introduction of occasional verses, many of them in hymn meter. These songs of *Pilgrim's Progress,* one of the most apparent features of the book, are to be interpreted not as the overflow of literary high spirits but as propaganda for church singing."[20] A split in Bunyan's church over the matter of singing was not compromised until 1691 (after Bunyan's death), when it was decided that those who were conscientiously opposed to song could either remain silent or wait in the vestibule until the singing was over.[21]

Benjamin Keach is usually given credit for introducing singing among the Particular Baptists. The first to substitute the hymn for the metrical song in the service, Keach had started his campaign around 1673;[22] by 1690 his congregation in Southwark was singing hymns every Lord's-Day. Though violently attacked by members of his own group, Keach laid the foundation for Baptist hymn-singing.

Joseph Stennett carried on the work begun by Keach. By 1690 he too was circulating manuscript copies of hymns in his meeting. His first hymnal was published in 1697, *Hymns in Commemoration of the Sufferings of our Blessed Saviour Jesus Christ, composed for the Celebration of his Holy Supper.* Watts probably did not think highly of the efforts of Bunyan and Keach in divine poetry,[23] but he appropriated several lines from

14

Stennett and used him as a model in the renovation of church
song. The simplicity in verse and the direct appeal through
imagery and content to the lower classes as exemplified in this
early Baptist divine poetry probably contributed more to
Watts's hymn style than he himself realized. The same sort of
appeal, though on a higher plane, is found in Watts's works.[24]

In spite of individual successes like those mentioned above,
there was not much hymn-singing among the Baptists. The
same was true among the Independents; single churches
adopted hymn-singing but the practice was generally frowned
upon. Sporadic as they were, however, all of these efforts helped
to make men conscious of the growing importance of the hymn
in public worship.

Thus by 1707 the stage had been set for the entrance of a
genius who could capitalize the partial success of the efforts
to foster hymn-singing and, at the same time, unite the two
streams of church song—the metric Psalm and devotional
poetry. The age found such a genius. As Dr. Benson has stated:

> With the work of Isaac Watts . . . a new epoch began in Eng-
> lish church song. Behind it was a great personality, clear of vision,
> fertile of resource, dominant in leadership. And no small part of
> his equipment was his youthfulness. He planned and began his
> work in the ardor of youth, its singleness of conviction, its pref-
> erence of radical remedies over compromise, its comparative dis-
> regard of other people's feelings.[25]

When Watts "in the ardor of youth" began his renovation
of congregational song, he found that most of the churches
sang only metrical Psalms and these in the Sternhold and Hopkins or some similar pure version; the singing was in the
hands of a precentor, usually not a person versed in music; the
whole book of Psalms was gone through in sequential order
without regard for special occasions or conditions. There were
only a few tunes—some churches used only three—to which the
Psalms were set. The Psalms were "lined out" by the precentor.

The whole procedure was reduced to a drab, uninspired meaningless ritual.

Enoch Watts's letter to his brother Isaac gives an excellent picture of the condition of congregational song:

Dear Brother,

In your last you discovered an inclination to oblige the world by showing it your hymns in print; and I heartily wish, as well for the satisfaction of the public as myself, that you were something more than inclinable thereunto. I have frequently importuned you to it before now, and your invention has often furnished you with some modest reply to the contrary, as if what I urge was only the effect of a rash and inconsiderate fondness to a brother; but you will have other thoughts of the matter when I first assure you that that affection, which is inseparable from our near relationship, would have had in me a very different operation, for instead of pressing you to publish, I should with my last efforts have endeavoured the concealment of them, if my best judgment did not direct me to believe it highly conducing to a general benefit, without the least particular disadvantage to yourself. This latter I need not have mentioned, for I am very confident whoever has the happiness of reading your hymns (unless he be either sot or atheist), will have a very favourable opinion of their author; so that, at the same time you contribute to the universal advantage, you will procure the esteem of men the most judicious and sensible.

In the second place you may please to consider, how very mean the performers in this kind of poetry appear in the pieces already extant. Some ancient ones I have seen in my time, who flourished in Hopkins and Sternhold's reign, but Mason now reduces this kind of writing to a sort of yawning indifferency, and honest Barton chimes us asleep. There is, therefore, great need of a (pen),[26] vigorous and lively as yours, to quicken and revive the dying devotion of the age, to which nothing can afford such assistance as poetry, contrived on purpose to elevate us even above ourselves. . . .

And as for those modern gentlemen, who have lately exhibited their version of the Psalms; all of them I have not seen I confess, and, perhaps, it would not be worth while to do it, unless I had a mind to play the critic, which you know is not my talent; but those I have read, confess to me a vast deference to yours, though they are done by persons of no mean credit. Dr. Patrick most certainly has the report of a very learned man, and, they say, understands the Hebrew extremely well, which indeed capacitates him for a translator, but he is thereby never the more enabled to versify. Tate and Brady still keep near the same pace. I know not what sober beast they ride (one that will be content to carry double), but I am sure it is no Pegasus: there is in them a mighty deficiency of that life and soul, which is necessary to raise our fancies and kindle and fire our passions, and something or other they have to allege against the rest of adventurers; but I have been persuaded a great while since, that were David to speak English, he would choose to make use of your style. If what I have said seems to have no weight with you, yet you cannot be ignorant of what a load of scandal lies on the dissenters, only for their imagined aversion to poetry. You remember what Dr. Speed says:

> 'So far hath schism prevail'd, they hate to see
> Our lines and words in couplings to agree,
> It looks too like abhorr'd conformity:
> A hymn, so soft, so smooth, so neatly drest,
> Savours of human learning and the beast.'

And perhaps, it has been thought there were some grounds for his aspersion from the admired poems of Ben. Keach, John Bunyan, etc., all flat and dull as they are; nay, I am much out if the latter has not formerly made much more ravishing music with his hammer and brass kettle.

Now when yours are exposed to the public view, these calumnies will immediately vanish, which methinks, should be a motive not the least considerable . . . .[27]

Note that although Enoch urges his brother to publish a volume of hymns, he is also highly dissatisfied with the Psalms then in popular use. In 1700 Watts had done more work on his hymns than on his Psalm-versions. The latter task, however, he considered the more important of the two, for he realized that only a renovated Psalmody could prepare the way for hymnody. Let us then consider first the *Psalms of David Imitated* although it was published after the hymns.

The primary cause of the general dissatisfaction with the Psalmody in his day, Watts felt, was the non-Christian content of the versions then in use:

I have long been convinced, that one great occasion of this evil arises from the matter and words to which we confine all our Songs. Some of 'em are almost opposite to the spirit of the gospel: many of them are foreign to the state of the New-Testament and widely different from the present circumstances of christians.[28]

The Psalms of David Imitated in the Language of the New Testament, and applied to the Christian State and Worship answered the challenge implied in this criticism. In order to Christianize the Psalms, Watts carried to their logical conclusion the innovations of Tate and Brady and Patrick. He omitted whole Psalms that did not lend themselves to his Christian purpose; he left out parts of others. Evangelical and New Testament themes were introduced in the place of the "dark sayings" of David. He changed the names of Judah and Israel to England and Scotland and the names of Jewish kings to those of Great Britain. The pious reader was probably shocked to find his Psalm 147:

> Praise ye the Lord: for it is good to
> sing praises unto our God; . . . .
> The Lord doth build up Jerusalem:
> he gathered together the outcasts of Israel; . . .

changed to "A Song for Great Britain":

> O Britain, praise thy mighty God,
> And make his honours known abroad;
> He bid the ocean round thee flow;
> Not bars of brass could guard thee so.

Watts's preface to *The Psalms of David Imitated* was just as daring as the imitations. With spirit he tells the reader that he, Isaac Watts, a Christian, knows far more about salvation than David could have possibly known. As a sort of parting challenge, he invites the reader to look in his *Hymns and Spiritual Songs* for any thought or attitude not expressed in the present work. It is hard in our age to conceive the anger aroused among the orthodox by such a stand.[29]

Psalms of David Imitated contains one hundred and thirty-eight of the one hundred and fifty Psalms. Many are translated into several different metres, and the preface gives specific directions concerning the singing of them.[30] The work also contains critical notes, often in the first person, telling from whom Watts borrowed or why he used a certain word or phrase. The work—preface and content—reveals that Watts knew the subject of Psalmody intimately. His approach showed not only a scholarly mind but a deep understanding of the forces which would work against acceptance of his version.

He had toiled over nineteen years on this work. We do not know when he began; but by 1700, as the letter from Enoch attests, he had already finished a number of Psalms. He included four in *Horae Lyricae* (1706) and fourteen in *Hymns and Spiritual Songs* (1707). In 1717 he sent some of his imitations in manuscript to Cotton Mather for comment or criticism, and in 1719 the great work appeared. Watts was confident that his work was good. The conclusion of the preface contains a degree of justifiable smugness:

Though there are many gone before me, who have taught the Hebrew psalmist to speak English, yet I think I may assume this pleasure of being the first who hath brought down the royal author into the common affairs of the christian life, and led the psalmist of Israel into the church of Christ, without anything of a jew about him.[31]

Watts's efforts to introduce hymns and hymn-singing were

so closely connected with his work on the Psalms that it is difficult to separate the two. But certain problems not found in revising the Psalms were presented by the introduction of hymns. Hymns were purely man-made; the Psalms, even in imitations, had a basis of inspiration. Moreover, metrical Psalm-singing was an established practice in the churches; hymns had yet to make their way. Realizing the difficulty of his task, Watts appended to the first edition of *Hymns and Spiritual Songs* an "Essay towards the Improvement of Psalmody" in which he reviews all of the objections to hymns. He vindicates the making and using of hymns on five counts: one, since a Psalm properly translated for Christian use is no longer an inspired work, it is just as lawful to use other scriptural thoughts for spiritual songs; two, the end of Psalmody demands songs to respond to God's revelation of Himself in all ages; therefore God's revelation of Christ must also be sung; three, the Scriptures—Eph. V: 19-20 and Col. III: 16-17—command us to sing with "spiritual songs" and hymns unto the Lord; four, Psalms, as they are in the Bible, do not provide for all the occasions, shades, and nuances of Christian experience; and, five, the primitive "Gifts of the Spirit" covered preaching, prayer, and song. If one has to acquire the art of preaching, why not that of making and practicing the art of song?

Watts probably spent twelve years writing the hymns included in *Hymns and Spiritual Songs*. Tradition tells us that the first hymn in that work, "Behold the glories of the Lamb", was composed in 1694-5 in protest against the ugliness of praise in his father's church. We know from Enoch's letter that Watts by 1700 had completed a number of hymns. *Horae Lyricae* (1706) contains twenty-five hymns. In the preface to the latter work Watts tells the reader that there are two hundred similar pieces ready for publication if the public wants them. *Hymns and Spiritual Songs,* published in 1707, contains two hundred and ten hymns in addition to several doxologies.

Arranged to suit as many tastes as possible, the work contains seventy-eight paraphrases, twenty-two communion hymns, and one hundred and ten "free composures." Three metres are used—long, common, and short. And the hymns are written down to the "level of vulgar capacities." In order not to disturb the devotions of weaker intellects, Watts "wilfully effaced" many of the lines.[32]

During the process of composition, he invited criticism of his pieces. A letter to his friend Samuel Say describes his manner of revision:

The method I took was, to collect all the remarks together, that several friends had made by word or letter, and got a friend or two together, and spent a whole day in perusing and considering the remarks; . . . .[33]

The second edition of *Hymns and Spiritual Songs* (1709)[34] shows the result of such a thorough-going revision. About fifty of the original lines were altered; one hundred and forty-five new hymns added; and many improvements in phraseology and imagery effected. After this edition, Watts made no further changes in the work. Of the hymns appearing later in *Sermons* (1721), (1723), (1729), in *Reliquiae Juveniles* (1734), and in *Remnants of Time* (1753), none was added to *Hymns and Spiritual Songs*.[35] He sold the copyright to the work presumably in 1709.[36]

The "System of Praise" was completed in 1719, when Watts was in his forty-sixth year. He felt that his work in church song was sufficient to "answer most occasions of the Christian life." It was with satisfaction that he wrote in 1720:

And, if an Author's own Opinion may be taken, he esteems it the greatest Work that ever he has publish'd, or ever hopes to do, for the use of the churches.[37]

And Watts had reason to be proud of his achievement, for he had done an excellent job. He understood more clearly than any before him the possibilities and limitations of church song.

Knowing his audience as few writers ever knew theirs, he set to work to edify that audience. At an early period in his career, he discovered that the key to universal acceptance was the reproduction of the thoughts, desires, aspirations, and hopes of the humblest Protestant Christian. He tells us in the Preface to *Hymns and Spiritual Songs* that he wrote down to the capacity of the most humble; he "aim'd at ease of numbers and smoothness of sound, and endeavoured to make the sense plain and obvious." He adds that if the verses often seem feeble he has labored to make them so by throwing out lines that were "too sonorous" and purposely spoiling the beauty of others. He wants nothing in these hymns that will in any wise disturb the devotion of the "weakest souls." And in carrying out this design, he omitted many pieces originally written for the work because they were too poetic. He put them in later editions of *Horae Lyricae,* which was written for the "politer part of mankind."

This democratic purpose accounts for the form, the imagery, and the themes of Watts's hymns. Far too practical to adopt many new forms, he improved within the limits of the old. He realized that enough opposition would be aroused by the use of hymns themselves. His concern with the "meanest capacities" also made him avoid all excess baggage of intricate form as well as of poetical adornment. Watts's hymns generally follow a simple pattern. The opening line is striking and appealing: "Our God, our help in ages past." This line sets the tone of the complete poem. The hymn progresses swiftly from the opening to a strong climax:

> Be thou our guide while life shall last,
> And our eternal home!

The whole hymn usually contains but one evangelical idea; metre, diction, and imagery all subserve this theme. Each hymn becomes therefore an epitome of some important Christian thought. The net result of these practical considerations made

for the permanently simple, but satisfying poetic form of the
English hymn. John Julian thinks that Watts's place in
hymnody is to be "estimated by his enduring influence on the
structure of our hymns." [38]

The imagery of Watts's hymns is largely scriptural in
origin.[39] Many of his pieces are simply verse transcriptions of
the better known and often quoted evangelical passages found
in the *Epistles, Isaiah, Revelation,* and the *Psalms.* For instance,
Rev. xiv: 13:

And I heard a voice from heaven saying unto me, Write, Blessed
are the dead which die in the Lord from henceforth: Yea saith the
Spirit, that they may rest from their labours; . . . .

becomes in *Hymns and Spiritual Songs*:

> Hear what the voice from heav'n proclaims
>   For all the pious dead,
> Sweet is the savour of their names
>   And soft their resting bed.

In his hymns Watts uses the language and figures made common to pious Protestants of his day by the pulpit and by two
centuries of metrical Psalms. Even when he becomes (to us)
quaintly physical as in the following passage:

> Blessed are the men whose bowels move
> And melt with sympathy and love,

he is still using Biblical language. This scriptural flavor accounted in large measure for the widespread acceptance of
his works. The secret of his appeal was that he expressed, in
phraseology and images already a part of the heritage of the
average Protestant, the various experiences of religious life so
lucidly, that the pious found in Watts's lines a mirror to their
own thoughts.[40]

The themes of the hymns were likewise such as all orthodox
Protestant Christians of Watts's day could accept. There were
a few pieces on "Hell, or, the Vengeance of God," [41] "Divine

Wrath and Mercy," "Original Sin, or, the First and Second Adam," "Justification by Faith, not Works" and "Election Sovereign and Free" that would repel the too sensitive Churchman; but even a superficial reading of Watts's work will show that such hymns are rare. The typical themes of the hymns are "The Shortness and Misery of Life," "The Holy Scriptures," "The Invitation of the Gospel," "The Excellency of the Christian Religion," "The Strength of Christ's Love," "The Redemption by Christ," "The Triumph over Death," and "The Blessed Society in Heaven." His characteristic theme was Christ's suffering and dying for sinful men. He sang primarily of the saving power of the Christian faith and the joys of the saints in this world and in the world to come. Avoiding controverted points of Christianity, he took the common ground of Protestant belief, and, in the words of Benson:

He produced a whole cycle of religious song which his own ardent faith made devotional, which his manly and lucid mind made simple and strong, which his poetic feeling and craftsmanship made rhythmical and often lyrical, and which his sympathy with the people made hymnic [42]

In a work of this sort it is difficult to discuss adequately the musical element of Watts's hymns, but since hymns must be sung, and since the use of a hymn depends to a large extent upon the tune to which it is set, a word of comment is necessary. One must always remember that a fine song can come only from a fine poem; the composer cannot rise above the author. It attests the intrinsic worth of Watts's message to find that many of his best devotional poems have finally secured appropriate tunes.

Nowadays we expect every hymn to have its own tune, but in the early days of Psalm-singing three or four tunes were frequently used for the whole book of *Psalms*. This was the situation in many churches when Watts wrote *Hymns and Spiritual Songs* (1707), and it accounts for his strict adherence to the three conventional metres in this work. The tunes that were sung in church were Psalm-tunes. Watts wrote words to fit them. Inspired by these verses, church composers have from Watts's own age down to the late nineteenth century supplied music appropriate to the style and content of his poems.

The standards by which we judge a good hymn tune are few and simple. It must, first of all, be tuneful, that is, have a distinctive melody. It must be able to bear constant repetition without becoming trite. It must possess a moderate range, have few or no extreme intervals and florid counterpoint beyond the capacity of the average congregation. It must fit the poem in form (that is, accents and notes coinciding) and in spirit.

Watts's pieces have been fortunate in their tunes. They have been set to some of the noblest melodies found in our church music. Several like "I'll Praise my Maker while I've breath" (Old 113th) and "Before Jehovah's awful Throne" (Old 100th) come from the *Strasburg Psalter* (1542) and the *Geneva Psalter* (1551). Others like "Our God our help in Ages past" (St. Anne) come from composers like William Croft (1678-1727), who lived in Watts's own age. Still others like "Joy to the World" (Antioch) and "Sweet is the work" (Canonbury) have been arranged from works by great musicians like Handel and Schumann. And finally as late as the nineteenth century, composers like John B. Dykes, who supplied the tune (St. Agnes) for "Come, Holy Spirit, Heavenly Dove"; George M. Garrett, who composed the tune (Beulah) for "There is a land of pure delight"; and others have taken Watts's best poems and given them effective musical settings. In a few cases, it is possible that the tunes are now keeping alive poems whose doctrines would otherwise have sent them into oblivion.[43]

Space will not permit any extended consideration of the fortunes of the "System of Praise" among the various denominations. It is, however, a fascinating but intricate study, for reports conflict. From some we get the impression that the works were immediately popular; others give the opposite view. Extant letters from Doddridge, the Countess of Hertford, and Hervey seem to indicate that the dissenting and Evangelical congregations during Watts's lifetime received his work enthusiastically. Writing against the dominance of Wattsian Psalmody in 1755, William Romaine asked the following revealing question:

Why should Watts, or any hymnmaker not only take the precedence of the Holy Ghost, but also thrust him entirely out of the church? [44]

It is interesting to note that to Romaine, as early as 1755, Watts was symbolical of hymn-making.

But on the other hand, we have Walter Wilson, historian of the dissenters, writing in 1808 that among the Independents:

The poetry of Watts was received but slowly into most of our congregations. It is only of late years that it has acquired so general a patronage, and even in the present day there are many who prefer the rhyming of Tate and Brady, or the bald version of the Scotch. The reason is mankind are afraid of innovation, and it is only by degrees that their prejudices are loosened. [45]

The "System of Praise" made its way into each sect, church by church. There was at first no official adoption by the denominations as a whole. The more liberal churches used Watts; the more conservative tended to cling to the old Psalm versions. In some cases churches were split and ministers ousted over the issue of church song. But the editions indicate the general popularity of Watts's works. There were seven editions of the *Psalms* by 1748 (the year of Watts's death) and sixteen of the *Hymns*. The greatest aid which the "System" received came from the Methodist Revival. The Psalms and hymns of Watts (particularly the latter) rode to the dominating position they ultimately held on the wings of the Revival. One must add, however, that there was an element of reciprocity in the situation; for the eighteenth century hymns, primarily those of Isaac Watts, were one of the important aids in establishing Evangelicalism.[46]

Among the Congregationalists (eighteenth century Independents), Watts attained complete dominance by 1836. In that year Josiah Conder's *Congregational Hymn Book,* one of the church's greatest hymnals, appeared as a supplement to Watts's *Psalms and Hymns.* After the middle of the nineteenth century, the influence of Watts tended to wane in the denomination, but he dominated their hymnody so long that he fixed the evangelical tone of their hymnody.

Watts's influence among the orthodox eighteenth century Presbyterians parallels that among the Independents, for the two groups were not so clearly distinguished then as now. But among the heterodox, the hymns and Psalms of Watts became entangled in the mazes of the Unitarian Controversy. One of his earliest tilts with heterodoxy came, as we have seen, with Martin Tomkins. In the latter part of the century Priestley, Andrew Kippis, and other Unitarian hymn-writers began to "accommodate" Watts. Their efforts to free Watts's work of its Calvinism aroused a storm of protest.[47] As a result of the controversy[48] over the use and abuse of Watts, the Unitarians began writing their own hymns. By 1837 they had achieved a fine collection in John R. Beard's *A Collection of Hymns for Public and Private Use.*

Among the Anglicans,[49] Watts's influence from the beginning was connected with that of the Wesleys. The first hymn-book in the eighteenth century Church was John Wesley's *Collection of Psalms and Hymns* (Charles-town 1737). Of the seventy hymns that it contained over one-third were by Watts. The most important advances in hymn-singing in the Church, however, were made under the influence of the Evangelical Revival. The first in the series of important Evangelical hymnals was Madan's *A Collection of Songs and Hymns, Extracted from Various Authors* (1760). Watts and Wesley are naturally the most extensively represented of the "various authors." In 1776 Augustus M. Toplady published the famous *Psalms and Hymns for Public and Private Worship*. Although he added several new authors, Toplady also leaned heavily upon Watts and Wesley. The publication of the *Olney Hymns* (1779) marked the height of the Evangelical influence.

Between 1785 and 1819 the efforts of the Evangelicals to foster hymn-singing brought about the so-called "Period of Compromise" when many individual churches gave the hymns equal recognition with the Psalms. The remaining opposition to hymns among the Anglicans was brought to a head in 1819 when Thomas Cotterill attempted to force the use of his hymnal, *A Selection of Psalms and Hymns . . .* , upon his congregation at St. Pauls, Sheffield. The attendant lawsuit, which was finally decided by the Archbishop of York, left the church of England free to place hymns beside the *Book of Common Prayer* in the service.

But the years 1821 to 1850 saw the full flowering of the church's hymnody. Many new Anglican writers came into prominence and hymn-book publishing flourished as never before. Most important of all, the Oxford Movement led to the introduction of hymns translated from German and Latin. According to Julian, the dissenting element (that is, Watts and the Wesleys mainly) "which up to this period constituted nearly two-thirds of the total contents of the hymn-books in use in the Church of England, gave place, in some cases altogether, and in all cases to a very great extent, to the Latin and German, and to new hymns of a higher and more definite Church tone." [50]

In 1861 the great work *Hymns Ancient and Modern* was published. Its appearance marked the end of the Watts-Wesley domination of Anglican hymnody. Wesley, however, has fared better in the Church than Watts. The 1909 edition of *Hymns Ancient and Modern* includes twenty-five hymns by Wesley, and only nine by Watts. Wesley ranked second in the matter of contributions, Watts eleventh. Watts's Calvinism (mild as it was) and his homiletical approach both worked against a continued predominance in Anglican church song.

Watts's influence among the Baptists, especially among the Particular Baptists, was second only to that among his own group. The Baptists liked the homiletical aspect of Watts's hymns and used them as supplements to the sermon. This practice led in their own denomination to a homiletical hymnody, and one of the great Baptist hymnals, John Rippon's *A Selection of Hymns from the best Authors, intended to be an Appendix to Dr. Watts's Psalms and Hymns* (1787), shows this trend. The influence of Watts created in the early nineteenth century a "Baptist School of Watts" with a very numerous following.[51]

With such popularity among the dissenting sects[52] in the eighteenth century, it was only natural that a "School of Watts"[53] should appear. The first student in the school in point of time was Simon Browne (1680-1732). In 1720 he published *Hymns and Spiritual Songs* as a supplement to Watts's works. Doddridge (1702-51) was an early pupil and perhaps the greatest. His work was published posthumously in 1755 under the title: *Hymns founded on various texts in the Holy Scriptures*. Several of these hymns have become classics. Browne and Doddridge were members of Watts's own group —the Independents.

Among the Baptist followers of Watts, Samuel Stennett (1727-95) and Anne Steele (1716-1778) are best known. To her imitation Anne Steele added a new note of introspection. Her work, *Poems on Subjects chiefly devotional, by Theodosia* (Bristol, 1760), became very popular, and she still ranks among the foremost Baptist hymn-writers. Other members of the "School of Watts" were Thomas Gibbons, Watts's friend and biographer, President Davies of Princeton, Daniel Turning of Reading, Benjamin Wallin, Mrs. Anne Dutton, Benjamin

Beddome, John Ryland, John Fellows, John Fawcett, Richard Burham, Joseph Swain, Samuel Medley, Ralph Erskine in Scotland, Joseph Grigg, and Mrs. Barbauld.

Addison's hymns in the *Spectator* were probably inspired by Watts, although Addison did not use the latter as a model. The Wesleys were associated with Watts in perhaps the same manner. John Wesley took the hymns of Watts to Georgia and a large part of his first hymnal in 1737 consisted of Watts's material. Though both Wesleys admired Watts greatly, neither directly imitated him.

Perhaps in one sense of the word all Protestant English hymn-writers who came after Watts are of his school, because he established a definite type of hymn. "Simplicity, clarity, dignity, and melody, rich ideas about the basic matters of life and death, with strong emotion under sure control" [54] —these are the elements of a good hymn; these are the qualities possessed by the typical hymn of Watts. Because of its essential fitness, the model was easy to follow, but its utter simplicity betrayed an imitator into banality if he did not have talent. That, I am afraid, was the trouble with many of the followers of Watts.

When we come nowadays to an estimate of Watts's position as a hymn-writer, we are inclined to be less ardent than our nineteenth century ancestors. To them he was the "inventor of hymns", or as expressed by Horder:

What Ambrose was to the Latins; what Clement Marot was to the French; what Luther was to the Germans; that, and perhaps more, was Watts to the English. [55]

We know that Watts did not make any unique contribution to the hymn, but this does not detract from his position in the field. His work shows a happy meeting of man and age. He brought to the field a combination of spiritual, practical, and intellectual resources not possessed by any of his predecessors.

15

The result of the impact of his mind upon hymnody was so impressive and lasting that in a restricted sense he may be called the "Father of English hymnody."

How has Watts stood the test of time? Of the approximately seven hundred hymns which he wrote, only about twenty-five are in regular use. This may seem an extremely small percentage, but of the 6,500 written by Wesley only a similar number remains current. Most of Watts's hymns are unfit for modern services. This is to be expected, for hymn-writing is a progressive art, and each age has to find its own interpreter. But our hymnals still carry the following pieces by Watts: "Our God our help in ages past" (England's second national anthem), "Come, let us join our cheerful Songs," "Give me the wings of faith to rise," "Behold the morning sun," "High in the heavens, eternal God," "Alas! and did my Saviour bleed," "Welcome, sweet day of rest," "Jesus shall reign where'er the sun," "Sweet is the work, My God, my King," "Joy to the world, the Lord is come," "How bright these glorious spirits shine," "How beauteous are their feet," "The heavens declare thy glory, Lord," "Lo, what a glorious sight appears," "From all that dwell below the skies," "God of the morning at whose voice," "God is the refuge of his saints," "Come, dearest Lord, descend and dwell," "My soul repeat his praise," "Behold what wondrous grace," "Lord of the worlds above," "My God, my King, thy various praise," "To God the only wise," "This is the day the Lord hath made," "Come, Holy Spirit, heavenly Dove," "My God the spring of all my joys," "When I can read my title clear," "When I survey the wondrous cross" (Matthew Arnold thought this the best hymn in the language), "Am I a Soldier of the Cross," "There is a land of pure delight," and "Before Jehovah's awful throne." These hymns, and perhaps a score more not quite so popular, are still in fairly regular use.

If one were to make a graph of Watts's popularity, the line would rise steadily up to about 1865. Sixty thousand copies of

Psalms and Hymns were sold that year, and an examination of 750 hymnals made then, gave Watts two-fifths of all the hymns commonly used in the English-speaking world.[56] In 1898 an examination of 107 hymn books made by Benson to find the most popular hymns in the language showed that of the thirty-two most popular, five were by Watts (the largest number for any single writer); Wesley came next with three plus one in collaboration.[57]

The perennial quality of Watts's hymns was interestingly shown in a controversy in the columns of the New York *Herald-Tribune* for January 26 to 28, 1933. Organist Harold V. Milligan of the Riverside Baptist Church asserted that "Alas! and did my Saviour bleed" was old-fashioned and hence objectionable for modern church song. Watts-devotees heatedly attacked this statement. It is significant that after two hundred years men still become aroused over the hymns of Isaac Watts.

From a statistical point of view (and this is not the real measure of popularity), Watts ranks today very high among the hymn-writers of the English tradition. An analysis of seventeen hymnals (picked because of their recent publication and representative quality) gives the following figures: *The New Baptist Hymnal* (1926, Nashville), Watts, twenty-three hymns for first place, Wesley, fifteen for second; *The New Baptist Praise Book* (Phila., 1922), Watts, twenty-three for first place, Wesley, sixteen for second; *The Church Hymnary* (Oxford, 1927), Wesley and Neale tie for first place with twenty-three each, Watts in fifth place with sixteen;[58] *The Hymnary* (Presybterian Church of the U.S.A., Phila., 1923), Watts first with forty-nine, Wesley second with twenty-four; *The Methodist Hymnal* (New York, 1935), Wesley first with fifty-six and Watts second with eighteen; *The Congregational Hymnary* (Congregational Union of England and Wales, London, 1916), Wesley first with thirty-four, Watts second with twenty-five; *The Pilgrim Hymnal* (Boston, 1931), Wesley eleven, Watts, ten;[59] *Hymns Ancient and Modern* (London,

1909), Neale, first, with sixty-two hymns and translations, Wesley, second with twenty-five, Watts, eleventh with nine; *The English Hymnal* (Oxford, 1928), Neale first, Wesley second with twenty, and Watts third with ten; *The New Hymnal* (P. E. Church, U. S. A., 1916), Neale, thirty-three, Ellerton, nineteen, Wesley, eighteen, Montgomery, seventeen, and Watts, thirteen; *Hymns of the Spirit* (Boston, 1937), Wesley, six and Watts, five;[60] *The Oxford Hymn Book* (Clarendon Press, 1920), Wesley, twenty-nine and Watts, twenty-one; *The New Church Hymnal* (Appleton-Century, 1937), Wesley, twelve, Neale eleven, and Watts ten; *The Harvard University Hymn Book* (Cambridge, 1926), Watts sixteen and Wesley fourteen; *The Hymns of the Christian Life,* (New York, 1925), Wesley eleven and Watts, nine; *Hymns of the United Church* (Chicago, 1922), Watts fourteen, Wesley twelve; and *The Inter-Church Hymnal* (Chicago, 1930), Watts twenty-three and Wesley eighteen.

We can see from the above figures that Wesley tends to surpass Watts in present popularity, assuming of course that the hymnals selected are representative. One must bear in mind, however, that Wesley wrote 6,500 hymns and Watts 697. Moreover, the number of hymns found in hymnals is not the only index to a writer's position in the field; the power, popularity and influence of particular hymns must also be considered. Every generation or so, some critic tries to evaluate hymn-writers on the latter basis. In such evaluations, Watts usually takes precedence over all others as we saw in the 1865 and 1898 appraisals mentioned above. From the *Presbyterian Hymnal* (*1920*), Mr. Philo Adams Otis selected in 1928 the seventy-one hymns which he felt were the most important in the language. In this group Watts had four, the highest number of any single author; Wesley was second with three.[61]

Who then is the greater—Watts or Wesley? This question arouses little or no interest nowadays, but it was bitterly contested in the nineteenth century. For this reason, I feel obliged to touch on it briefly before I end the consideration of Watts as a hymn-writer. In 1825 James Montgomery's classic work on hymnody, *The Christian Psalmist,* awarded the palm unreservedly to Watts. There was immediate and violent opposition on the part of the Methodists who of course claimed for Charles Wesley this distinction. The controversy between the two groups, the Congregationalists[62] and the Methodists, was featured in their official publications down to the twentieth century. Neither side changed its original position.

The final answer to the question is irrevocably tied up in the individual view of the requirements a hymn should possess. Watts is the classic, objective "founder" of modern English hymnody; Wesley the poetic, highly emotional, romantic continuator of the tradition. The influence of both was vast; the present popularity of both is practically equal. Of the two, if for historical consideration alone, Watts is the more important. I feel with Frederic Palmer that

He was the first Englishman who set the gospel to music, and in his special field of song he has never been surpassed.[63]

The words of an 1874 commentator are still appropriate:

It may be that the power of Watts is somewhat waning; that as his voice is heard in the assembly less often than of old, so he is less powerful over the life . . . . Still I cannot conceive of Watts ceasing to be a potentate and a benefactor as long as men have spiritual needs and aspirations, and as long as the English language endures.[64]

CHAPTER IX

Character and Influence: A Summary

FROM his day down to ours, the character of Isaac Watts has received its full share of praise. To his contemporaries he was

> . . . the gentle Watts; in him we find
> The fairest pattern of an humble mind;
> In him the softest meekest virtue dwells
> As mild, as slight, as soft as evening gales.[1]

The Anglicans found Watts learned and charitable. Possessing few, if any of the qualities attributed by popular literature to the tub-thumping sectarian, he showed none of the rancour towards the Establishment so often voiced in the dissenting pulpits. To many nonconformists he was the perfect pattern of a minister of God. Gibbons describes him as being "pious without ostentation; devout without enthusiasm; humble without disguise; patient without fainting or complaint; faithful without morosity; firm without rigour; zealous without fury; and studious without gloom or stiffness."[2] Evangelical biographers since Gibbons have placed far more emphasis on the saintliness of Watts's life than on his works.

To be sure, there were a few of Watts's contemporaries who did not find him at all saintly. Bradbury certainly did not. There was also an anonymous author of a pamphlet, *Achates to Varus* (which I shall discuss later), who accused Watts of rather ugly hypocrisy. But, considering the latter's popularity and his connection with a disesteemed group, it is surprising that he was not attacked more often. The wits of the Queen Anne period enjoyed ridiculing the saints. The saints also indulged in vicious attacks upon each other; witness the many pamphlets directed against Bradbury. Both wits and saints were unusually considerate of Watts.

The reader of Watts's works is usually struck by the constant praise of charitableness which he finds. "Charity in man," Watts once wrote, "is a grace of that alluring sweetness, that . . . I would have it look thru my eyes continually, and it should be ever ready upon my lips to soften every expression of my tongue . . . ."[3] He possessed a large share of this grace. Thinking it tragic that men should be divided by trivial points of sectarian theology, he tried all of his life to reconcile Christians who differed on minor points of religion. God, he felt, left some things "dark" in religion in order to test man's charity. After reading Watts's *Orthodoxy and Charity United,* Johnson concluded that: "It was not only in his book, but in his mind that orthodoxy was united with charity."[4] To some of Watts's contemporaries, this charity seemed to be criminal heterodoxy; to us it represents a spirit of Christianity that was far too rare among the eighteenth century sects.

Watts possessed more than his share of piety of a type that is difficult for the average modern reader to conceive and to understand. It covered his every thought and act; poetry, art, religion, travel, and every human activity were viewed through a veil of piety with which he surrounded himself. The older he became the more he insisted that all actions should have a heaven-wards tendency or be eschewed. This kind of piety accounted for Watts's success as an evangelical writer. It was so vitally a part of him that we cannot question his sincerity even when he says, "I had rather be the author of Mr. Baxter's *Call to the Unconverted,* than the author of Milton's *Paradise Lost.*" [5] Literary fame meant nothing when compared with the evangelical aim of saving the humblest human soul.

Johnson's comment on this quality in Watts is well-known: "As piety predominated in his mind, it is suffused over his works; . . . it is difficult to read a page without learning, or at least wishing to be better. The attention is caught by indirect instruction, and he that sat down only to reason is on a sudden compelled to pray. . . . Few men have left behind such purity of character, or such monuments of laborious piety." [6]

That Watts's devoutness was not a passive acceptance of orthodox dogma we have already seen. Inheriting the Puritan's independence of mind, he called no man master in matters of religion. Like Sir Thomas Browne, he felt that God expected us to use our reason in discovering any mysteries left hidden in the Scriptures. Watts therefore sought spiritual truth through every means at his disposal and was unwilling to accept at face value any non-scriptural dogma; as a consequence, he was seldom guilty of bigotry. "I ever own myself a protestant," he once wrote Colman, "and claim a right to think freely and judge for myself." [7] In spite of objections from friends and attacks from enemies, he exercised that right to his dying day.

This persistent search after truth shocked some of his orthodox biographers. Southey primly remarks that

Watts had inherited a large share of the original temptation,— that inward and spiritual temptation whereby man is incited to pluck the forbidden fruit. He approached too near the veil; and confiding in his own natural and cultivated acuteness, endeavoured sometimes strictly to define what the scriptures have left indefinite, as if he were possessed of an intellectual prism with which he could decompose the Light of Lights.[8]

The poet-laureate then pontifically adds that in the course of an innocent and otherwise peaceful life, Watts "seems never to have been assailed by any other temptation than this of the intellect, ..." Southey, I am afraid, could not appreciate the intensity of Watts's conviction that religion should be a "plain and easy path" leading all to God. He sought that path.

In his quiet compromising way, Watts was at heart a rebel. His questioning attitude was not confined solely to things spiritual. His innovations in education, poetry, and hymnody show that he was not willing to accept things because usage had made them sacrosanct. He made reason corroborate the testimony of custom. This quality, it seems to me, was the outstanding and most productive characteristic of his career.

Our knowledge of Watts's character in private life is comparatively limited, but we are able to glean a few facts from the early biographies and from contemporary letters. Gibbons tells us that Watts never "discovered in his behaviour or conversation any thing like an high opinion of himself." [9] He was always considerate of his inferiors, and letters from Lady Hertford and Doddridge show that he was especially interested in the religious improvement of his friends' servants. A generous person, he devoted one-fifth of his income to "charitable uses." [10] Watts was "nobly avaricious of his time" and tried therefore to employ every waking moment in a worthwhile manner. [11] Some books which he left show that until late in life he used the laborious interleaving method of study which he had learned in the academy. But he also found time to make sketches of distinguished persons, to carry on a voluminous correspondence, to collect autographs and pictures of famous persons, and to entertain his numerous friends.

Watts was a cheerful host and an excellent talker. [12] As he did not possess a "furious zeal" or a "narrow decisive spirit," he welcomed cordially all true Christians regardless of their denominational bias. [13] Intensely loyal to his friends, he defended them vigorously whenever occasion arose. In his conversation he was also charitable towards opponents. Gibbons, however, confesses that Watts was not perfect:

He sometimes discovered a quick emotion and hastiness of temper, and would speak with a manifest degree of keenness and poignancy, but effervescences of this kind might, at least in part, be owing to the disagreeable sensations occasioned by the weakness and disorder of his body; however, they were quite momentary, and he soon returned to his former possession and placid dignity of soul. On the whole, if he had his spots, they were, like those of the sun, abundantly compensated by superior glories.[14]

The effect of ill health on Watts's character is a subject about which one can only conjecture, but a reading of his letters shows that he was not only a sick person but one obsessed with the idea of sickness. He harps continually upon his disabilities, and from his descriptions of these fits of illness, he must have suffered greatly. Constant ill health probably played a large part in causing the occasional "waspishness" which his friends reluctantly attributed to him, and which was seen in his differences with Bradbury. Considering the state of his health, the wonder is that he was not more acrimonious.

Jennings, the writer of the brief memoir attached to the authorized works, tells us that Watts's "humility was like a deep shade, . . . that set off his other graces and virtues, and made them shine with a brighter lustre."[15] This quality exhibits itself in an objectionable way, it seems to me, in many of Watts's prefaces. He is far too apologetic to ring true. In these introductions, he protests to the reader time after time his inability to write on the subject in question, states that he wishes some greater genius to take the subject and improve upon it, and asserts that the particular work is merely the result of spare hours and has "lain" by him for "above twenty years." Watts was both writer and preacher, and it was dissimulation to explain that authorship was not his field. He must have known his worth as a writer; his many editions were adequate proof of that. He probably considered his statements proper humility, but false humility is often irritating.

An interesting example of this tendency may be found in a

letter which Watts wrote to the *Spectator*, August 17, 1712. The following passages are pertinent:

Upon reading the hymns that you have published in some late papers, I had a mind to try yesterday whether I could write one . . . .

If the following essay be not too incorrigible, bestow upon it a few brightnings from your genius, that I may learn how to write better, or to write no more.[16]

In order to appreciate this letter, one has to remember that by 1712 three editions of *Hymns and Spiritual Songs* and two of *Horae Lyricae* had come off the press. The best hymn-writer in England had no need of such a peculiar sort of modesty to get a poem printed in the *Spectator*. Some writers consider this an example of Wattsian humor. Somehow it does not strike me that Watts was joking.

Watts liked the smell of printer's ink. It would probably be gentler to say that he was a practical person and knew how to meet the demands of his public. In any case he brought out edition after edition of works, a few on subjects in which he was not eminently qualified. He was probably acting from purely unselfish motives, but some of his contemporaries felt differently. In 1769, John Wesley made the following observation in his *Journal*:

Fri. Feb. 17 (Yarmouth).—I abridged Dr. Watts's pretty "Treatise on the Passions." His hundred and seventy-seven pages will make a useful tract of four and twenty. Why do persons who treat the same subjects with me, write so much larger books? Of many reasons, is not this the chief—we do not write with the same view? Their principal end is to get money; my only one to do good.[17]

I cannot agree with Wesley's insinuation that Watts was primarily interested in money. He was evidently a good business man, but his generosity in dealing with his New England friends and with local charities shows that he was definitely not mercenary.

Another contemporary work, the scurrilous *Achates to Varus,* which was published by E. Curll in 1746, accused Watts rather violently of publishing too much and too often:

Admit a writer is capable of giving us some valuable Lessons in *Logick,* Divinity, or sacred *Odes:* Does it therefore follow he is to be heard in every Science, or is a Master of All Subjects he is pleased to fancy himself acquainted with: . . . ?[18]

The writer then satirized Watts's penchant for advertising;[19] he poked fun particularly at an advertisement from the year 1744-5 in which Watts promised his public, even from a bed of illness, more works "as fast as the Providence of God shall restore my health." Whatever Watts's motives were, at least one of his contemporaries felt that he was too anxious to rush into print.

Watts, as we have seen, was often inconsistent in his various beliefs, for he was an ingrained compromiser. He confided too often in the pragmatic explanation to rescue him from a philosophical dilemma. But his impulses were usually right even if he failed on occasion to justify them rationally. Watts accepted Locke's philosophy, but he also clung to the theory of "innate ideas"; he wrote a *Guide to Prayer* to tone down dissenter enthusiasm in prayer, but he published *An Exhortation to Ministers* to arouse more warmth in nonconformist preaching; he rejected the Trinity of the Athanasian Creed because it was illogical; yet he refused to be classed with the Unitarians; he exalted reason in his non-religious essays and depreciated the sufficiency of reason in the religious; he had the usual Neo-classic horror of enthusiasm, but he spent a lifetime trying to infuse it into the religion of his age; he believed in the certain election of a chosen few, but at the same time he insisted that all men have free will. Watts probably never felt the inconsistency of these opposing views, because he could defend each of them to his own satisfaction on what were to him perfectly rational grounds. As Southey observed, he depended too much upon his "own natural and cultivated acuteness."

The mind of Watts impresses one with its quickness, its keenness, and its versatility rather than with its depth. He had a broad and ample store of knowledge gained from a lifetime of study; he possessed an excellent memory, indefatigable industry, and inexhaustible energy. But he was not highly original. A facile writer, a quick thinker, a shrewd observer, and an apt learner, he was perhaps handicapped by his own facility. It was too easy for him to improve and to perfect the ideas of others; he did not often bother to attempt original creation himself. But he was an excellent and ingenious improver. Watts did not possess great genius, but he used that which he had with an industry and devotion to an ideal rarely equalled.

I conclude this review of Watts's character feeling that in spite of the few failings which he possessed, he was essentially an admirable person. Charitable, pious, gentle—his saintliness was tinged with just enough worldliness to make him human. Very few figures in his century have been so universally beloved, and few have been so worthy of such love.

The influence of Watts has been tremendous, but it has been of a type hard to measure. The first and simplest influence was that exerted by his evangelical works in his own lifetime. By the end of the third decade of the century, Watts's name had become the theme of literally hundreds of religiously sentimental anecdotes. Drunkards saved, sinners stopped in their headlong flight, even Jews converted through the influence of Watts's works—stories such as these grew into a Watts religious saga. The pages of Wesley's *Journal* contain detail after detail of death-bed scenes in which the dying person passed with Watts's hymns on his lips.[20]

This kind of influence is difficult to measure, but it is none the less real. Moreover, it was effective in aiding the general softening of eighteenth century religion. In the Preface to the *Rise and Progress,* Doddridge evaluates this service:

Such is the improvement you have made of your capacities for service that I am fully persuaded heaven has received very few in these latter ages who have done so much to serve its interests here below; . . . .

I congratulate you, dear sir, while you are in a multitude of families and schools of the lower class, condescending to the humble yet important work of forming infant minds to the first rudiments of religious knowledge and devout impressions, by your various catechisms and divine songs, you are also daily reading lectures of logic and other useful branches of philosophy to studious youth; and this not only in private academies but in the most public and celebrated seats of learning, not merely in Scotland, and in our American colonies, . . . but, through the amiable candour of some excellent men and accomplished tutors, in our English universities too. I congratulate you that you are teaching no doubt hundreds of ministers and private Christians by your sermons, and other theological tracts, so happily calculated to diffuse through their minds that light of knowledge, and through their hearts that fervour of piety, which God has been pleased to enkindle in your own. But above all, I congratulate you that by your sacred poetry, especially by your psalms and your hymns, you are leading the worship, and, I trust also, animating the devotions of myriads in our public assemblies every Sabbath, and in their families and closets every day . . . . Every word which you drop from the pulpit has now surely its peculiar weight. The eyes of many are on their ascending prophet eagerly intent that they may catch if not his mantle, at least some divine sentence from his lips, which may long guide their ways and warm their hearts.[21]

This contemporary and personal influence is again attested by the number of recommendations for popular religious works that Watts wrote. He knew the value of his name in a "recommendatory preface," and he was always willing to lend his name to any work assisting the cause of religion and virtue. "Bibliography I" gives a partial list of works recommended by Watts. The authors of these volumes were connected with practically all of the evangelical movements of the day.

A consideration of Watts's literary influence introduces a problem. It bears repeating that Watts was not a part of the polite world of his day. He read and praised Pope and Young; he admired the *Spectator* above all contemporary lay works; he knew Richardson and remonstrated with him about the effects of *Pamela* on youth; but he was not a part of the life of these men. Since he was opposed both to the novel and to the stage and disliked personal satire, he could have but little immediate effect upon the current literature of his day. The influence that he exerted was felt principally among those who, like him, were writing for the religious element that lived beyond the influence of the Neo-classic compromise.

To his contemporaries Watts was an excellent religious poet. In the preface to the 1718 edition of his poems Blackmore voiced the consensus of the age:

Hitherto, as I have said, but few of the wits of this kingdom, . . . have thought fit to exercise their pens expressly and directly in cultivating divine and moral poetry but only in an allegorical and disguising dress. Some persons of great virtue and piety have attempted it; but these having neither poetical genius nor judgment, . . . have only written indifferent prose in the poorest verse; and though they deserve the honour of good men, they must be contented with the character of bad poets. This, I think, is a just censure on the greatest part of those who have written religious books in English verse; but I except from this number the ingenious Mr. Watts, whose divine poetry is very laudable, and much superior to all who have gone before him in the lyric kind.[22]

Cave, too, considered Watts a writer of merit and in 1734 asked him to serve as judge in a poetry contest conducted by *Gentleman's Magazine*.[23] In his letter of acceptance Watts admonished the publisher concerning the absence of religious poetry in the periodical. A diplomatist as well as a good business man, Cave announced in the July (1734) issue of *Gentleman's* a new contest with the following theme: "Life, Death,

Judgment, Heaven and Hell." Watts was gracefully invited to contribute:

> With regard to what you have added in the postscript to your letter, I must allow, Sir, there has been too much reason for the censure you have passed on the magazine; but it shall be my future care to let nothing pass of that kind, and to convince the world I am much better pleased with ingenuity of a more serious turn, I have proposed a considerable reward for poems on five sublime subjects; on which, if it suited your leisure, and you have not taken absolute leave of the Muses, I should be proud of a poem from Dr. Watts.[24]

Watts's influence as a religious poet was supreme among the dissenters, both in England and in America. Dr. Watts, Johnson felt, was one of the first nonconformists to teach his group "to write and speak like other men, by showing them that elegance might consist with piety." The dissenter poets, Johnson added, "have had Dr. Watts before their eyes, a writer who, if he stood not in the first class of genius, compensated that defect, by a ready application of his powers to the promotion of piety." [25]

Mrs. Rowe was a disciple of Watts in an interesting way. She used lines and phrases from the latter's works as themes for her rhapsodies. Her respect for Watts and Watts's connection with the *Devout Exercises,* I have already mentioned in Chapter III.

Doddridge, another dissenter whom I have already discussed, was an ardent disciple and protégé of Watts, who imitated not only the latter's hymns and children's poetry but his prose as well. *The Rise and Progress of Religion in the Soul* was Watts's original idea which Doddridge developed, as it were, under Watts's guiding hand. Watts even attempted to mold the prose-style of his friend.[26]

Thomas Gibbons, Watts's first biographer, also modelled his verses on those of Watts. Gibbons' *Juvenilia* (1750) are highly

Wattsian in content and form; and in his "Elegiac Poem to the Memory of the Rev. Isaac Watts, D.D.," the disciple acknowledges his indebtedness to the master:

> But still a Muse that Watts has deign'd to hear,
> A Muse, that his celestial Fires have warm'd
> And kindled into song, with bold Essay
> Would tell how rich a Treasure left our World.[27]

Joseph Mitchell (1684-1738), a Scotch poet of unsavory reputation, shows in his work some traces of Watts's influence. In the "Muses Original" and in the "Ode on the Power of Musick," both from *Poems on Several Occasions* (1729), there are evidences of the Dennis-Watts-Blackmore theory of divine poetry. Mitchell's *Lugubres Cantus* (1719) contains a laudatory "Ode to the Reverend Mr. Watts," and *Jonah* (1720) is addressed to Watts. Professor Fairchild thinks that Watts may have been useful in helping Mitchell to publish *Lugubres Cantus.*[28]

Ralph Erskine (1685-1752), Scotch Presbyterian minister and author of the popular *Gospel Canticles,* also looked to Watts for guidance in writing religious verse. The Preface to his *Paraphrase, or Large Explicatory Poem upon the Song of Solomon, . . .* (1736) states that the work had been submitted to Watts who read part of it and suggested certain revisions.

Thomas Harrison (1693-1745), a Baptist minister who conformed and became vicar of Radcliffe-on-the-Wreke, Leicestershire, published in 1719 *Poems on Divine Subjects.* The Preface to the work justifies divine poetry after the manner of *Horae Lyricae* to which the reader is referred. Watts's influence is strong throughout the book.

Moses Browne (1704-87),[29] Hervey's curate who later succeeded to the living at Olney, published in 1739 *Poems on Various Subjects.* In the preface Browne commends the work of Watts and his efforts to rescue the age from its "degenerate taste" in poetry. It is noteworthy that Browne and Hervey, both of whom played significant parts in the Evangelical Movement, expressed profound respect for Watts's works and aims.[30]

But Watts's influence touched better poets than Browne. Robert Blair, author of "The Grave," wrote Doddridge in 1742:

I was urged by some friends here, to whom I showed it ["The Grave"], to make it public; nor did I decline it, provided I had the approbation of Dr. Watts, from whom I have received many civilities, and for whom I ever entertained the highest regard.[31]

Although Watts was unsuccessful in procuring a publisher for this famous poem, the letter reveals in no uncertain way his prominence as a religious poet. Incidentally, Blair borrowed a figure, that of death shooting his arrows upon unsuspecting mortals, from Watts's "To Mitio."

I have already noted Cowper's imitation of Watts's "Day of Judgment" in his poem, "Lines Written during a Period of Insanity." Cowper was also indebted to Watts's *Hymns* for the following lines in "Truth":

A Truth the brilliant Frenchman never knew:
And in that charter *reads with sparkling eyes
Her title to a treasure in the skies.*[32]

Cowper revered the name of Watts, and in all probability the latter's influence upon him was more general than one can readily trace. They are both important figures in the same movement.

William Blake, too, shows the influence of Watts in *Songs of Innocence*. "Watts is the only author we can positively name," states S. Foster Damon, "whose writings may have affected these *Songs* even slightly." [33] Most critics agree that Blake's "A Cradle Song" was inspired by "Hush! my dear, lie still and slumber." [34] One of the illustrations (plate 4) in the *Visions of the Daughters of Albion* was inspired by Watts's poem, "To Mitio". It is a pictorial representation of the arrow-shooting episode which Blair also used.

The poetry of Watts was extremely popular for over a century after his death. There were ninety-five English editions of *Divine Songs* by 1810, twenty-five editions of *Horae Lyricae* by 1850, eleven publications of "collected poetry" in editions of British poetry by 1851, and numerous publications of the *Beauties of Watts* in both America and England. The traces of such a popularity, I feel certain, are reflected in the poetry of the late eighteenth and nineteenth centuries, but the search would be hardly worth the effort. I have chosen rather to touch only those poets whom Watts directly influenced in some definite way.

Attempting a final evaluation of Watts's position in our tradition, I am forced to admit that his sermons are read no more and that his educational texts and theories, although influential for over one hundred years, are now outmoded. I must admit also that his essays and treatises deal with issues that are no longer vital. Nevertheless, Watts will live in our tradition. His fame is assured because of efforts in three fields: evangelical poetry, children's poetry, and hymnody. Though inferior to Herbert and Cowper, Watts is a not unworthy kinsman of these evangelical poets. *Horae Lyricae* has become a minor classic in the field. Scholars interested in the eighteenth century have recently discovered the work's great value in illustrating pre-romantic tendencies. They are consulting it more and more frequently, not only because of its historical significance, but also because of its intrinsic excellence. In the field of children's poetry, Watts merits the title of epoch-maker. Though not a pioneering effort, *Divine Songs* was so superior to all previous work of its kind that it usurped the field of eighteenth century children's poetry. A definite literary landmark, it was the source of practically all late eighteenth and early nineteenth century children's verse and hymns. Watts's greatest contribution to our tradition was of course his "System of Praise." *Hymns and Spiritual Songs* and *Psalms of David Imitated* changed the course of English-speaking congregational praise.

Watts's entire range of activities must be considered as one many-sided effort to touch and influence that vast group of religious persons left outside by the Neo-classic compromise. His sermons, poems, essays, and hymns all contributed to the making of the religious temper from which sprang the Methodist Revival. As a precursor of that movement, he influenced its three great leaders—Wesley, Whitefield, and Edwards. Through Watts the evangelical tendencies inherent in seventeenth century Puritanism were transmitted to the new Puritanism of the eighteenth; and though there were other similar transitional figures, Watts's eminence in so many different fields distinguished him above the rest.

APPENDIX A

LETTERS OF ISAAC WATTS

The following abbreviations have been used for sources which appear often in this list: *C. H. S.* for *Transactions, Congregational Historical Society;* Dod. for *The Correspondence . . . Philip Doddridge* (London, 1830); Gib. for Gibbons' *Memoir of Isaac Watts;* *M. H. S. Proc.*[1] and *M. H. S. Coll.* for the *Proceedings* and the *Collections* respectively of the Massachusetts Historical Society; Mil. for Milner's *Life . . . of Isaac Watts; Post. II* for *The Posthumous Works of Isaac Watts,* Vol. II; and Wms. for the unpublished letters of Watts in Dr. Williams' Library, London.

DATE	TO	WHERE PRINTED OR FOUND
1691, Sept. 20	Enoch Watts (Latin Verse)	Gib., 64; Mil., 116
1692	His Father (?) (Verse)	*Works,* IV, 571
1693, Feb. 1	Richard Watts (Latin Verse)	Gib., 68; Mil., 119
1695, June	Horatio	*Works,* IV, 571
1696, —	Pocyon	*Works,* IV, 531
1698, —	David Polhill	Mil., 176; *Works,* IV, 410
1698, —	Pocyon	*Works,* IV, 533
1700, Jan.	Arthur Shallet	*Works,* IV, 447
1701, July	Lady Abney	Mil., 179; *Works,* IV, 437
1702, —	Church, Mark Lane	Gib., 98; Mil., 187
1702, Feb. 8	Church, Mark Lane	Mil., 181
1704, June 15	Sarah and Mary Watts	Gib., 249; Mil., 225
1705, Aug. 24	Henry Bendish	Mil., 226; *Works,* IV, 407
1707, Dec. 22	John Shower	Mil., 227; *Works,* IV, 433

DATE	TO	WHERE PRINTED OR FOUND
1708, Dec. 23	Samuel Say	Mil., 228
1709, Mar. 12	Samuel Say	Mil., 229
1709, Nov. 1	Samuel Say	Mil., 231
1712, —	Church in Bury Street	Mil., 327
1712, Aug. 19	*The Spectator*	Mil., 325
1713, Nov. 4	Church in Bury Street	Mil., 327; *C. H. S.,* I, 95
1713, Nov. 5	Church in Bury Street	*Christian Observer* (London), XXXII, 648
1714, Apr 3.	Church in Bury Street	Wms.
1715, Aug. 6.	Church in Bury Street	Wms.[2]
1716, Apr. 14	Church in Bury Street	Wms.
1716, Nov. 21	Church in Bury Street	Wms.
1717-8, Jan. 29	Church in Bury Street	Wms.
1717-8, Feb. 12	Church in Bury Street	Wms.
1717-8, Mar.	Cotton Mather	Mass. Historical Society, unpublished
1717-8, Mar. 17	Cotton Mather	Geo. Hood, *History of Music in New England,* 155 n.
1719, Jan. 9	Sir R. Blackmore	Gib., 299; Mil., 333
1719, May 2	A Friend	*Works,* IV, 607
1719-20, Feb. 1	Sir Thomas Abney	*Works,* I, 144
1719-20, Feb. 10	Benjamin Colman	Unpub., Mass. Historical Society, (Colman papers)
1719-20, Feb. 11	Cotton Mather	In part, *M. H. S. Coll.*
1720, July 31	The Misses Abney	Gib., 148; *Works,* IV, 647
1721, Feb. 21	Church in Bury Street	*Works,* I, xix
1722, Feb.	Lady Abney	*Works,* IV, 545
1722, Apr. 7	Samuel Rosewell	Mil., 411
1722, May 24	Mrs. Rosewell	Mil., 412
1722, July 6	Sir John Hartopp	*Works,* II, 131

DATE	TO	WHERE PRINTED OR FOUND
1722, Aug.	Mrs. Mary Abney	British Museum, unpub.
1722, Aug. 4	Hubert Stogdon	Mil., 405
1723, Apr. 11	Benjamin Colman	*M. H. S. Proc.*
1724, Aug. 24	Sir John Hartopp	*Works* (1810 ed.), V, 3
1725, Feb. 26	Thomas Bradbury	*Post. II,* 168
1725, June 11	John Eames	*Works,* V, 411
1725, Nov. 1	Thomas Bradbury	Mil., 391; *Post. II,* 229
1726, —	A Lady (Sister of Dr. Share)	*Gospel Magazine* (1779), 657
1726, Jan. 24	Thomas Bradbury	*Post. II,* 177; Mil., 395
1726, Feb. 2	Thomas Bradbury	*Post. II,* 191
1726, Mar.	Dr. Nathaniel Lardner	Wright's *Life of Watts,* 162
1726, Mar. 6	Mrs. Rosewell	Mil., 444
1726, Mar. 15	Thomas Bradbury	*Post. II,* 209, Mil., 393
1726, Mar. 18	Thomas Bradbury	*Post. II,* 219
1726, July 6	Benjamin Colman	*M. H. S. Proc.*
1727, Feb. 2	Samuel Say	Mil., 451
1727, July 28	Benjamin Colman	*M. H. S. Proc.*
1727, Aug. 10	Samuel Say	Mil., 455
1727, Sept. 12	Samuel Say	Mil., 456
1727, Dec. 26	Mr. Ford, Bookseller	*Notes and Queries,* 3rd Series, IX, 493
1727-8, Feb. 2	Samuel Say	Bodleian, unpub.
1728, Apr. 11	Samuel Say	Mil., 457
1728, May 8	Benjamin Colman	*M. H. S. Proc.*
1728, June 7	Benjamin Colman	*M. H. S. Proc.*
1728, Nov. 7	Mrs. Sewall	*M. H. S. Coll.* Series 5, V, 149n.
1728, Dec. 3	Mrs. Richier, Bath	Unpub. In 1914 owned by W. H. Watts, Liverpool.[3]
1728, Dec. 9	Mrs. Richier, Bath	Rix Manuscripts, unpub.[4]

DATE	TO	WHERE PRINTED OR FOUND
1728-9, Feb. 22	Samuel Mather	Mass. Historical Society, unpub.
1728-9, Mar. 19	H. Francis	*C. H. S.* III, 241
1729, Apr. 25	Mather Byles	*Notes and Queries,* 4th Series, VIII, 414
1729, Apr. 26	Benjamin Colman	*M. H. S. Proc.*
1729, Oct. 7	Lady Hertford	R. B. Adam Collection, University of Rochester, Rochester, N. Y., unpub.
1729-30, Feb. 14	Parents and Family Heads, Bury St.	*Works,* V, 411
1729-30, Mar. 4-5	Benjamin Colman	*M. H. S. Proc.*
1730, Aug. 4	Mrs. Sarah Abney	British Museum, unpub.
1730, Sept. 28	Thomas Prince	Mass. Historical Society, unpub.
1731, July 31	The Misses Abney	Gib., 148
1731-2, Feb. 2	Elisha Williams	A. S. Pratt, *Isaac Watts and His Gifts of Books to Yale College,* 18
1731-2, Feb. 3	Samuel Say	*M. H. S. Proc.*
1731-2, Mar. 21	Mrs. Richier	Rix MSS., unpub.
1732, Apr. 28	Lady Abney	*Works,* I, 560
1732, May 3	Samuel Mather	Mass. Historical Society, unpub.
1732, Sept. 7	Samuel Say	Cozens-Hardy MSS., unpub.[5]
1732, Nov. 20	Samuel Say	Cozens-Hardy MSS., unpub.
1733, June 29	Benjamin Colman	*M. H. S. Proc.*
1733, Sept. 6	Elisha Williams	A. S. Pratt, *op. cit.,* 23
1733-4, Feb. 28	Samuel Say	Cozens-Hardy MSS., unpub.

DATE	TO	WHERE PRINTED OR FOUND
1734, Mar. 26	Samuel Say	Cozens-Hardy MSS., unpub.
1734, May 8	Friend in New England	*M. H. S. Coll.*, 2nd Series, X, 39-40
1734, Aug. 16	Elisha Williams	A. S. Pratt, *op. cit.*, 25-26
1734, Nov. 1	Wm. Duncombe	Mil., 505
1734, Sept. 7	A Young Gentleman	*New Spiritual Mag.* (Oct. 1783), 163
1734, Dec. 26	Edward Cave	Gib., 139; Mil., 508[6]
1735, Jan. 21	A Friend	Mil., 512
1734-5, Jan. 30	Mr. and Mrs. Duncombe	Pa. Historical Society, unpub.
1735, Apr. 29	Benjamin Colman	*M. H. S. Proc.*
1735, May 13	Unknown (at Harvard?)	Pa. Historical Society, unpub.
1735, May 16	Benjamin Colman	*M. H. S. Proc.*
1735, May 23	Wm. Duncombe	Gib., 87; Mil., 517
1735, June 14	Joseph Highmore	*Gentleman's Magazine*, LXXXVI, 10
1735, June 21	Benjamin Colman	*M. H. S. Proc.*
1735, Aug. 21	Benjamin Colman	*M. H. S. Proc.*
1736, Jan. 28	Samuel Say	Mil., 538
1736, Mar. 9	Wm. Duncombe	National Library of Scotland, unpub.
1736, Sept. 13	Benjamin Colman	*M. H. S. Proc.*
1736, Sept. 22	Benjamin Colman	*M. H. S. Proc.*
1736, Oct. 2	John Hallet	British Museum, unpub.
1737, Feb. 8	Isaac Watts the elder	Gib., 2; Mil., 53
1736-7, Feb. 28	Benjamin Colman	*M. H. S. Proc.*
1737, Apr. 2	Benjamin Colman	*M. H. S. Proc.*
1737, Oct. 13	Benjamin Colman	*M. H. S. Proc.*
1738, May 31	Benjamin Colman	*M. H. S. Proc.*
1738, June 1	President Holyoke	*Four Letters of Dr. I.*

DATE	TO	WHERE PRINTED OR FOUND
		Watts, Mass. Historical Society
1738, June 7	Elisha Williams	*M. H. S. Proc.*
1738, Aug. 28	Bishop of London	Harvard Library, unpub.
1738, Sept. 22	Benjamin Colman	*M. H. S. Proc.*
1738, Dec. 21	A Friend in America	*Congregational Mag.* (Dec. 1836)[7]
1739, Apr. 4	Benjamin Colman	*M. H. S. Proc.*
1739, June 6	Benjamin Colman	*M. H. S. Proc.*
1739, June 7	President Holyoke	*Four Letters etc.*
1739, July 18	Unknown	R. B. Adam Collection, University of Rochester, Rochester, N. Y., unpub.
1739, Aug. 15	Bishop of London	Mil., 637
1739, Sept. 17	Benjamin Colman	*M. H. S. Proc.*
1739, Oct. 12	Benjamin Colman	*M. H. S. Proc.*
1739, Nov. 13	Benjamin Colman	*M. H. S. Proc.*
1739, Dec. 1	Philip Doddridge	Dod. III, 406
1739-40, Feb. 8	Dr. Lardner	*Gentleman's Mag.,* LXVII, 12 and 655
1740, Feb. 17	Philip Doddridge	Dod. III, 414
1740, Feb. 25	Philip Doddridge	Dod. III, 419
1739-40, Mar. 1	Philip Doddridge	Bodleian, unpub.
1740, May 23	Benjamin Colman	*M. H. S. Proc.*
1740, May 29	Benjamin Colman	*M. H. S. Proc.*
1740, June 28	Philip Doddridge	Dod. III, 475
1740, July 16	Benjamin Colman	*M. H. S. Proc.*
1740, Sept. 18	Philip Doddridge	Dod. III, 514
1740, Sept. 18	Benjamin Colman	*M. H. S. Proc.*
1740-1, Mar. 18	Benjamin Colman	*M. H. S. Proc.*
1741, Apr. 14	Philip Doddridge	Dod. IV, 14
1741, May 18	Benjamin Colman	*M. H. S. Proc.*
1741, May 30	President Holyoke	*Four Letters etc.*
1741, May 30	Elisha Williams	A. S. Pratt, *op. cit.,* 59.

DATE	TO	WHERE PRINTED OR FOUND
1741, June 2	Benjamin Colman	*M. H. S. Proc.*
1741, July 14	Benjamin Colman	*M. H. S. Proc.*
1741, Aug. 18	Benjamin Colman	*M. H. S. Proc.*
1741, Aug. 19	Benjamin Colman	*M. H. S. Proc.*
1741, Oct. 24	John Mason	*Select Remains of Rev. John Mason*, Second Ed., (1742)
1741, Nov. 11	Benjamin Colman	*M. H. S. Proc.*
1741, Dec. 24	Philip Doddridge	Dod. IV, 61
1741-2, Feb. 24	Benjamin Colman	*M. H. S. Proc.*
1742, Feb. 26	Philip Doddridge	Dod. IV, 75
1741-2, Mar. 1	Bishop of Oxford	*Phonetic Journal* (Oct. 9, 1886), 484
1742, Apr. 7	Unknown	T. Foxcroft, *An Apology etc.* (Boston, 1745)
1742, Apr. 8	Unknown	T. Foxcroft, *An Apology etc.* (Boston, 1745)
1742, Apr. 16	Benjamin Colman	*M. H. S. Proc.*
1742, May 25	Philip Doddridge	Bodleian, unpub.
1742, July 3	Benjamin Colman	*M. H. S. Proc.*
1742, Oct. 22	Benjamin Colman	*M. H. S. Proc.*
1742, Nov. 15	Benjamin Colman	*M. H. S. Proc.*
1742, Nov. 15	President Holyoke	*Four Letters etc.*
1742, Dec. 26	Philip Doddridge	Mil., 629
1743, Jan. 27	Philip Doddridge	Dod. IV, 187
1742-3, Feb. 5	Benjamin Colman	*M. H. S. Proc.*
1743, Feb. 24	Philip Doddridge	Dod. IV, 208; Mil., 629
1743, Mar. 31	Philip Doddridge	Dod. IV, 230; Mil., 629
1743, Sept. 14	Benjamin Colman	*M. H. S. Proc.*
1743, Sept. 20	Philip Doddridge	Dod. IV, 269
1743, Dec. 14	Philip Doddridge	Dod. IV, 295; Mil., 629

DATE	TO	WHERE PRINTED OR FOUND
1744, —	D. Longueville	Gib., 309
1744, Jan. 17	Philip Doddridge	*Gentleman's Mag.*, LX, 1085
1743-44, Feb. 28	Benjamin Colman	*M. H. S. Proc.*
1744, Apr. 9	Benjamin Colman	*M. H. S. Proc.*
1744, May 4	Benjamin Colman	*M. H. S. Proc.*
1744, Sept. 13	Philip Doddridge	Dod. IV, 353 (in part)
1744, Oct. 30	Benjamin Colman	*M. H. S. Proc.*
1744-5, Mar. 20	Benjamin Colman	*M. H. S. Proc.*
1745, Mar. 30	Benjamin Colman	*M. H. S. Proc.*
1745, Dec. 10	Enoch Watts	British Museum, unpub.[8]
1745, Dec. 14	Philip Doddridge	Dod. IV, 420; Mil., 689
1746, Jan. 26	Philip Doddridge	Dod. IV, 516
1747, Jan. 13	Church in Bury St.	*Works,* II, v.
1746-7, Feb. 11	Benjamin Colman	*M. H. S. Proc.*
1747, Oct. 18	Philip Doddridge	Dod. IV, 514
1747, Nov. 21	Philip Doddridge	Dod. V, 23
1748, July 14	Society for Promoting Christian Knowledge	Stoke Newington Public Library, unpub.
N. D.	To a Lady	British Museum, unpub.
N. D.	Enoch Watts	Mil., 189
N. D.	A Minister in Affliction	Gib., 117
N. D.	Countess of Hertford	*Works,* IV, *Rel. Juv.* (1734), 455
N. D.	Mrs. Rowe (Philomela)	*Works,* IV, *Rel. Juv.* (1734), 563
N. D.	To Lucius	*Works,* IV, *Rel. Juv.* (1734), 554

APPENDIX B

THE POETRY OF THE POSTHUMOUS WORKS

In 1779 there appeared *The Posthumous Works of the late Reverend and Learned Isaac Watts, D.D. in Two Volumes. Compiled from papers in possession of his immediate successors: Adjusted and published by a Gentleman of the University of Cambridge.* Volume I contains poems, translations, and a brief memoir of Watts; Volume II consists of five sermons and correspondence. This publication has been neglected by most of the biographers since Gibbons because of his assertion that only ten[1] of the hundred or more poems and translations found in Volume I were the work of Watts. And in fairness to Gibbons one must admit that the first volume is a shoddy production. The compiler placed the same poem in two places, assigning it first to Watts and later to the poet's father. He senselessly mixed translations and original poems under the heading, "Translations." And he included in the memoir some utterly fantastic biographical material. The work was obviously a bookseller's attempt to capitalize the fame of Watts.

Granting this, I feel, however, that the publication should not be summarily rejected as Gibbons has done. He dismisses the work on four counts: first, that the poems are not *posthumous* because the first nine are to be found in a more finished condition in *Hymns and Spiritual Songs* (1707); second, that their quality is inferior to that of all of the acknowledged poems of Watts; third, that the latter wrote no poems after 1737, and there are pieces in Volume I from later dates;[2] and, fourth, that these poems if written by Watts would have been printed during his lifetime.[3]

These reasons are not convincing; the last one is particularly weak, and Gibbons is not too definite about the third.[4] There is one poem in the work, "On the Death of my Sister, Elizabeth Watts, who deceased November 11, 1691, aged Two Years," which in date, style, and content points to the youthful Watts as author, but Gibbons rejects it also. He argues that if Watts had written on the death of a sister he "would undoubtedly have clothed her verse with the deepest gloom, and most solemn pomp of melancholy,

... such as we find in the elegies ... on the deaths of Mr. Gouge and Mr. Gunston, ..." [5]

Such criticism is hardly worthy of consideration, but every biographer since 1780 has accepted Gibbons' conclusions, namely that all of the poems and translations except the ten mentioned above were written by another person, probably the elder Watts. Although I cannot prove beyond all doubt that Gibbons was in error, I do feel that his contentions are open to question.

In the first place, Gibbons infers that all of the poems except ten are by the same hand. I submit that the poet who wrote the following lines:

> 'Tis true, that in the legal dispensation,
> Which only did concern the Jewish nation,
> Religious rites were constantly maintain'd
> By such, and only such, as Heav'n ordain'd;[6]

did not write this translation from Horace:

> Why stay we at all, let us drink while we may,
> Our life is as brief as a short winter's day:
> Hang thoughts of tomorrow, awhile we'll be merry,
> And drown all our cares with Falernum and Sherry.[7]

The person who wrote the first wooden stanza and many others like it would not be likely to achieve, even in a translation, the sprightliness of the second. There are obviously two different hands represented in Volume I. Because some of these poems resemble in style and content the known poems of the elder Watts, I agree with Gibbons that they were written by the poet's father. But the second hand is that of Isaac Watts in his younger years.

This contention is based upon a series of verbal similarities between certain poems in *Horae Lyricae* and in *Posthumous Works*. "The Adventurous Muse" (*Horae Lyricae*), a Pindaric eulogy of Milton, is one of Watts's best-known poems. In the *Posthumous Works*, there is a rhymed résumé of *Paradise Lost* written in labored Pindarics in which the following line occurs:

> My *muse, adventurous,* soared upright.

In the former poem, Watts describes his muse as springing "upward to eternal day." In both poems the idea of an "adventurous muse" is associated with Milton and with the Pindaric metre.

Compare the following lines from the poem, "Sincere Praise" (*Horae Lyricae*):

> The *lark* mounts up the sky,
>   With unambitious song,
> And bears her *Maker's Praise* on high
>   Upon her artless tongue;[8]

with these from "The Lark" (*Posthumous Works*):

> And flying, sings a morning hymn
> Which sweetly meant her Maker's praise.[9]

In the "Life of Man" (*Posthumous Works*) the poet writes:

> This life's a tragedy, the world's a stage,
> The actor's man, each several scene's an age . . .

> At length he lays him down and death draws nigh,
> Stabs him at heart, and ends the tragedy.[10]

Watts writes in the "Mourning Piece" (*Horae Lyricae*):

> Life's a long tragedy: This globe the stage.
> . . . . The actors many:
> The plot immense: a flight of daemons sit
> On every sailing cloud with fatal purpose;
> And shoot across the scenes ten thousand arrows
> Perpetual and unseen, headed with pain,
> With sorrow, infamy, disease and death.

There are several other verbal similarities one could list, but these are sufficient for our purpose. The two different poets, if there were two, write somewhat alike, and this similarity occurs too often to be mere coincidence. Since there are ten acknowledged poems of Watts in this work, and since the letters in Volume II of this collection are genuine, is it not possible that these poems could be the juvenile efforts of Watts which he never intended to publish, but which were exploited after his death? Is it not possible that the inferior quality of these pieces caused Watts to with-hold publication, but did not prevent his borrowing lines and ideas from them?

One notes also that the best pieces in the work are translations from the sensual portions of both Latin and Greek poets—Juvenal, Vergil, Ovid, and Theocritus. Could not he have made these trans-lations as a schoolboy when he studied the classics? After dedi-cating himself to the religious muse, he had no desire to publish the pieces, but he probably liked them too well to destroy them.

This is all mere conjecture, but, on the basis of verbal and struc-tural similarity and on the presence of other authentic material in the work, I feel that of the poems and translations in Volume I of *Posthumous Works,* about twenty-five, or roughly one-fourth, may be assigned to Watts's father. The rest, I believe, were written by Watts in his younger years. The man who made verses prac-tically from the cradle to the grave would of a necessity write many that were unworthy of publication.

NOTES

CHAPTER I

[1] The birthplace of Watts, according to tradition, was the house later known as 41 French Street. Thomas Wright, *The Life of Isaac Watts* (London, 1914), p. 7.

[2] *The Works of . . . . Isaac Watts* (London, 1753), Vol. IV, p. 436. This is the authorized edition. All references to *Works,* unless otherwise specified, indicate this edition.

[3] F. J. S. Hearnshaw and F. Clarke, *A Short History of Southampton* (Oxford, 1910), p. 231.

[4] Thomas Gibbons, *Memoirs of the Rev. Isaac Watts, D.D.* (London, 1780), p. 1 n.

[5] H. H. Carlisle, *Honour to Whom Honour* (London, 1874), p. 15. This is a brief sketch of Watts's life taken in part from the church records.

[6] Johnson in the *Lives of the Poets* gives the occupation of the father as that of shoemaker. I cannot find the source of Johnson's information. See *Gentleman's Magazine,* Vol. LVII (1787), p. 99, for a letter on this matter.

[7] Some of the older historians of dissent trace the origin of Independency to Robert Browne and Henry Barrowe, but Champlin Burrage (*The Early English Dissenters,* Cambridge, 1912, p. 281) designates Henry Jacobs (d. 1624) as the founder. The first Independent church on English soil, says Burrage, was established by Jacobs in London in 1616. Bogue and Bennett (*History of Dissenters, etc.* 2nd Ed., London, 1808, p. 176) say that the name "Independent" was first used by John Robinson. A. H. Drysdale (*History of the English Presbyterians,* London, 1889, p. 5n) claims that Jacobs gave the name.

[8] The two names were used interchangeably. For a technical distinction between the two, see R. W. Dale, *History of English Congregationalism* (London, 1907), pp. 374 ff.

[9] W. Haller, *The Rise of Puritanism* (New York, 1938), p. 176.

[10] *Ibid.,* p. 16.

[11] *Ibid.,* p. 174.

[12] W. Haller, *Tracts on Liberty in the Puritan Revolution* (New York, 1934), Vol. I, p. 34.

[13] Cf. pp. 15-17 *infra* for Watts-Say friendship.

[14] S. Stainer, *History of the Above Bar Congregationalist Church* (Southampton, 1909), pp. 16-18.

[15] A lecturer was a special preacher to a congregation. His pay was raised usually by popular support or through patronage. He preached at unprescribed times, i.e. week-days and Sunday nights.

[16] Stainer, *op. cit.,* p. 17.

[17] *Ibid.*, p. 18.

[18] By 1719 the group had raised enough money to buy the land from Watts's father, *ibid.*, p. 11.

[19] This fund, started by Robert Thorner, the wealthy senior elder of Above Bar Church, provided (and still provides) support for "elderly women of slender means." Thorner left a bequest to Harvard for which Isaac Watts later became trustee.

[20] This MS., which was discovered in the early nineteenth century, is in Watts's hand. It is written in two columns. On one side he has a table of "coincidents"; on the other, "Memorable Affairs in My Life." The MS. is a valuable biographical aid; but, unfortunately, it stops at 1711. It is printed (with a facsimile of the first page) in E. Paxton Hood's *Isaac Watts; His Life and Writings, His Times and Friends* (London, 1875).

[21] Printed in Thomas Milner, *The Life, . . . of the Rev. Isaac Watts, D.D.* (London, 1834), pp. 36-44.

[22] See pp. 171-3, *infra*.

[23] For examples of this verse, see Milner, *op. cit.*, pp. 47-53. See also "Appendix B" for further comment.

[24] The dates of birth are taken from the Watts family Bible. See transcription of this material in *Transactions, Congregational Historical Society*, Vol. I (London, 1901), pp. 275 ff.

[25] Gibbons, *op. cit.*, p. 5.

[26] *Ibid.*

[27] "Memorable Affairs".

[28] *Ibid.*

[29] *C. H. E. L.*, Vol. IX, p. 382.

[30] The portrait now hangs in the Above Bar Church, Southampton.

[31] *Works*, Vol. IV, p. 427.

[32] Translated in Gibbons, *op. cit.*. p. 19.

[33] Cf. pp. 159-62, *infra*.

[34] Irene Parker, (*Dissenting Academies in England*, Cambridge, 1914, p. 51), distinguishes three periods of development in the history of academies: the first from 1663 to 1690; the second from 1690 to 1750; and the third from 1750 on.

[35] *Ibid.*, p. 57.

[36] *Historical View of the State of the Protestant Dissenters in England* (London, 1814), pp. 225 ff.

[37] Parker, *op. cit.*, p. 70. Watts used most of these books at Newington Green. Enoch Watts gave Gibbons an abridgment of Burgersdicius' work made by Watts when a student (Gibbons, *op. cit.*, p. 59).

[38] This was the academy attended by Defoe and Samuel Wesley.

[39] This account is given in Palmer's *Defense of the Dissenters' Education in their Private Academies* (London, 1703).

[40] Gale was the author of the *Court of the Gentiles* (1669-78), a work which attempted to prove that *all* learning came from the Jews, hence the superiority of the Christian tradition. Gale left his estate as a fund to educate

dissenting ministers. He left all of his books, except those on philosophy, to Harvard.

[41] It was customary for the tutor to have a meeting also.

[42] W. Wilson, *The History and Antiquities of Dissenting Churches in London* . . . (London, 1808), Vol. III, p. 171.

[43] H. McLachlan, *English Education under the Test Acts* (Manchester, 1931), p. 52.

[44] The term was probably taken from Joseph Glanvill's essay, "Anti-Fanatical Religion and Free Philosophy" (1676).

[45] A. Gordon, *Addresses Biographical and Historical* (London, 1922), pp. 203-4.

[46] W. Wilson, *op. cit.*, Vol. III, p. 171.

[47] These books were given to Gibbons by Enoch Watts. They contain twenty-four dissertations—twenty-two in Latin, two in English. Gibbons transcribed the English and translated two of the Latin. See his work, *op. cit.*, pp. 20 ff.

[48] *The Works of Samuel Johnson* (Troy, N. Y., 1903), Vol. XI, pp. 41-42.

[49] *Works*, Vol. IV, p. 393.

[50] *Works*, Vol. IV, p. 532.

[51] Cf. Chapter IV, *infra*.

[52] For a discussion of Watts's mystical poetry, see pp. 175 ff. *infra*.

[53] Cf. p. 177, *infra*.

[54] Hughes was the author of the *Siege of Damascus*. He contributed to the *Tatler* Nos. 644, 73, 113; to the *Spectator* Nos. 33, 53, 66, 91, 104, 141, 210, 220, 230, 231, 237, 252, 302, 311, 375, 525, 537, 541, 554; to the *Guardian* No. 37.

[55] They are found principally in *The Correspondence of John Hughes, Esq. . . . in Two Volumes* (Dublin, 1773).

[56] *Ibid.*, Vol. I, p. 132. Say in "Die Natali 23° Mar 1702" decided that he would dedicate his poetry to God alone. See H. N. Fairchild, *Religious Trends in English Poetry* (New York, 1939), p. 144.

[57] Quoted in Milner, *op. cit.*, p. 131.

[58] Hughes's *Correspondence, op. cit.*, Vol. I, p. 156.

[59] *Ibid.*, p. 133.

[60] *Ibid.*, pp. 9 ff.

[61] Cf. the character of Watts in Chapter IX.

[62] Gibbons, *op. cit.*, p. 87.

[63] Hughes's *Correspondence, op. cit.*, Vol. I, p. 161-2.

[64] This intimacy is clearly shown in a MS. collection of Watts's letters now in the possession of Basil Cozens-Hardy, Esq., of Norwich, England. See "Appendix A."

[65] For comment on Say as a divine poet, see Fairchild, *op. cit.*, pp. 144-6.

[66] *Works*, Vol. IV, p. 425.

[67] A rare example, or rather the only example of a direct attack on the Establishment by Watts is to be found in a curious book, *Some Cursory Remarks on Reading the Book of Common-Prayer*, 1704. By Isaac Watts, D.D. (Bath, 1801). This book is a copy of a Prayer-Book in which Watts had jotted

down some rather bitter and sarcastic criticisms of the Liturgy. Watts never intended it for publication; it was simply an 1801 bookseller's exploitation of the fame of Watts, but it does show that Watts could be satirical and was in 1704 inclined to ridicule the Church. This trait does not appear again in any of his printed works.

[68] *A Letter from a Country Divine, . . .* , 3rd Ed. (London, 1706), p. 4.

[69] The Schism Act provided that persons acting as schoolmasters or tutors before subscribing to the Church of England and obtaining a license from the bishop should be imprisoned for three months in the common gaol. Queen Anne died on the morning (August 1, 1714) when it was to go into effect and practically no attempts were made to enforce it.

[70] This controversy produced among others: Defoe's *More Short Ways With the Dissenters* (London, 1704); Samuel Palmer's *A Defense of the Dissenters' Education in their Private Academies; . . .* (London, 1703); Wesley's reply to Palmer, *A Defense of a letter concerning the Education of Dissenters in their Private Academies; . . .* (London, 1704); another answer from Palmer, *A Vindication of the Learning, Loyalty, Morals, and Most Christian Behavior of the Dissenters towards the Church of England; . . .* (London, 1705); and Wesley's *A Reply to Mr. Palmer's Vindication, . . .* (London, 1707).

[71] This anecdote was told to Gibbons by Price, the co-pastor at Bury Street.

[72] Organized in London in 1695.

[73] "Original Minutes" of the board transcribed in *Transactions, Congregational Historical Society*, Vol. V (1911-12), p. 139.

[74] Watts wrote an "Elegiac Essay" on Gouge which was dedicated to Arthur Shallet. See *Works*, Vol. IV, p. 447.

[75] B. K. Gray, *History of English Philanthropy* (London, 1905), p. 103.

[76] J. P. Wright, "Some Forgotten London Benefactors," *Transactions, Congregational Historical Society*, Vol. X (London, 1927), pp. 75 ff.

CHAPTER II

[1] *Works*, Vol. I, p. 440.

[2] V. de Sola Pinto, "Isaac Watts and His Poetry," *Wessex* (Southampton, 1935) Vol. III, p. 2, pp. 27-36.

[3] Fairchild, *op. cit.*, p. 121.

[4] *Works* (London, 1825), Vol. II, p. 314.

[5] Fairchild, *op. cit.*, p. 121.

[6] *D. N. B.*

[7] Many of Owen's sermons were preserved in this manner by Hartopp. They were published in 1756 by Hartopp's granddaughter.

[8] Because of a defect in the will, only £5,000 was finally allocated to this purpose.

[9] *Works*, Vol. II, p. 129, *Death and Heaven*. This funeral sermon was one of Watts's most popular works.

[10] *Works*, Vol. IV, pp. 413 and 415.

[11] Wright, *op. cit.*, p. 44, states that Watts preached at Freeby, Leicestershire and also at the Independent chapel in Epsom Street adjoining the Hartopp city home.

[12] The meeting was originally in Leadenhall St. After Owen's death David Clarkson became pastor. He was succeeded by Isaac Loeffs under whom the church moved to Mark Lane. Chauncy succeeded Loeffs in 1687.

[13] Watts dedicated a poem in *Horae Lyricae* ("Against Tears") to Mrs. Bendish. Other members of the Cromwell clan to whom Watts dedicated poems were Nathaniel Gould (Fleetwood's son-in-law); "Mr. C. and S. Fleetwood (the grandchildren of General Fleetwood); Henry Bendish (son of Bridget Bendish); David Polhill (the grandson of Lord Deputy Ireton); and John Hartopp (Fleetwood's grandson).

[14] Richard Cromwell lived near Watts in Newington. The two are supposed to have met at John Howe's deathbed, but Cromwell could have known Watts through his wife's family connections in Southampton.

[15] Many of the ejected turned to medicine as a means of living.

[16] W. Wilson, *The History and Antiquities of Dissenting Churches . . . in London* (London, 1808), Vol. I, p. 290.

[17] The greater portion of the original *Register of the Bury Street Church* is to be found in Memorial Hall, London. The MS. is incomplete because it was once sold for fire-paper and partly used as such. Fortunately, however, John Rippon had seen the MS. and copied it before it was so abused. He printed portions of it in *The Baptist Register* (Vol. IV, 1800-1, pp. 593 ff.). These parts were again printed in *Transactions, Congregational Historical Society* (Vol. VI, No. 5, pp. 333 ff.). The present work makes use mainly of the original MS.

[18] *Register*, p. 78.

[19] See next chapter for Bradbury-Watts differences.

[20] *Register*, p. 79.

[21] Milner, *op. cit.*, p. 181.

[22] In 1658 the Independents drew up at the Savoy Conference "a Declaration of the Faith and Order owned and practiced in the Congregational Churches in England." The committee who composed the declaration were Caryl, Nye, Bridge, Greenhill, Thomas Goodwin, and Owen. The faith and order of this declaration were generally, though not universally, adhered to and practiced by Independent churches throughout the eighteenth century. See R. W. Dale's *History of English Congregationalism* (London, 1907), pp. 386-90 for a full text of this declaration.

[23] Some of the early Independent churches had an officer called the "widow" whose duty it was to visit the sick.

[24] *Register*, pp. 84 ff.

[25] Milner, *op. cit.*, pp. 187-8.

[26] *Register*, pp. 86-90. Benoni Rowe was the brother of Watts's tutor, Thomas, and father of Thomas, the husband of Elizabeth Singer.

[27] After ordination, Watts sat for a portrait which he sent to Pinhorne. This portrait hangs yet in Above Bar Church, Southampton.

[28] "Memorable Affairs in My Life."

[29] J. Quincy, *History of Harvard University* (Cambridge, 1840), Vol. I, p. 399.

[30] Samuel Price, born in Wales and educated under Timothy Jollie at Attercliffe, Yorkshire, was a good, solid preacher who possessed, though no outstanding abilities, a special gift in prayer. He was made co-pastor of Watts in 1713, and remained a staunch, admiring friend of the great doctor all of his life. At his death in 1756, his one request was that his grave be placed as near that of Watts as possible.

[31] Pinners Hall, used in 1580 by a Venetian glass-blower, was leased in 1610 by the Pinners Company. It was let to a Baptist group in Cromwell's time, and in 1661 to Independents. It was pulled down in 1800.

[32] The new building cost £620 exclusive of the pews. The plan and subscription-list of the pews may be found in *Transactions, Congregational Historical Society*, Vol. III (1907-8), pp. 117 ff. See also Vol. V (1911-12), pp. 92 ff. for a description of the church, its size, its cost, etc.

[33] Note Dunton's rhyming of "can" with "town" and "gown", "Watts" with "notes," and "Thames" with "strains."

[34] From Watts's Poem to Elizabeth Singer, afterwards Mrs. Rowe.

[35] *Life and Errors of John Dunton, Citizen of London, . . .* (London, 1818), Vol. II, p. 722.

[36] *C. H. E. L.,* Vol. IX, p. 430.

[37] Milner, *op. cit.,* p. 232.

[38] The Abneys evidently had a city home in Lime Street, London, from which many of Watts's letters were sent. But in 1733-4, Watts moved with the Abneys from Theobalds and Lime Street to the Abneys' new home in Stoke Newington. There he remained the rest of his life. See two letters in Anne S. Pratt's *Dr. Watts and His Gifts of Books to Yale College* (New Haven, 1938), pp. 23 and 26.

[39] *The Works of Augustus Toplady*, A.B., 2nd Ed. (London, 1794), Vol. IV, p. 117.

[40] *D. N. B.* and Jeremiah Smith's *The Magistrate and the Christian*, 2nd Ed. (London, 1722), Abney's funeral sermon, have supplied the facts for this account of Abney's life.

[41] One of Watts's closest friends was the younger Sir Thomas Gunston, brother of Mrs. Abney. See *Works*, Vol. IV, p. 437 for funeral ode on Sir Thomas, which is one of Watts's best odes. See also the poem, "Happy Solitude" (*Works*, Vol. IV, p. 414), dedicated to Gunston.

[42] W. Wilson, *Memoirs of the Life and Times of Daniel Defoe* (London, 1830), Vol. II, pp. 36 ff.

[43] See dedication to *The Art of Reading and Writing English* (*Works*, Vol. IV, p. 647). This work was written to be used in teaching the Abney girls and was affectionately dedicated to them.

[44] An unpublished collection of these letters is to be found in Dr. Williams' Library, London. See "Appendix A."

[45] From an unpublished letter in Dr. Williams' Library, London.

[40] *Ibid.*

[47] Jeremiah Smith, *op. cit.*, pp. 40-5.

[48] Max Weber, *The Protestant Ethic and the Spirit of Capitalism* (London, 1930). Cf. also R. H. Tawney, *Religion and the Rise of Capitalism* (New York, 1926).

[49] An unpublished letter written in 1741 and found in the collection of the Rev. Mr. Rix, Ealing, London. In the first part of the letter, Doddridge stated that three men had been put out of church at that meeting for bankruptcy.

CHAPTER III

[1] The grant, later raised to £1000, was continued until 1851 (Dale, *op. cit.*, p. 520).

[2] *A view of the Dissenting Interest in London of the Presbyterian and Independent Denominations from the year 1695 to the 25th of December 1731. With a Postscript of the Present State of the Baptists.* This survey was made by a person who signed himself simply "A.B." It is still in manuscript form in Dr. Williams' Library, London.

[3] Daniel Neal discovered that in 1716 there were only 1107 nonconformist congregations in England and Wales, whereas over two thousand ministers were ejected in 1662.

[4] *An Enquiry . . .* (London, 1730), p. 26.

[5] See pp. 142-3, *infra.*

[6] See H. W. Clark, *History of English Nonconformity* (London, 1911-13), Vol. II, pp. 246-50 for Methodist influence among Independent congregations.

[7] See "Bibliography I" for works during this period. See also pp. 225-6, *infra,* for his position as divine poet in correspondence with Cave.

[8] The dissenters usually received degrees either from Dutch or Scotch universities. The latter were particularly useful to dissent in this respect.

[9] See "Appendix A" for a list of the persons with whom Watts corresponded.

[10] *Posthumous Works of the late Reverend and Learned Isaac Watts, D.D. Adjusted and published by a Gentleman of the University of Cambridge. Two Vols.* (London, 1779), Vol. II, p. 62, (hereinafter, *Post. Works*).

[11] Gibbons, *op. cit.*, p. 434.

[12] A. A. Perdeck, *Theology in Augustan Literature* (Groningen, Den Haag, 1928), p. 73.

[13] N. Curnock (ed.), *The Journal of the Rev. John Wesley, A.M.* (London, 1913), Vol. II, p. 82.

[14] John Telford (ed.), *The Letters of the Rev. John Wesley, A.M.* (London, 1931), Vol. IV, p. 294. See also Vols. III, p. 232; VII, p. 21; and VIII, p. 89 for references to Watts.

[15] See Curnock, *op. cit.*, Vols. I, pp. 139 and 243; II, pp. 82 and 511; III, pp. 529 and 537; IV, pp. 125 and 69; V, pp. 106, 300, and 360; VI, p. 278; and VII, pp. 413, 377, and 527 for further references to Watts.

[16] The work appeared originally in 1756.

[17] Gibbons, *op. cit.*, p. 398. One notes in passing that the Countess also knew the Countess of Huntingdon and Whitefield. The latter preached in her home.

[18] *Post. Works,* Vol. II, p. 112.

[19] Watts's poetic name for Lady Frances.

[20] The poem had also a letter to Philomela (Mrs. Rowe) appended.

[21] Contrast, however, his attitude towards the Great Awakening in New England (see p. 52, *infra*).

[22] The Rev. L. Tyerman, *Life of the Rev. George Whitefield* (London, 1876), Vol. I, p. 162.

[23] Milner, *op. cit.,* p. 638.

[24] *Ibid.,* p. 646.

[25] *Massachusetts Historical Society Proceedings,* 2nd Series, Vol. IX (Boston, 1895), p. 374, (hereinafter, *M.H.S. Proc.*). This is the Belknap Collection of letters written by Watts to Colman between 1723 and 1748. The letters—over fifty in number—throw new light on many Colonial figures and are an excellent index to English-American cultural relations in the eighteenth century.

[26] *Ibid.,* pp. 381-2.

[27] *Ibid.,* pp. 382-3.

[28] *Ibid.,* p. 379.

[29] *Ibid.,* pp. 387 ff.

[30] *Ibid.,* p. 391.

[31] *Ibid.,* p. 392.

[32] *Ibid.,* p. 394.

[33] *An Apology in Behalf of the Revd. Mr. Whitefield: . . . by Thomas Foxcroft, A.M. . . . The Second Edition to Which is Prefix'd Dr. Watts's Opinion of Mr. Whitefield* (Boston, 1745).

[34] *Ibid.*

[35] *Ibid.*

[36] Tyerman, *op. cit.,* Vol. II, p. 72.

[37] *M.H.S. Proc.,* 2nd Series, Vol. IX, p. 404.

[38] *Ibid.,* p. 407.

[39] The last letter mentioning Whitefield is dated Feb. 11, 1746/7.

[40] Toplady claims that Whitefield visited Watts while the latter was on his death-bed. Gibbons denies this. See the *Gospel Magazine* (1776), p. 30 and Gibbons, *op. cit.,* p. 316, for this minor debate.

[41] See Robert Philip, *The Life and Times of the Reverend George Whitefield, M.A.* (New York, 1838), pp. 242 ff. for letters to Doddridge concerning his relations with Whitefield. Philip also states that the dissenters were cool towards the Methodists because they were trying to revive the comprehension scheme which Baxter once promoted. They therefore did not wish to be connected with the enthusiastic Methodists at the time.

[42] For a fuller account of these relations, see the Belknap Collection of Watts's correspondence (*M.H.S. Proc.,* 2nd Series, Vol. IX) referred to above.

See also Anne S. Pratt, *Isaac Watts and his Gifts of Books to Yale College* (New Haven, 1938).

[42] See the *New England Historical and Genealogical Register,* Vol. I (1847), p. 191.

[44] *Mass. Historical Society Collections,* 7th Series, Vol. VIII (1912), p. 142.

[45] *Ibid.,* p. 242.

[46] The letter accompanying these Psalms is printed in George Wood's *History of Music in New England* (Boston, 1846), p. 155 n.

[47] An unpublished letter now in the library of the Mass. Historical Society, Boston.

[48] *Mass. Historical Society Collections,* 1st Series, Vol. V (Boston, 1798), p. 200.

[49] The first of the *Three Dissertations on the Trinity* (1724).

[50] See pp. 113-4, *infra.*

[51] John D. Humphreys (ed.), *The Correspondence and Diary of Philip Doddridge* (London, 1830), Vol. IV, p. 187 (hereinafter, Doddridge's *Correspondence*).

[52] T. H. Johnson, "Jonathan Edwards' Background of Reading," *Publications Colonial Society of Mass.,* Vol. XXVIII (1935), pp. 193 ff.

[53] John Guyse (1680-1761), Independent pastor, Coward and Merchants' lecturer.

[54] See A. S. Pratt, *op. cit.,* pp. 41-47 for a full account of this publication.

[55] *M.H.S. Proc.,* 2nd Series, Vol. IX, p. 361.

[56] *Ibid.,* p. 400.

[57] Cf. pp. 138-9, *infra.*

[58] Wright, *op. cit.,* p. 188.

[59] *Ibid.*

[60] *D. N. B.*

[61] Quoted in *D.N.B.* under Barrington.

[62] *The Works of the Rev. Dr. Edward Young* (Charlestown, 1811), Vol. I, p. 145. The poem quoted was first published in 1728.

[63] Anon., "Dr. Watts's Hymns," *Hours at Home,* Vol. VII (1868), p. 512.

[64] Jeremy Belknap, *Memoirs of the Lives, Characters, and Writings of . . . Dr. Isaac Watts and Dr. Philip Doddridge* (Boston, 1793), p. 20.

[65] Prior's *Poetical Works* (London, 1835), p. 54.

[66] E. P. Hood, *Isaac Watts: His Life and Writings* (London, 1875), p. 186.

[67] Watts also has a poem in *Horae Lyricae,* dated 1706, dedicated "To Mrs. Singer. On the Sight of some of her divine Poems, never printed." She, in return, wrote in the same year a dedicatory poem to this work—"To Dr. Watts, on his Poems Sacred to Devotion."

[68] *M.H.S. Proc.,* 2nd Series, Vol. IX, p. 361.

[69] *Devout Exercises of the Heart* (London, 1737), Preface.

[70] See pp. vii and viii, *supra,* for comment on Gibbons' life of Watts.

[71] Gibbons published *Juvenilia: Poems on various Subjects of Devotion and Virtue* in 1750 and a *Rhetoric* and *Memoirs of Eminently Pious Women* in

1767. For Watts's influence on Gibbons' hymns and poetry, see pp. 210 and 226.

[12] Cf. p. 65, *infra*.

[13] Published in *Transactions, Congregational Historical Society*, Vols. I and II.

[14] G. B. Hill (ed.), *Boswell's Life of Johnson* (New York, 1891), Vol. IV, p. 146.

[15] *D.N.B.* states that he probably quoted the text in conversation rather than from the pulpit. By special arrangement with Burnet, Bradbury was the first minister in London to proclaim the Queen's death.

[16] Wilson, *op. cit.*, Vol. III, p. 514.

[17] See *An Appeal to the Dissenting Ministers, occasioned by the Behaviour of Mr. Thomas Bradbury* (London, 1722).

[18] The Harburgh Lottery scandal mentioned above. Shute used the name of Watts in his effort to regain his seat in Parliament. Bradbury felt that a minister should not have been involved in such secular matters.

[19] *Post Works*, Vol. II, p. 168.

[20] When Bradbury's clerk "lined-out" one of Watts's hymns for the congregation, Bradbury is said to have stopped him with the admonition: "Let us have none of Watts's (w)hims."

[21] *Post. Works*, Vol. II, p. 170.

[22] *Ibid.*, p. 173.

[23] *Ibid.*, p. 189.

[24] Lady Abney wanted Doddridge to write a biography of Watts; for some reason, lack of material ostensibly, Doddridge refused. David Jennings the other literary executor refused also although he wrote a "memoir" which was attached to the authorized works.

[25] Gibbons, *op. cit.*, p. 309.

[26] Doddridge's *Correspondence, op. cit.*, Vol. III, p. 74. As early as Nov. 17, 1725, Doddridge was mentioning Watts in his correspondence and seeking then to know him (see *Correspondence*, Vol. II, p. 77).

[27] See p. 48, *supra*.

[28] His scheme was set forth in the pamphlet, *The Evil and Danger of Neglecting the Souls of Men* (1742).

[29] See p. 40 *supra*.

[30] J. H. Colligan, *Eighteenth Century Nonconformity* (London, 1915), p. 49.

[31] See Chapter V.

[32] Doddridge's *Correspondence, op. cit.*, Vol. IV, p. 506.

[33] *Ibid.*

[34] Gibbons, *op. cit.*, p. 313 n.

[35] Doddridge's *Correspondence, op. cit.*, Vol. IV, p. 519.

[36] *M.H.S. Proc.*, 2nd Series, Vol. IX, p. 409.

[37] *Post. Works*, Vol. II, p. 177.

[38] MS. letter in the British Museum.

[39] *The Watchful Christian . . . A Sermon on Occasion of the Decease of Mrs. Sarah Abney . . .* (London, 1732), p. 23.

[100] This collection is owned by the Rev. Mr. Wilton Rix, M.A., pastor of the Ealing Congregational Church, Ealing, London. The Rev. Mr. Rix is a lineal descendant of Joseph Parker, five generations removed.

[101] Wright, *op. cit.*, p. 250.

[102] Unpublished MS. letter in the Rix collection. Note that Doddridge wrote so hurriedly that he forgot his capitals. This is typical of his letters.

[103] Doddridge's *Correspondence, op. cit.*, Vol. V, p. 80.

[104] *Ibid.*, p. 82.

[105] MS. letter in Dr. Williams' Library, London.

[106] The monument on which the above inscription was placed was erected by Sir John Hartopp, Bart. and Dame Mary Abney. There is also a monument in Westminster Abbey.

[107] This eulogy appears again in *Gentleman's Magazine*, Vol. LXXXVI (1816), p. 11.

[108] *A Sermon Occasioned by the Death of the late Reverend Isaac Watts, D.D. . . . To which is added the Funeral Oration . . .* (London, 1749).

[109] *Reflections on the Fall of a Great Man. . . .* 2nd Edition (London, 1749).

[110] *The Rest and Reward of Good Men at Death . . .* (London, 1749).

[111] See Doddridge's *Correspondence, op. cit.*, Vol. V, pp. 94 ff.

[112] Transcribed in *Transactions, Congregational Historical Society*, Vol. III (1907), p. 2.

[113] See Milner, *op. cit.*, pp. 729 ff.

[114] Doddridge sold Watts's "Copies" to one Mr. Waugh for £600, (see his *Correspondence*, Vol. V, p. 157).

[115] See Gibbons, *op. cit.*, pp. 340-3, 291, and 205.

[116] *Ibid.*, p. 325.

[117] *A Poem Sacred to the Memory of the . . . Isaac Watts, D.D.* (London, N.D.), p. 12.

[118] *The Gentleman's Magazine*, Vol. XVIII (1748), p. 525.

CHAPTER IV

[1] Both Milner and Wright enter this work in their bibliographies under the date 1725, but the authorized edition (*Works*, Vol. V, title-page) expressly states that it was published for the first time in that edition.

[2] All of the editions up to 1750 contained this dedication. Note also that the present title of the work: *Divine and Moral Songs*, was not used until 1785.

[3] Jas. Janeway, *A Token for Children* (Leeds, 1793), Preface.

[4] F. J. Harvey Darton, *Children's Books in England* (Cambridge, 1932), pp. 55-56.

[5] *Ibid.*, pp. 53-64.

[6] *Ibid.*, p. 61.

[7] *Ibid.*, p. 66.

[8] Wm. York Tindall, *John Bunyan Mechanick Preacher* (New York, 1934), p. 204.

[9] Professor Tindall thinks that the poems of Abraham Cheare directly inspired Bunyan to attempt his work for children (*ibid.*, pp. 206-7).

[10] Cf. Wither's "Rocking Hymn" in *Hallelujah* and Watts's "A Cradle Hymn" in *Divine Songs*.

[11] Cf. Chapter VIII for a similar procedure with the hymns of Patrick and others.

[12] This poem is somewhat similar to "A Rocking Hymn" in George Wither's *Hallelujah*. Watts knew the works of Wither. He probably borrowed the idea from the latter poet.

[13] *Works*, Vol. IV, p. 312.

[14] They are: "Solemn Thoughts of God and Death", "The Danger of Delay", "Heaven and Hell", "Against Lying", "Against Scoffing", "Against Cursing", "Against Evil Company", and "Obedience to Parents".

[15] Daniel Waterland, D.D., Chaplain in Ordinary to His Majesty, *Religious Education of Children: . . . a Sermon . . .* (London, 1723).

[16] W. M. Stone, *The Divine and Moral Songs of Isaac Watts* (New York, 1918), p. 10. See also Stone's "A Brief List of Editions of Watts's *Divine Songs* located since 1918 (Oct. 1929)" [Harvard Library MS.].

[17] Stone, *op. cit.*, p. 17.

[18] *Ibid*.

[19] *Ibid.*, p. 19. The Taylor sisters played an important rôle in the Sunday School movement.

[20] See, for example, the 1787 edition edited by "A Lady".

[21] See Julian's *Dictionary of Hymnology* (London, 1907), pp. 221 ff.

[22] See the 1781 edition (Boston).

[23] Stone, *op. cit.*, p. 35.

[24] *Ibid*.

[25] Darton, *op. cit.*, pp. 109-11.

[26] *Ibid.*, p. 111.

[27] This book ran to eight editions by 1751. It should be better known by students of the history of the language, because its tables illustrate excellently eighteenth century pronunciation and usage.

[28] *Works*, Vol. IV, p. 651.

[29] Dyche was a popular London school master.

[30] The second edition is dated 1710.

[31] These MSS. are now in the possession of the Reverend Mr. Milton Rix, M.A., Ealing, London.

[32] Shallet, a candidate for the ministry, was the son of the Arthur Shallet mentioned earlier.

[33] Father Ignatius Pardies' work was translated into English in 1701. Watts's MS. is dated 1706.

[34] Johnson's *Works, op. cit.*, Vol. XI, p. 48.

[35] Johnson's copy of *Logic* marked for quotation is to be found in the British Museum. The work is 365 pages in length, and at least one word is

marked on every page and some pages have as high as eleven words marked for quoting. Johnson also quoted from *The Art of Reading . . . , The Improvement . . . ,* and the poems of Watts.

[36] Watts wrote to Colman: "Even Oxford and Cambridge break thru their bigotry and hatred of ye Dissenters, and use my Logic, Astronomy, & my Poems" (*M.H.S. Proc.,* 2nd Series, Vol. IX, p. 341).

[37] See Paul J. Fay, "Isaac Watts—An Unsung Singer of Education," *School and Society,* Vol. XXVIII, pp. 217 ff. and Robert F. Seybolt, "Student Libraries at Harvard, 1763-4," *Publications, Colonial Society of Massachusetts,* Vol. XXVIII, pp. 449 ff.

[38] I am indebted to Dr. Jan Schilt, Rutherfurd Professor of Astronomy at Columbia University, for the appraisal of this text.

[39] *Works,* Vol. V, p. 414.

[40] *Ibid.,* p. 637.

[41] Johnson's *Works, op. cit.,* Vol. XI, p. 48.

[42] Joseph Emerson, *Questions and Supplements, to Watts on the IMPROVEMENT OF THE MIND* (Boston, 1831), pp. 3 and 4.

[43] The *Shorter Catechism* was an abbreviated version of the *Westminster.*

[44] One of Watts's friends, Sir Gilbert Elliott, Bart., persuaded him to adapt the catechism to the various age levels (see letters in Milner, *op. cit.,* pp. 456-7). Watts sent his Catechisms around to friends of varying shades of opinion for corrections, compiled their views, and wrote to please all (MS. letter dated Sept. 28, 1730, and sent to Thomas Prince; Mass. Historical Society, Boston).

[45] For a study of New England catechisms see Wilberforce Eames, "Early New England Catechisms," *American Antiquarian Society Proceedings,* Vol. XII (Worcester, 1897-8), pp. 76-182.

[46] The work was published in 1715, but it was originally written for a group of younger persons whom Watts taught when he was assistant to Dr. Chauncy at Mark Lane.

[47] *Works,* Vol. III, p. 105.

[48] See p. 18 n., *supra.*

[49] *Works,* Vol. III, p. 137.

[50] See P. L. Ford, *The New England Primer* (New York, 1897), p. 46 and elsewhere for Watts's prominent position in the *Primer* after 1740.

[51] *The Short View* had 25 editions by 1818.

[52] As late as 1836 we find the work used as a basis for similar new works. See J. Stephenson, *Sacred History* (London, 1836), Preface.

[53] See p. 143, *infra.*

[54] See Rev. J. Evans, A. M., *A Compendious View of the Proofs of the Authenticity and Inspiration of the Old and New Testaments* (Oxford, 1831).

[55] D. Gardiner, *English Girlhood at School* (Oxford, 1929), p. 300. Miss Gardiner feels that this period vies in importance with the Tudor which saw the rise of grammar schools and universities. Note also that the "Academies" came from this period.

[56] *Transactions, Congregational Historical Society,* Vol. X (1927), pp. 73 ff.

[57] *Spectator*, Nos. 294, 380, 430; *Tatler*, Nos. 138, 261, 372.

[58] Boyer's *Annals of Queen Anne's Reign*, Vol. X, p. 221.

[59] Gardiner, *op. cit.*, p. 305. No returns were made by county agents after 1735.

[60] See the following sermons: *Danger of Hard-heartedness to the Poor* by Geo. Stanhope, D.D., Dean of Canterbury (London, 1705); *The Peculiar Excellency and Reward of Supporting Schools of Charity* by Bishop Edmund Gibson (London, 1716); and Bishop Butler's Sermon for the year 1745 in his *Works* (Oxford, 1896), Vol. II, pp. 339 ff.

[61] *The Method of Education in the Charity Schools of the Protestant Dissenters* by Daniel Neal, M.A. (London, 1723) is an excellent example of the dissenter type.

[62] F. B. Kaye (ed.), *The Fable of the Bees* (Oxford, 1924), Vol. I, pp. lxx-lxxii.

[63] Some other answers to the *Fable of the Bees* were made by John Dennis (*Vice and Luxury, Public Mischiefs*, 1724); Bishop Berkeley (*Alciphron* Dial. ii, 1732); William Law (*Remarks on the Fable of the Bees*, 1724); and Archibald Campbell (*Aretelogia*, 1728).

[64] For a discussion of these abuses see M. Dorothy George, *London Life in the Eighteenth Century* (London, 1925), Chap. V. See also Gardiner, *op. cit.*, p. 322.

[65] *Works*, Vol. II, p. 732.

[66] See *Twenty-Five Sermons Preached at the Anniversary Meetings of the Children Educated in Charity-Schools . . . 1704, to 1728 inclusive, . . .* (London, 1729). See also Robert Nelson's *Address to Persons of Quality* (1715).

[67] Children in the century were put to work in the work-schools as young as four years. See B. K. Gray, *A History of English Philanthropy* (London, 1905), p. 104.

[68] *Works*, Vol. V. p. 390.

[69] *Ibid.*, p. 373.

[70] *Short View of the English Stage* (1698).

[71] Gardiner, *op. cit.*, p. 373.

[72] Established in 1695. See *Transactions, Congregational Historical Society*, Vol. V (1911), pp. 134 ff.

[73] *Ibid.*, Vol. XII (1929), pp. 34 ff.

[74] *Ibid.*, Vol. VI (1914), pp. 229 ff.

[75] *Ibid.*, Vol. XII (1929), pp. 346 ff.

[76] See H. MacLachlan, *English Education under the Test Acts* (Manchester, 1931), for texts used in various schools.

[77] See E. E. Brown, *The Making of our Middle Schools* (New York, 1910), p. 166 and Vivian T. Thayer, "The Misinterpretation of Locke as a Formalist in Educational Philosophy," *University of Wisconsin Studies in the Social Sciences and History* (Madison, 1921), No. 3.

[78] For Watts's influence in America—which was considerable—see Paul

J. Fay, "Isaac Watts—An Unsung Singer of Education," *School and Society*, Vol. XXVIII, pp. 217-24.

[79] *Christian Discipline and Theological Review* (Boston) n.s. Vol. II (1820), p. 461.

[80] *Christian Witness* (London), Vol. XV, No. 178 (1858), p. 471.

[81] See Julian's *Dictionary of Hymnology* (London, 1907), pp. 220-3.

CHAPTER V

[1] *Works*, Vol. IV., p. 532.

[2] Haller, *Rise of Puritanism*, p. 370; see also p. 360.

[3] Toulmin, *op. cit.*, pp. 180-1.

[4] Tindall, *op. cit.*, p. 44. Professor Tindall also cites Baxter as an example of this attitude (p. 44n).

[5] John Wesley's tract, *The Doctrine of Original Sin . . .* (1757), was another answer to John Taylor. Wesley's work incorporated sections of Watts's *Ruin and Recovery*.

[6] See *Post. Works*, Vol. II, p. 134.

[7] See tables of publications on the Controversy in Leslie Stephen's *English Thought in the Eighteenth Century* (London, 1927), Vol. I.

[8] See Mark Pattison's "Tendencies of Religious Thought in England, 1688-1750," *Essays and Reviews* (London, 1860), pp. 256 ff. for a full discussion of these orthodox attitudes.

[9] Watts felt that virtuous heathen would be mercifully dealt with by God (*Works*, Vol. II, p. 216). In this he was following the best Puritan precedent (see Perry Miller and T. H. Johnson, *The Puritans*, New York, 1938, p. 22).

[10] *Works*, Vol. III, p. 731.

[11] *Ibid.*, pp. 761-2.

[12] *Works*, Vol. III, p. 725. In the *World to Come* (*Works*, Vol. I, p. 514), he again strikes at Shaftesbury, claiming that the doctrines of rewards and punishments were the "noblest and most effectual springs of true and vital religion." Watts refers to Shaftesbury as "Rhapsodus."

[13] Miller and Johnson, *op. cit.*, pp. 42 ff. The Puritans, Miller and Johnson assert, believed in the Bible as the only revelation and as the guide in all matters of life. The Anglicans, on the other hand, believed in a multiform revelation. It was to be found in reason, in nature, in proverbs, in civil law, and in poetry as well as in the Bible. The teachings of the Bible must be accepted not merely because they come from the Bible but because they agree with other sources of immutable wisdom. Contrast these two views in Thomas Hooker's *The Saints' Dignities* (London, 1651) and Jeremy Taylor's *Ductor Dubitantium* (London, 1659).

[14] Lois Whitney, *Primitivism and the Idea of Progress* (Baltimore, 1934), p. 16.

[15] *Works*, Vol. VI, pp. 287 ff.

[16] *Ibid.*

[17] *Works*, Vol. III, p. 566.

[18] See p. 14, *supra.*

[19] See Haller, *op. cit.*, pp. 195 ff. for an account of the beginnings of Anti-Trinitarianism in England.

[20] This Act condemned all persons found guilty of writing or preaching against the doctrine of the Trinity to practically a total loss of citizenship. A second offense would give not only civil disability but also a prison sentence of three years.

[21] See *C. H. E. L.*, Vol. X, pp. 376 ff. and Toulmin, *op. cit.*, pp. 172-87 for full discussions of this controversy.

[22] The "happy union" was formed in 1691. It was dissolved in 1695 by the dissension caused by the "Neonomian Controversy."

[23] *C. H. E. L.*, Vol. X, p. 378.

[24] For a full discussion of this controversy, see A. Gordon, *Addresses Biographical and Historical* (London, 1922), pp. 123 ff.

[25] Cf. Milner, *op. cit.*, p. 583 and J. M. Robertson, *A Short History of Free Thought* (London, 1915), Vol. II, pp. 201-2.

[26] He wrote to Colman in 1723 concerning Salters' Hall: "As I have always been a neuter in the controversie I have attempted to be a reconciler, and attempt it still where I have opportunity" (*M. H. S. Proc.* 2nd Series, Vol. IX, p. 339).

[27] The Son is inferior to the Father and derives from Him. He was with the Father before the world was created and was united with the Father and so "dwelt in him" that he became "one with God."

[28] *Post. Works*, Vol. II, p. 206.

[29] *Ibid.*, p. 112.

[30] Robertson (*op. cit.*, Vol. II, p. 201) claims that this exchange between Watts and Tomkins started the Unitarian controversy. Tomkins' work was highly influential throughout the century.

[31] *Works*, Vol. VI, p. 497.

[32] *Massachusetts Historical Society Collections*, 7th Series, Vol. VIII (1912), pp. 816 ff. The letter was dated Jan. 24, 1726-27.

[33] *Works*, Vol. VI, p. 548.

[34] Belknap, *op. cit.*, p. 29.

[35] *M.H.S. Proc.* 2nd Series, Vol. IX, p. 340.

[36] *Works*, Vol. I, p. 140. The original sermon was inspired by an essay on the Trinity written by John Howe in 1694.

[37] This controversy is contained in a volume, *Correspondence between the Rev. Dr. Isaac Watts, and the Rev. Martin Tomkins, concerning the Worship of the Holy Spirit, . . .* (London, 1803).

[38] Found in the *Correspondence between the Rev. I. Watts and the Rev. Martin Tomkins, . . .*

[39] In the British Museum there is also an undated version of the work with notes presumably in Watts's writing. The corrections pointed to republication. The catalog gives the date: 1745.

[40] That Watts's dereliction from the orthodox aroused accusations of dotage and insanity is evident from the violent attacks found in a book, *Achates to Varus,* published in London by E. Curll in 1746.

[41] Rev. George Burder (ed.), *Works of the Reverend and Learned Isaac Watts, D.D.* (London, 1810), Vol. I, p. xxxvi.

[42] *Works,* Vol. VI, pp. 713 ff.

[43] *Ibid.,* p. 854.

[44] Caleb Fleming (1698-1779), pastor of Bartholomew Close, was a prolific Anti-Trinitarian writer. He was a friend of Lardner, an enemy of Bradbury.

[45] *Works,* Vol. VI, p. 856. The quotations by Watts came from Goodwin's *Works* (London, 1704), Book III in Vol. II.

[46] See Haller, *Rise of Puritanism,* pp. 75 ff. and 94 ff. for an evaluation of Goodwin's contributions to the Puritan reform movement.

[47] *Works,* Vol. VI, p. 690.

[48] Belknap, *op. cit.,* p. 90.

[49] *Works,* Vol. IV, pp. 640 ff.

[50] *Ibid.,* pp. 640-1.

[51] *Ibid.,* p. 641.

[52] *Ibid,* p. 643.

[53] Lindsey (1723-1808) was founder of the famous Unitarian Essex Street Chapel. He was associated with Priestley in Unitarian activities.

[54] Theophilus Lindsey, M. A., *A Second Address to the Students of Oxford and Cambridge, . . .* (London, 1790), pp. 3 ff.

[55] See Joseph Priestley, *Dr. Watts's Historical Catechisms, with Alterations,* 2nd Ed. (Birmingham, 1783).

[56] See Belknap, *op. cit.,* pp. 116-118, 134-39, for a fuller discussion of this problem.

[57] *The Sacred Classics* (London, 1834), Vol. IX, p. lix.

[58] Nathaniel Lardner (1684-1768) was the author of the *Credibility of the Gospel History* (1727-55). He was a friend of Watts and Barrington.

[59] *A Solemn Address . . . ,* Printed and sold by the Unitarian Association (London, 1840), p. xxxvii.

[60] *Ibid.*

[61] *Ibid.*

[62] *Ibid.*

[63] Jeremy Belknap, *Memoirs of . . . Dr. Isaac Watts and Dr. Philip Doddridge* (Boston, 1793), pp. 115-16. Belknap took the material from Palmer's *Life of the Rev. Isaac Watts, D.D.* by Samuel Johnson L.L.D. with notes (1785).

[64] To be found in Belknap, *op. cit.,* pp. 76 ff.

[65] *Ibid.,* p. 84.

[66] *Ibid.,* pp. 136 ff.

[67] *The Monthly Repository of Theology and General Literature,* Vol. VIII (Hackney, 1813), pp. 322 ff and pp. 683 ff.

[68] Boston, New Series II (1820), pp. 461 ff.

[69] See "Preface."

[70] London, 1835, Vol. II, p. 164.

[71] *Notes and Queries* had a running debate in its pages lasting roughly speaking from Vol. V to Vol. VIII (1860).

CHAPTER VI

[1] Only those essays which have not been considered elsewhere will be discussed in this chapter.

[2] Watts had nine sermons in this collection. See "Bibliography I". Associated with him were Neal, Guyse, Price, Hubbard, and D. Jennings.

[3] In 1812 John Pye Smith published *Nine Sermons, Preached in the years 1718-19, By the late Isaac Watts, D.D.* (Oxford, 1812). These sermons are characteristic of Watts but do not compare favorably in form and expression with those that he prepared for the press. In *Post. Works*, Vol. II, pp. 241 ff. and 293 ff. there are two series of sermons preached by Watts in 1707 at Pinners' Hall.

[4] *Works*, Vol. I, p. ix.

[5] Johnson's *Works*, *op. cit.*, Vol. XI, p. 46.

[6] Gibbons, *op. cit.*, p. 142.

[7] Quoted in the *Christian Observer*, Vol. XII (London, 1813), p. 720.

[8] See Milner, *op. cit.*, p. 639; see also p. 502.

[9] Cf. especially the "Charges" for the year 1727.

[10] Found in *An Humble Attempt* (1731) which will be discussed later in this chapter. Watts also had sections on the art of preaching in *The Improvement of the Mind* and in the *Rational Foundation of a Christian Church*. In the latter work he justifies the Puritan-dissenter manner of preaching.

[11] For the Puritan origin of this type of soul-analysis, cf. Haller, *Rise of Puritanism*, pp. 90-91.

[12] *Works*, Vol. III, p. 22. Contrast this advice with that given by Swift to a young clergyman: "But I do not see how this talent of moving the passions can be of any use towards directing Christian men in the conduct of their lives, at least in these northern climates, where I am confident the strongest eloquence of that kind will leave few impressions. . . ." in *Swift's Writings on Religion and the Church*, Temple Scott, ed. (London, 1898), Vol. I, p. 205.

[13] Haller, *Rise of Puritanism*, p. 20.

[14] The remarks on seventeenth century preaching are taken largely from the following secondary works: Perry Miller, *The New England Mind* (New York, 1939), W. F. Mitchell, *English Pulpit Oratory from Andrewes to Tillotson* (London, 1932), and William Haller, *The Rise of Puritanism* (New York, 1938).

[15] Haller, *Rise of Puritanism*, p. 22.

[16] *Ibid.*, p. 25.

[17] *Ibid.*, pp. 134-5.

[18] See Mitchell, *op. cit.*, p. 99.

[19] See Miller, *op. cit.*, p. 335.

[20] *Works*, Vol. II, p. 156.

[21] There were four editions by 1737. The sixteenth edition came out in 1818. In 1727 it was translated into German by Professor John Jacob Rambach of Halle.

[22] Cf. Baxter's *The Saints' Everlasting Rest* (1649). Although the world to come was a typical Puritan theme, it is highly probable that Watts took some hints from Baxter's work.

[23] *The End of Time*, one of the discourses appended to *The World to Come*, has often been published separately. It is one of Watts's most popular works.

[24] See *Works*, Vol. I, pp. 686 ff.

[25] Cf. pp. 175-8, *infra*.

[26] See p. 146, *infra*.

[27] *Works*, Vol. I, p. 24.

[28] This letter, written in 1732, is found in the MS. collection of Basil Cozens-Hardy, Norwich, England.

[29] *Works*, Vol. I, p. 1.

[30] *Ibid.*, p. 20.

[31] *Ibid.*, p. 22.

[32] *Ibid.*, p. 27.

[33] Frank A. Patterson (ed.), *The Student's Milton* (New York, 1931), p. 1041.

[34] See Umphrey Lee, *Historical Background of Early Methodist Enthusiasm* (New York, 1931).

[35] *Works*, Vol. III, p. 179.

[36] *Ibid.*, II, p. 95.

[37] *Ibid.*, p. 97-8.

[38] From a MS. sermon in the library of the Massachusetts Historical Society, Boston, Mass.

[39] *Works*, Vol. II, p. 102.

[40] *Ibid.*, p. 101.

[41] L. Stephen, *op. cit.*, Vol. II, p. 386.

[42] The "Bills of Mortality" report 59 cases of suicide in London in 1725, besides 74 drowned and 43 found dead of causes unknown.

[43] J. H. Harder, *Eighteenth Century Tendencies in Poetry and Essay* (Amsterdam, 1933), pp. 120-141.

[44] See *Works*, Vol. II, pp. 637-8.

[45] Edwards' final position is found in *A Treatise Concerning Religious Affections* (1746). To Edwards, religion was primarily a matter of the affections. Compare also Baxter's *Directions for the Use of the Passions* found in his *Christian Directory*. Baxter's work in aim and content foretokens Watts's essay.

[46] There were many answers to this pamphlet. Among them were: *A Letter to the Author of the Enquiry*, . . . (London, 1730); *The Methods to be taken by Ministers for the Revival of Religion* . . . by David Some (London,

1730); *Some Observations upon the Present State of the Dissenting Interest* (London, 1731); and *An Apology for the Church of England* (London, 1732). One of the best answers was that by Philip Doddridge, *Free Thoughts on the most Probable Means of Reviving the Dissenting Interest* (1730).

[47] *Works*, Vol. III, p. xi.

[48] *Works*, Vol. II, p. 345.

[49] This particular section was answered in 1740 by Robert Cornthwaite in a tract, *An Essay on the Sabbath;* . . . .

[50] One of Watts's members refused to take communion at noon because it was called "supper" in the Bible.

[51] Watts's translation or rather "imitation" of the *Psalms* was done in this spirit. See next chapter.

[52] See H. F. R. Smith, *The Theory of Religious Liberty in the Reigns of Charles II and James II.* (Cambridge, 1911).

[53] Dale, *op. cit.*, pp. 519-21.

[54] *Works*, Vol. VI, p. 134. Watts set out to draw up this scheme without consulting any authors, but he stated that he had read Locke's *Charter for the State of North Carolina* and Puffendorf's *The Relation between Church and State*.

[55] This argument was found in practically all of the Puritan writers on toleration. See the essays on John Goodwin, Henry Parker, Walwyn, and Henry Robinson in Haller's *Tracts on Liberty in the Puritan Revolution*, Vol. I.

[56] *Works*, Vol. VI, p. 137.

[57] *Works*, Vol. VI, p. 168.

[58] Miller, *op. cit.*, pp. 185-6.

[59] This was an answer to Stillingfleet's *Unreasonableness of Separation* (1680).

[60] When two objects are so similar that choice of either could not be made on the grounds of "apparent goodness," then man exercises freedom of the will in taking one or the other.

[61] The influence of John Locke may be seen not only here but in Watts's educational theories (see p. 101) and also in his *Essay on Civil Power* (see p. 145 n).

[62] *Works*, Vol. V, p. 503.

[63] Watts tells us in a letter dated May 13, 1735 (unpublished and found in the Pennsylvania Historical Society's collection), that he regretted not having read Bishop Berkeley's works in his "Philosophical age of Life". They were considered then too "whimsicall and chimerick."

[64] Stephen, *op. cit.*, Vol. II, p. 386.

[65] Note that both Wesley and Edwards had the same reaction to Locke's philosophy. Cf. Wesley's *An Earnest Appeal to Men of Reason and Religion.*

[66] Cf. p. 107, *supra*.

[67] R. S. Crane and M. E. Prior, "English Literature, 1660-1800: A Current Bibliography," *Philological Quarterly*, Vol. XI (1932).

[68] See Miller, *op. cit.*, p. 186.

[69] *Works*, Vol. V, p. 583.

[70] *Ibid.*, p. 576.

[71] Jonathan Edwards' beliefs were essentially similar to those of Watts.

[72] There were five editions of *Philosophical Essays* by 1800.

[73] James P. R. Lyell, *Mrs. Piozzi and Isaac Watts, being annotations in the Autograph of Mrs. Piozzi on a copy of the First Edition of the Philosophical Essays of Watts* (London, 1934).

[74] *Ibid.*, p. 23.

[75] *Ibid.*, p. 24. Beattie's *Essay on Truth* (1761) was a very popular orthodox philosophical work of the day.

[76] *Ibid.*, p. 44.

[77] *Ibid.*, p. 26.

[78] *Ibid.*, p. 42.

[79] This work was dedicated to the "Right Honourable the Countess of Hertford." See p. 44, *supra*.

[80] *Works*, Vol. IV, p. 512.

[81] Compare "To Velina, on the Death of Several Young Children" with "The Hazard of Loving the Creatures" (*Horae Lyricae*) and "The Day of Judgment" (*Horae Lyricae*) with "Distant Thunder".

[82] See Nos. 37 and 61 of the Religious Tract Society (London) publications.

[83] Johnson's *Works, op. cit.*, Vol. XI, p. 50. Johnson himself was guilty on the same score; see the *Rambler*.

[84] *Works*, Vol. V, p. 233.

[85] *Ibid.*, pp. 326-9.

[86] *Monthly Review*, Vol. X (1754), p. 93.

[87] *Works*, Vol. I, p. 702.

[88] Quoted in Louis F. Benson, *The Hymnody of the Christian Church* (New York, 1927), p. 111.

CHAPTER VII

[1] According to Nichols' *Literary Anecdotes*, Vol. V (1812), pp. 218-9, Watts is supposed to have remonstrated with Pope who consented to change the line. The original appeared only in surreptitious editions.

[2] L. F. Salzman, "The Little Busy Watts," *Cornhill Magazine*, n.s., Vol. XLIX, pp. 472-8.

[3] Johnson's, *Works, op. cit.*, Vol. XI, p. 50.

[4] J. G. Frazier, *Letters of William Cowper* (London, 1912), Vol. I, p. 146. The letter was addressed to Newton.

[5] *Specimens of the Later English Poets* (London, 1807), Vol. II, p. 96.

[6] Geo. Saintsbury, *A History of English Prosody* (London, 1908), Vol. II, p. 508.

[7] *The Nation* (March 16, 1937), art., "Homage to Isaac Watts," p. 280.

[8] A. E. Housman, *The Name and Nature of Poetry* (Cambridge, 1933), p. 30.

[9] V. de Sola Pinto, "Isaac Watts and His Poetry," *op. cit.*

[10] Fairchild, *op. cit.*, p. 123.

[11] Legouis and Cazamian, *History of English Literature* (New York, 1930), p. 819.

[12] W. J. Courthope, *A History of English Poetry* (London, 1919), Vol. V, pp. 273 ff. and 327 ff.

[13] The word is used here not to denote the party of the English Church which did not come into existence until the third or fourth decade of the century, but as a generic term for all the dissident emotional and religious forces of the age.

[14] *Works*, Vol. IV, p. 317.

[15] *Ibid.*, p. 318.

[16] See Basil Willey, *The Seventeenth Century Background* (London, 1934), p. 227; also Spingarn's *Critical Essays of the Seventeenth Century* (Oxford, 1908), Vol. II, p. 89.

[17] See *Works of Giles and Phineas Fletcher* (Cambridge, 1908), Vol. I, pp. 10-13.

[18] *Works*, Vol. IV, p. 323.

[19] *Ibid.*, p. 323.

[20] *Ibid.*, p. 327.

[21] For a full discussion of this subject, see H. G. Paul, *John Dennis* (New York, 1911), pp. 120-44. For other examples, see Flecknoe's *Discourse on the English Stage* (1664); Rymer's *Tragedies of the Last Age* (1678); Baxter's *Poetical Fragments* (1681); Nahum Tate's *On the Present Corrupted State of Poetry* (1684); John Norris's Preface to *A Collection of Miscellanies* (1687); and Jeremy Collier's *Short View* (1698).

[22] See especially *Reason of Church Government* and *Paradise Lost*, Books I and VII.

[23] The theory is presented in the preface to Blackmore's *Redemption* (1722) and *A Paraphrase on the Book of Job* (1700); Dennis's *The Advancement and Reformation of Modern Poetry* (1701) and *The Grounds of Criticism in Poetry* (1704).

[24] See Sister M. Kevin Whelan, *Enthusiasm in English Poetry of the Eighteenth Century* (Washington, 1935), pp. 51-73 for a fuller discussion of the evidences of this critical theory in the late eighteenth century.

[25] See p. 108, *supra*.

[26] Eleanor M. Sickels, *The Gloomy Egoist* (New York, 1932), pp. 35-6.

[27] Amy Reed, *Background of Gray's Elegy* (New York, 1924), p. 47.

[28] Cf. "Afflictions by divine influence purge out sin, and promote holiness; *loosen from the world* and prepare for leaving it." (*The Magistrate and the Christian . . . by Jeremiah Smith*, London, 1722).

[29] Cf. this poem with Drummond's "This World a hunting is". Note also its influence on Blair's *Grave* and on Blake (see pp. 228-9, *infra*).

[30] Note the resemblance to Shelley's "Ozymandias".

[31] Reed, *op. cit.*, p. 94. It is possible that all of these "last day" poems have a common inspiration in the very popular *Theory of the Earth* (1684) by

Thomas Burnet. It is filled with conflagration and "last day" imagery. A fifth edition of the work came out in 1722 as *The Sacred Theory of the Earth.*

[32] J. W. Draper, *The Funeral Elegy and the Rise of English Romanticism* (New York, 1929), p. 92.

[33] *Ibid.*, p. 75.

[34] *Works*, Vol. IV, p. 437.

[35] R. D. Havens, *Influence of Milton on English Poetry* (Cambridge, 1922), p. 425.

[36] See p. 228, *infra.*

[37] *Works*, Vol. IV, p. 462.

[38] *Ibid.*

[39] Courthope, *op. cit.*, Vol. V, p. 21.

[40] *Works*, Vol. IV, pp. 410-12. Polhill was one of the five gentlemen who presented the famous "Kentish Petition" to Parliament in William's Reign.

[41] This is Watts's only attempt in poetical satire.

[42] Matthew Casimir Sarbiewski (1595-1640), commonly called "Casimir," was a Polish Jesuit who wrote exclusively in Latin. He was known in his day as the "Christian Horace." His poetry tended to the moral.

[43] Translated by Gibbons, *op. cit.*, p. 12.

[44] In 1708 Watts wrote a poem on "Burning several Poems of Ovid, Martial, Oldham, Dryden, etc.," (*Works*, Vol. IV, p. 401).

[45] Translated by Gibbons, *op. cit.*, p. 12.

[46] *Works*, Vol. IV, pp. 608-9.

[47] Cowley and Denham introduced this type of translation to England. See *C.H.E.L.*, Vol. VII, pp. 298-9.

[48] *Oxford Book of English Mystical Verse* (Oxford, 1916), p. vii, the definition of a mystical poem. "The Incomprehensible" is one of the four poems listed for the eighteenth century (before Blake).

[49] There are thirteen of these poems in Book I of *Hymns and Spiritual Songs* and twenty-two in *Horae Lyricae.*

[50] *Works*, Vol. I, p. 687.

[51] *Devout Exercises of the Heart* (London, 1826), p. xv.

[52] *Ibid.*, p. xiv.

[53] "The Mystical Element in English Poetry," *Essays and Studies*, Vol. VIII (1922), pp. 90-108.

[54] *Works*, Vol. IV, p. 326.

[55] *Ibid.*, p. 582, essay on "The Cadence of Verse."

[56] *Ibid.*, p. 585.

[57] Watts's position on this matter was one commonly held in his age. See Whelan, *op. cit.*, pp. 121-27 for a discussion of this critical attitude.

[58] Watts implies in his poem "The Adventurous Muse" that "coupled sound" cannot climb to sublimity.

[59] George N. Shuster, *The English Ode from Milton to Keats* (New York, 1940), pp. 154-6.

[60] Enid Hamer, *The Metres of English Poetry* (New York, 1930), pp. 306-9.

[61] Havens, *op. cit.*, p. 62. Havens feels that there is a correlation, exempli-

fied by Watts, Say, Grove, and Standen, between the piety of dissent and the use of blank verse.

⁶² *Miscellaneous Poems* (London, 1729), p. iv.

⁶³ V. de Sola Pinto, "Isaac Watts and His Poetry," *op. cit.*, p. 35.

⁶⁴ George Saintsbury, *A History of English Prosody* (London, 1908), Vol. II, p. 508.

⁶⁵ *Works*, Vol. IV, p. 458.

⁶⁶ *Theology in Augustan Literature* (Groningen, 1922).

⁶⁷ *Op. cit.*

⁶⁸ *Protestantismus und Literatur* (Leipzig, 1922).

⁶⁹ *Op. cit.*

⁷⁰ *Works*, Vol. IV, p. 593.

⁷¹ Doddridge's *Correspondence, op. cit.*, Vol. III, pp. 389-90. The letter is dated July 9, 1739.

⁷² See Chapter IX for a résumé of Watts's influence as a religious poet.

CHAPTER VIII

¹ I am indebted for the general facts and method of treatment in this chapter to *The English Hymn* (London, 1915) by Prof. Louis F. Benson of Princeton Theological Seminary. Prof. Benson's work, the result of twenty-five years of research, is a classic on this subject.

² The Bohemian Brethren had a hymn book as early as 1505, Benson, *op. cit.*, p. 21.

³ To Luther the hymns of the old church and folk songs were alike beautiful, and he used both freely.

⁴ *The Bay Psalm Book* and *Rous's Version* were thought to be "purer" than Sternhold and Hopkins'.

⁵ See *Works*, Vol. IV, p. xii.

⁶ There were two later enlarged editions of Barton's work appearing in 1668 and 1688.

⁷ Benson, *op. cit.*, p. 63.

⁸ Two of Wither's hymns are still in modern use: "Come, O come with pious lays" and "Behold the sun that seemed but now."

⁹ Benson, *op. cit.*, p. 65.

¹⁰ Watts, however, did not acknowledge this indebtedness in his works, although he was usually generous in this respect.

¹¹ Two of Crossman's hymns now in current use are "My song is love unknown" and "My life's a Shade, my daies."

¹² For an evaluation of Ken as a divine poet, see Fairchild, *op. cit.*, pp. 98-106.

¹³ The *Manual* first appeared in 1674. It originally contained only the injunction to sing hymns mornings and evenings. The hymns were evidently circulated among the students in manuscript. They were first published, without Ken's knowledge, in 1692.

[14] Watts published Mason's *Remains* in 1741.

[15] Watts was also indebted to Denham. See the *Christian Observer* (London, 1835), pp. 17 ff. for a detailed account of Watts's borrowings from the latter.

[16] John Playford's first book came out in 1671, *Psalms and Hymns in Solemn Musick of foure Parts on the common Tunes to the Psalms in Metre.*

[17] Benson, *op. cit.*, p. 81.

[18] The General Baptists opposed "promiscuous singing" until 1733. See Benson, *op. cit.*, pp. 91-94.

[19] Crosby's *History of the English Baptists* (London, 1738-40), Vol. I, p. 378.

[20] W. Y. Tindall, *John Bunyan Mechanick Preacher* (New York, 1934), p. 66-7. "He who would valiant be," "He that is down needs fear no fall," and "Let the most blessed be my guide" are three of Bunyan's hymns still in use.

[21] *Ibid.*

[22] His earliest printed hymns appeared in *War with the Power of Darkness*, 4th Ed. (1676).

[23] See letter from Enoch, p. 198, *infra.*

[24] Watts in *Divine Songs* was definitely following a Puritan tradition in which both Bunyan and Keach were important. See pp. 74 ff., *supra.*

[25] Benson, *op. cit.*, p. 108.

[26] "Piece" in Milner but certainly a misprint.

[27] Milner, *op. cit.*, pp. 176-9.

[28] *Works*, Vol. IV, p. 147.

[29] See *A Vindication of David's Psalms, from Mr. J. Watts's Erroneous Notions and Hard Speeches of Them* (London, 1727) and *Reasons wherefore Christians ought to Worship God in Singing his Praises; not with the Matter and Sense of Dr. Watts's Psalms and Hymns; . . .* (London, 1759).

[30] *Works*, Vol. IV, pp. xxii and xxiii.

[31] *Works*, Vol. IV, p. xxi.

[32] *Works*, Vol. IV, p. 149.

[33] Milner, *op. cit.*, p. 229. The letter is dated, Mar. 12, 1709.

[34] For a detailed study of the differences among these editions, see Louis F. Benson, *The Early Editions of Dr. Watts's Hymns* (Phila., 1902).

[35] In 1806 John Dobell printed *Dr. Watts's Fourth Book of Spiritual Hymns*, composed of the hymns from the above-mentioned works. This volume had great vogue (Benson, *op. cit.*, p. 121).

[36] See p. 116, *supra.*

[37] *Works* (1810 ed.), Vol. IV, p. 256.

[38] *Dictionary of Hymnology*, Revised Ed. (London, 1908), art., "Early English Hymnody."

[39] The imagery of Watts's hymns also owes much to the seventeenth century poetic tradition in which he was nourished. This has been discussed, pp. 161 ff., *supra.*

[40] John Wesley's *Journal* contains many accounts of Christians repeating or singing Watts's hymns on their dying beds.

[41] In the early editions of *Hymns and Spiritual Songs*, each hymn had its own title.

[42] Benson, *op. cit.*, p. 206.

[43] The material for these paragraphs on music has come in large part from H. B. Marks, *The Rise and Growth of English Hymnody* (New York, 1938).

[44] Wm. Romaine, *An Essay on Psalmody* (London, 1755), p. 106.

[45] W. Wilson, *The History and Antiquities of Dissenting Churches . . . in London, . . .* (London, 1808), Vol. III, p. 527.

[46] Frederic Palmer, "Isaac Watts", *Harvard Theological Review*, Vol. XII (1919), p. 371.

[47] See *Gentleman's Magazine*, Vol. LXV, (1795), p. 321 for a strong attack on Kippis's mangling of Watts. See also Vol. LXVI, p. 295; p. 1068; Vol. LVII, p. 775; p. 1052; and p. 1151 for similar attacks on the Unitarian treatment of Watts.

[48] See, for example, *Inconsistency of Several Passages in Doctor Watts's Hymns, . . .* American Unitarian Tracts (Phila., 1807), pp. 233 ff.

[49] Julian, *op. cit.*, art., "Church of England Hymnody," has been the major source of material for this discussion.

[50] *Ibid.*

[51] See Benson, *op. cit.*, pp. 142-7.

[52] The influence of Watts on American hymnody was also exceedingly great. For treatment of this subject, see Benson, *op. cit.*, and E. S. Ninde, *Story of the American Hymn* (New York, 1921).

[53] See Benson, *op. cit.*, pp. 210-16 for a detailed consideration of this school.

[54] J. B. Reeves, *The Hymn as Literature* (New York, 1924), p. 6.

[55] W. G. Horder, *The Hymn Lover* (London, N. D.), p. 96.

[56] I. L. Bird, "Hymns of the English Nonconformists," *Littel's Living Age*, 4th Series, Vol. IX (1865), pp. 387 ff. The same article states that in 1865, from 80 to 100 thousand copies of *Divine Songs* were sold annually.

[57] David R. Breed, *The History and Use of Hymns and Hymn-Tunes* (New York, 1903), pp. 86-7.

[58] This is the Presbyterian hymnal for the Church of Scotland, the United Free Church of Scotland, and the Presbyterian Church of Ireland, England, Wales, Australia, New Zealand and South Africa.

[59] This work was sponsored by the National Council of Congregational Churches.

[60] Unitarian hymnal.

[61] P. A. Otis, *The Hymns You Ought to Know* (Chicago, 1928). The four hymns from Watts were: "Our God our help etc.," "When I survey the wondrous cross," "Jesus shall reign etc.," and "Behold what wondrous grace." See also *Literary Digest* (Jan. 11, 1930), p. 31 for the surveys conducted by the *Methodist Times* (London). Watts still has two of the twenty-five "favorite hymns," Wesley none.

[62] See Thomas H. Gill, "Watts and Wesley Compared," *The Congregationalist*, Vol. VII (1878), pp. 129 ff.

[63] "Isaac Watts," *op. cit.*, p. 403.

[64] Thomas H. Gill, "Isaac Watts," *The Congregationalist*, Vol. III (1874), p. 432.

CHAPTER IX

[1] "Verses made on the Dissenting Ministers . . ." by an anonymous satirist, quoted in John Stoughton, *Religion in England under Queen Anne and the Georges*, 2 vols. (London, 1878), Vol. I, p. 335.

[2] Gibbons, *op. cit.*, p. 324.

[3] *Works*, Vol. III, p. 668.

[4] Johnson's *Works, op. cit.*, Vol. XI, p. 48.

[5] Gibbons, *op. cit.*, p. 157.

[6] Johnson's *Works*, op. cit., Vol. XI, pp. 48-9.

[7] *M. H. S. Proc.*, 2nd Series, Vol. IX, p. 346.

[8] *Sacred Classics* (London, 1834), Vol. IX, p. lxi.

[9] Gibbons, *op. cit.*, p. 137.

[10] *Works*, Vol. I, Preface.

[11] *Ibid.*, p. 140.

[12] Gibbons, *op. cit.*, p. 153.

[13] *Ibid.*, p. 147.

[14] *Ibid.*, p. 165.

[15] *Works*, Vol. I, p. viii.

[16] Milner, *op. cit.*, pp. 325-6.

[17] P. L. Parker (ed.), *The Heart of John Wesley's Journal* (London, 1903), p. 344.

[18] *Achates to Varus* (London, 1746), p. ii.

[19] Watts used rather regularly the following papers for the purpose of advertising his own and recommending the works of others: the *Old Whig, Post Boy, Daily Post*, and *Hooker's Weekly Miscellany*. The *Old Whig* was evidently his favorite medium.

[20] Wesley himself sang a Watts hymn on his death bed.

[21] P. Doddridge, *Rise and Progress of Religion in the Soul* (London, 1745), pp. vi and xii.

[22] Quoted in Milner, *op. cit.*, p. 333.

[23] See *Post. Works*, Vol. II, pp. 131 ff. for Watts-Cave correspondence.

[24] *Ibid.*

[25] Johnson's *Works, op. cit.*, Vol. XI, p. 46.

[26] See letters in *Gentleman's Magazine*, Vol. LX (1790), pp. 1085 ff.

[27] *Juvenilia* (London, 1750), p. 173.

[28] Fairchild, *op. cit.*, p. 415.

[29] Browne wrote a poem on Watts's death, see p. 71, *supra*.

[30] See p. 43, *supra*, for Watts-Hervey relation.

[31] Doddridge's *Correspondence, op. cit.*, Vol. IV, p. 73.

[32] Cf. "When I can read my title clear
       To mansions in the skies."

[33] S. F. Damon, *William Blake his Philosophy and Symbols* (London, 1924), p. 41.

[34] Damon, *op. cit.*, p. 269.

APPENDIX A

[1] Unless otherwise stated, all "M. H. S. Proc." notations refer to the Belknap Collection of letters, 2nd Series, Vol. IX, pp. 331-410. The letters are arranged in chronological order.

[2] See p. 36, *supra.*

[3] See Wright, *op. cit.* pp. 173 and 274.

[4] In possession of Rev. Wilton Rix, Ealing, London.

[5] In possession of Basil Cozens-Hardy, Esq., Norwich, England.

[6] See p. 136, *supra.*

[7] Source indefinite, see Wright, *op. cit.*, p. 275.

[8] See p. 66, *supra.*

APPENDIX B

[1] Of the ten, nine are hymns and appear in *Hymns and Spiritual Songs* (1707). The other, "An Ode to the Lady Sunderland, 1712," is one of the very few examples of non-religious poetry to be found in Watts's works. It is a poetic compliment to the beauty of Lady Sunderland, the daughter of the Duke of Marlborough. She and her two sisters were at Tunbridge Wells while Watts was there. When they left some anonymous wit wrote a poem on their beauty. The verses, which were not very good, were attributed to Watts, who wrote in self-defense the poem in question. It does not appear in any of his works although Gibbons tells us that it was published (Gibbons, *op. cit.*, pp. 131-2).

[2] Gibbons claims that Watts's last poem was "On an Elegy written by the Right Hon. the Countess of Hertford, on the Death of Mrs. Rowe" (1737).

[3] *Ibid.*, pp. 481-91.

[4] *Ibid.*, p. 483.

[5] *Ibid.*, pp. 486-7.

[6] *Post. Works*, Vol. I, p. 50.

[7] *Ibid.*, p. 214.

[8] *Works*, Vol. IV, p. 349.

[9] *Post. Works*, Vol. I, p. 87.

[10] *Ibid.*, p. 159.

BIBLIOGRAPHY I

[1] Unless otherwise stated, all works were published in London.

BIBILIOGRAPHY I

WORKS OF ISAAC WATTS [1]

1706 Horae Lyricae. Poems chiefly of the Lyric Kind, in Three Books. Sacred I. To Devotion and Piety. II. To Virtue, Honour, and Friendship. III. To the Memory of the Dead. [The work actually appeared in 1705, although 1706 appears on title-page.]

1707 Essay against Uncharitableness, wherein the Secret Springs of that Vice are Traced and the Mischievous Effects of it briefly Surveyed.

1707 A Sermon Preached at Salters-Hall to the Societies for Reformation of Manners, in the Cities of London and Westminster, October 6th 1707.

1707 Hymns and Spiritual Songs. In Three Books. I. Collected from the Scriptures. II. Composed on Divine Subjects. III. Prepared for the Lord's Supper. With an Essay towards the Improvement of Christian Psalmody, by the use of Evangelical Hymns in Worship, as well as the Psalms of David.

1715 A Guide to Prayer: or, a Free and Rational Account of the Gift, Grace and Spirit of Prayer; with plain Directions how every Christian may attain them.

1715 Divine Songs attempted in Easy Language, for the use of Children. With some Additional Composures.

1719 The Psalms of David Imitated in the Language of the New Testament, and Applied to the Christian State and Worship.

1720 An Elegy on the much lamented Death of Mrs. Elizabeth Bury. [Published in *An Account of the Life and Death of Mrs. Elizabeth Bury*.]

1721 The Art of Reading and Writing English: or, the chief Principles and Rules of Pronouncing our Mother-Tongue, both in Prose and Verse; with a Variety of Instructions for True Spelling. Written at first for Private Use, and now published for the Benefit of all Persons who desire a better acquaintance with their Native Language.

1721 Sermons on Various Subjects; viz. I. II. III. The Inward Witness of Christianity. . . . XIII. XIV. Appearing before God. Wherein many Things relating to Christian Experience, and the Future State, are set in a Fair and Easy Light. Together with a Sacred Hymn annexed to each Subject.

1722 An Elegiac Ode written in the form of a Soliloquy or Mourning Meditation at the Death of Sir Thomas Abney, Knt. and Alderman of London, . . . In Two Parts. . . . [Published in *The Magistrate and the Christian* by Jeremiah Smith].

1722 The Christian Doctrine of the Trinity: or, Father, Son and Spirit, three Persons and one God, asserted and proved, with their Divine Rights and Honors vindicated by plain Evidence of Scripture, without the Aid or Incumbrance of Human Schemes. Written chiefly for the use of private Christians.

1722 Death and Heaven; or, the Last Enemy Conquered, and Separate Spirits made perfect: with an Account of the Rich Variety of their Employments and Pleasures; attempted in two Funeral Discourses, in memory of Sir John Hartopp, Baronet, and his Lady, deceased.

1723 Sermons on Various Subjects, viz. Christian Faith, I. II. III. A Rational Defence of the Gospel. . . . XVI. Courage and Honour. With Hymns suitable to every Subject. . . . Vol. II . . .

1723 A Hopeful Youth Falling Short of Heaven, exemplified in the Conduct of the Rich Young Man whom Jesus Loved.

1724 Three Dissertations relating to the Christian Doctrine of the Trinity, (viz.) I. The Arian invited to the Orthodox Faith. II. God and Man united in the Person of Christ. III. The Worship of Christ as Mediator founded on his Godhead.

1724 Logic: or the Right Use of Reason in the Enquiry after Truth with a Variety of Rules to guard against error in the Affairs of Religion and Human Life, as well as in the Sciences.

1725 Four Dissertations relating to the Christian Doctrine of the Trinity.

1726 The Knowledge of the Heavens and the Earth made easy: or the first principles of Astronomy and Geography explained by the use of Globes and Maps: . . . .

1726 A Defence against the Temptation to Self-Murther. Wherein the Criminal Nature and Guilt of it are displayed: the various Pretences for it are examined and answered: . . . . Together with some Reflexions on Excess in strong Liquors, Duelling and other Practices a-kin to this heinous Sin.

1727 The Religious Improvement of Public Events. A Sermon preached at Berry-Street, June 18, 1727. On Occasion of the Death of our late Gracious Sovereign George I. and the peaceful Succession of his present Majesty George II.

1728 Prayers Composed for the Use and Imitation of Children, suited to their different Ages and their various Occasions: together with Instructions to Youth in the Duty of Prayer, drawn up by way of Question and Answer. And a Serious Address to them on that Subject.

1728 An Essay towards the Encouragement of Charity-Schools, particularly those which are supported by Protestant Dissenters, for teaching the Children of the Poor to Read and Work; . . . to which is prefixed, an Address to the Supporters of those Schools.

1729 Sermons on Various Subjects, Divine and Moral: With a Sacred Hymn suited to each Subject. In Three Volumes. Design'd for the Use of Christian Families, as well as for the Hours of Devout Retirement. . . . Vol. III. . . .

1729 A Caveat against Infidelity: or the Danger of Apostasy from the Christian Faith: with an Answer to various queries concerning the Salvation of the Heathens, and the Hope of the Modern Deists upon their Pretences to Sincerity.

1729 The Doctrine of the Passions Explained and Improved; or, a brief and comprehensive Scheme of the Natural Affections of Mankind, and an Account of their Names, Nature, Appearances, Effects, and different Uses in Human Life; to which are subjoined Moral and Divine Rules for the Regulation or Government of them.

1729 Discourses of the Love of God and the Use and Abuse of the Passions in Religion, with a Devout Meditation suited to each Discourse. To which is Prefixed, A Plain and Particular Account of the Natural Passions, with Rules for the Government of them.

1730 To His Excellency, Jonathan Belcher, Esq.; in London, appointed by His Majesty King George II to the Government of New England, and now Returning Home. [This poem of forty-one lines was published in Boston, probably by Belcher. It does not appear in the collected works.]

1730 Catechisms; or, Instructions in the Principles of the Christian Religion, and the History of Scripture, composed for Children and Youth, according to their different Ages. To which is prefixed, a Discourse on the Way of Instruction by Catechisms, and the best Manner of Composing them.

1731 An Humble Attempt towards the Revival of Practical Religion among Christians, and particularly the Protestant Dissenters, by a Serious Address to Ministers and People, in some occasional Discourses.

1731 The Strength and Weakness of Human Reason: or, the Important Question about the Sufficiency of Reason to Conduct Mankind to Religion and Future Happiness, argued between an Inquiring Deist and a Christian Divine: and the Debate Compromised and Determined to the Satisfaction of both, by an impartial Moderator.

1732 The Watchful Christian Prepared for Early Death. A Sermon on occasion of the Decease of Mrs. Sarah Abney, . . . Preached . . . April 2, 1732.

1732 A Short View of the Whole Scripture History, with a Continuation of the Jewish Affairs, from the Old Testament, till the Time of Christ; and an Account of the Chief Prophecies that relate to him: represented in a way of Question and Answer. Illustrated with various Remarks on the History and the Religion of the Patriarchs, Jews and Christians; and on the Laws, Government, Sects, Customs, and Writings of the Jews; and adorned with Figures relating to their Camp, Tabernacle, and Worship.

1732 An Essay toward the Proof of a Separate State of Souls between Death and the Resurrection, and the Commencement of the Rewards of Virtue and Vice immediately after Death. [The second edition of this work, enlarged, formed part of *World to Come*.]

1732 An Essay on the Freedom of Will in God and in Creatures, and on various Subjects connected therewith: viz. the Ideas of Liberty and Necessity; the Causes of the Determination of the Will; the Use of the Understanding to direct, not to determine it; the Liberty of God as a Creator, a Governor, and a Benefactor; the Doctrine of Fatality; the Spring of Moral Good and Evil; the Difference between Moral and Positive Laws; the Sin and Fall of Man, and the Free Grace of God; the Rewardableness of Faith in the Gospel, and the criminal Nature of Infidelity. [This essay was usually bound with the *Separate State of Souls* (1732).]

1733 Philosophical Essays on Various Subjects, viz. Space, Substance, Body, Spirit, the Operations of the Soul in Union with the Body, Innate Ideas, Perpetual Consciousness, Place and Motions of Spirits, the Departing Soul, the Resurrection of the Body, the Production and Operation of Plants and Animals, with some Remarks on Mr. Locke's Essay on the Human Understanding. To which is subjoined a Brief Scheme of Ontology, or the Science of Being in General, with its Affections.

1734 Reliquiae Juveniles: Miscellaneous Thoughts in Prose and Verse, on Natural, Moral, and Divine Subjects; written chiefly in Younger Years.

1735 Faith and Practice Represented in fifty-four Sermons on the Principal Heads of the Christian Religion; Preached at Berry-Street, 1733. By I. Watts, D.D., D. Neal, M.A., J. Guyse, D.D., S. Price, D. Jennings, J. Hubbard. Published for the use of Families, especially on the Lord's-Day Evenings. [The

19

work appeared in two volumes. Watts wrote Sermons i, xi, xiii, xix, and xxv in Vol. I and xxxi, xxxvii, xlii, and xlix in Vol. II.]

1736 The Redeemer and the Sanctifier: or, the Sacrifice of Christ and the Operations of the Spirit Vindicated: with a free Debate about the Importance of these Doctrines, represented in a friendly Conversation between Persons of different Sentiments.

1737 Humility Represented in the Character of St. Paul, the chief Springs of it Opened, and its various Advantages Displayed; together with some occasional Views of the contrary Vice.

1738 The Holiness of Times, Places, and People under the Jewish and Christian Dispensations considered and compared, in several Discourses, viz. I. On the Perpetuity of a Sabbath, and the Observation of the Lord's-Day. II. The Administration of the Lord's-Supper, at noon or Evening. III. The Holiness and Consecration of Places of Worship, considered in a Sermon at the opening of a new meeting-place. IV. Forms of Worship, and Holy Things more exactly prescribed in the Old Testament than in the New. V. The difference between the Visible and the Invisible Church, the Jewish and the Christian; and the Holiness of each of them.

1739 The World to Come: or, Discourses on the Joys or Sorrows of Departed Souls at Death, and the Glory or Terror of the Resurrection. Whereto is prefixed, An Essay towards the Proof of a Separate State of Souls after Death.

1739 A New Essay on Civil Power in Things Sacred; or, an Inquiry after an Established Religion, consistent with the just Liberties of Mankind and practicable under every form of Civil Government.

1739 Self-Love and Virtue Reconciled only by Religion; or, an Essay to prove that the only Effectual Obligation of Mankind to practice Virtue depends on the Existence and Will of God; together with an occasional Proof of the Necessity of Revelation.

1740 The Ruin and Recovery of Mankind: or, an attempt to Vindicate the Scriptural Account of these great Events upon the plain Principles of Reason. With an answer to various Difficulties relating to Original Sin, the Universal Depravation of Nature, and the over-spreading Curse of Death; general offers of Grace to all Men, and the certain Salvation of some; the Case of the Heathen Nations, and the State of the Dying Infants. Whereto are subjoined three short Essays, viz. The Proof of Man's Fall by his Misery; The Imputation of Sin and Righteousness; and, The Guilt and Defilement of Sin.

1740 Questions Proper for Students in Divinity, Candidates of the Ministry, and Young Christians.

1741 The Improvement of the Mind: or, a Supplement to the Art of Logic: containing a Variety of Remarks and Rules for the Attainment and Communication of useful Knowledge in Religion, in the Sciences, and in Common Life.

1742 The Harmony of all the Religions which God ever Prescribed: containing a brief Survey of the several publick Dispensations of God towards Man, or his appointment of different Forms of Religion in successive Ages. Humbly proposed as an easy Clew to lead us through many difficulties of the Old Testament, and the New; and particularly to Explain and Reconcile the several Parts of St. Paul's Epistles on these Subjects to every Capacity.

1745 The World to Come. (Vol. II.)

1745 Orthodoxy and Charity United: in several Reconciling Essays on the Law and Gospel, Faith and Works; viz. Essay I. The Substance or matter of the Gospel. II. The Form of the Gospel. III. The use of the Law under the Gospel. IV. Mistaken ways of coming to God without Christ. V. A Plain and Easy Account of Saving Faith, or coming to God by Jesus Christ. VI. A Reconciling Thought on various Controversies about Faith and Salvation. VII. Against Uncharitableness. VIII. The Difficulties in Scripture, and the various opinions of Christians. IX. An Apology for Christians of Different Sentiments.

1745 [?] A Faithful Enquiry after the Ancient and Original Doctrine of the Trinity Taught by Christ and his Apostles. [I was unable to find a 1745 edition of this work. The title is taken from an 1802 reprint of the original work. See p. 117, *supra,* for a discussion of this edition.]

1746 Useful and Important Questions concerning Jesus the Son of God freely proposed: with a humble attempt to Answer them according to Scripture . . . To which is added, a Charitable Essay on the True Importance of any Human Schemes to explain the Sacred Doctrine of the Trinity.

1746 The Glory of Christ as God-Man Displayed, in Three Discourses. Viz. Disc. I. A Survey of the Visible Appearances of Christ, as God before his Incarnation, with some Observations on the texts of the Old Testament applied to Christ. Disc. II. An Inquiry into the Extensive Powers of the Human Nature of Christ in its present Glorified State, with several Testimonies annexed. Disc. III. An Argument tracing out the early Existence of the Human Soul of Christ, even before the Creation of the world. With an Appendix containing an Abridgment of Doctor Thomas Goodwin's Discourse of the "Glories and Royalties of Christ," in his Works in folio, Vol. II. Book 3.

1747 Evangelical Discourses on several Subjects. To which is added, an Essay on the Powers and Contests of Flesh and Spirit.

1747 The Rational Foundation of a Christian Church, and the Terms of Christian Communion. To which are added three Discourses, viz. Discourse I. A Pattern for a Dissenting Preacher. Discourse II. The Office of Deacons. Discourse III. Invitations to Church-Fellowship.

Posthumous Publications

1751 The Improvement of the Mind. The Second Part. [Published in 1751 by D. Jennings and P. Doddridge, the literary executors of Watts's estate.]

1753 The Works of the late Reverend and Learned Isaac Watts, D.D. Published by himself, and now Collected into Six Volumes. In which are also inserted The Second Part of The Improvement of the Mind, An Essay on Education, And some Additions to his Miscellaneous Thoughts in Prose and Verse. Now first Published from his Manuscripts, and, by the Direction of his Will, Revised and Corrected by D. Jennings, D.D. and the late P. Doddridge, D.D.

1779 The Posthumous Works of the late Learned and Reverend Isaac Watts, D.D. In Two Volumes. Compiled from Papers in Possession of his immediate Successors: Adjusted and Published by a Gentleman of the University of Cambridge. [See pp. 239 ff., *supra,* for comments on this work.]

1812 Nine Sermons Preached in the years 1718-19, by the late Isaac Watts, D.D. Now first Published from MSS. in the Family of a Contemporary Friend. Oxford, 1812, John Pye Smith, (ed.).

Recommendations and Prefaces

Recommendatory prefaces for the works given below were written by Isaac Watts. When it was not possible to find a first edition, I have given the date of the recommendation.

Memoirs of the Reverend, Learned, and Pious Mr. Thomas Halyburton, Professor of Divinity in the University of St. Andrews. With a large Recommendatory Epistle by Dr. Watts. Phila., 1796. [The Epistle is dated May 1, 1718.]

Disputes Reviewed in a Sermon Preached at the Evening Lecture in Salters' Hall, on Lord's-Day, July 23, 1710. By Matthew Henry. London, 1719.

The Great Concern of Salvation. By Thomas Halyburton. With a work of Recommendation by I. Watts. Edinburgh, 1721.

Two Discourses: the first, *Of Preaching Christ;* the Second, *Of Particular and Experimental Preaching* by the late Reverend Mr. John Jennings. With a Preface by the Reverend Dr. Isaac Watts. The Fourth Edition . . . Boston, 1740. [The preface is dated June 14, 1723.]

The Example of St. Paul represented to Ministers and to Private Christians . . . . Recommended by the Rev. Mr. Isaac Watts. . . . London, 1726.

A Sermon Preached at Chester, on Occasion of Opening the new

Meeting-house there, August 8, 1700. By the late Reverend Mr. Matthew Henry. London, 1726.

A Practical Discourse of Reconciliation between God and Man, . . . By the late Learned and Pious Mr. John Reynolds. With a Recommendatory Preface, by the Reverend Mr. Isaac Watts. London, 1729.

A Faithful Narrative of the Surprizing Work of God in the Conversion of many Hundred Souls in Northampton, and the Neighbouring Towns and Villages of New Hampshire in New England. . . . And Published, with a Large Preface, by Dr. Watts and Dr. Guyse. London, 1737. [By Jonathan Edwards.]

The Christian-Family Prayer Book: or, Family Prayers for Morning and Evening; with a Variety of Occasional Forms, Prefaced by a Discourse, Representing the Reasonableness, Beauty, Pleasure and Usefulness of Family Religion. By Samuel Bourn. Recommended by Dr. I. Watts. London, 1737.

Devout Exercises of the Heart, in Meditation and Soliloquy, Prayer and Praise. By the late Pious and Ingenious Mrs. Elizabeth Rowe. Reviewed and Published at her Request, by I. Watts, D.D. London, 1737.

Select Remains of the Reverend John Mason, M.A. Late Rector of Water-Stratford, in the County of Bucks, author of the Songs of Praise to Almighty God. . . . Recommended by the Rev. I. Watts, D.D. 2nd Ed. London, 1742. [The Recommendation is dated Oct. 24, 1741.]

The Distinguishing Marks of a Work of the Spirit of God applied to that uncommon Operation that has lately appeared in the Minds of many of the People of this Land . . . [This work by Jonathan Edwards was published in Boston in 1741. Watts reprinted it in London in 1742, adding to its preface some additional extracts of letters from Benjamin Colman and Mr. Parsons of Lyme.]

An Abridgment of the Life of the late Reverend and learned Dr. Cotton Mather, of Boston in New-England. Taken from the account of him published by his son, the Reverend Mr. Samuel Mather . . . By David Jennings. Recommended by I. Watts. . . . London, 1744.

The Testimony and Advice of an Assembly of Pastors of Churches in New England, at a Meeting in Boston, July 7, 1743. Occasioned by the late Happy Revival of Religion in many Parts of the Land. . . . With a Recommendation of it by the Revd. Dr. Watts, as the plainest and fullest Attestation to the late Work of Divine Grace in New England. By Order of the Assembly. Boston Printed: London Reprinted, . . . 1744.

The Religious Tradesman; or, Plain and Serious Hints of Advice for the Tradesman's Prudent and Pious Conduct; from his Entrance into Business to his leaving it off. A New Edition. Bath, 1802. [Written by R. Steele. The Preface, dated Jan. 24, 1747, was written by Gibbons for Watts who was ill at the time. Gibbons allowed his name to be suppressed. See Gibbons, *op. cit.,* p. 134.]

A Collection of the Promises of Scripture, under their Proper Heads. . . . By Samuel Clark, D.D. With a Recommendatory Preface by Dr. Watts. London, 1790. [The Preface is signed Newington, Jan. 14, 1750 (obviously a misprint). Watts refers in the Preface to a second edition of the work but gives no dates.]

BIBILIOGRAPHY II

GENERAL

This is primarily a list of the books cited in the present work. Some additional titles, however, have been added which will aid the student seeking further information about Isaac Watts.

A.B., A View of the Dissenting Interest in London of the Presbyterian and Independent Denominations from the year 1695 to the 25 of December 1731 [MS. in Dr. Williams' Library, London].

Abbey, C. J. and Overton, J. H., The English Church in the Eighteenth Century, London, 1878.

Anonymous, Achates to Varus. An Epistle: Describing some late Wonderful Appearances that Ensued from a Touch of Ithuriel's Spear, London, 1746.

Anonymous, "Dr. Watts's Hymns," *Hours at Home,* Vol. VII (1868), pp. 512 ff.

Anonymous, A Letter to the Author of the *Monthly Review,* on his Account of Dr. Watts's *Posthumous Works* and his Strictures upon Dr. Gibbons' *Memoirs of Watts,* London, 1781.

Anonymous, A Poem Sacred to the Memory of the Reverend and Learned Isaac Watts, D.D., London, (n.d.).

Anonymous, Reasons wherefore Christians ought to Worship God in singing His Praises; not with the Matter and Sense of Dr. Watts's Psalms and Hymns, London, 1759.

Anonymous, To His Excellency Jonathan Belcher Esq., Boston, 1730 [Fragment in Mass. Historical Society Library].

Anonymous, A Vindication of David's Psalms, from Mr. J. Watts's Erroneous Notions and Hard Speeches of Them, London, 1727.

Anonymous, Was Dr. Watts a Believer in the Supreme Deity of Jesus Christ?, Boston, (n.d.).

Ashton, John, Social Life in the Reign of Queen Anne, London, 1882, 2 Vols.

Ashworth, Caleb, Reflections on the Fall of a Great Man. A Sermon . . . on Occasion of the Death of the late Learned Isaac Watts, D.D., 2nd ed., London, 1749.

Babenroth, A. Charles, English Childhood, New York, 1922.

Barbauld, Mrs. Anna Letitia, Works, London, 1825, 2 Vols.

Baxter, Richard, The Practical Works, London, 1838, 4 Vols.

Belknap, Jeremy, Memoirs of the Lives, Characters and Writings of . . . Dr. Isaac Watts and Dr. Philip Doddridge, Boston, 1793.

Benson, Louis F., The Early Editions of Dr. Watts's Hymns, Philadelphia, 1902.

——————, The English Hymn, New York, 1915.

——————, The Hymnody of the Christian Church, New York, 1927.

Bird, Isabella L., "Hymns of the English Nonconformists," *Littel's Living Age,* 4th Series, Vol. IX (1868), pp. 387-393.

Blackmore, Sir Richard, Letters of Religion between Theophilus and Eugenia, London, 1720.

Bogue, David and Bennett, James, The History of Dissenters from the Revolution to . . . 1808, 2nd ed., London, 1833, 2 Vols.

Boswell, James, Boswell's Life of Johnson, ed. G. B. Hill, New York, 1891, 6 Vols.

Boyer, Abel, The History of the Reign of Queen Anne, Digested into Annals, London, 1703-13, 11 Vols.

Breed, David R., The History and Use of Hymns and Hymn-Tunes, New York, 1903.

Brown, E. E., The Making of our Middle Schools, New York, 1910.

Bury, Elizabeth, An Account of the Life and Death of Mrs. Elizabeth Bury . . . . Together with her Funeral Sermon, . . . And her Elegy by the Reverend Mr. J. Watts, 2nd. ed., London, 1721.

Butler, Joseph, The Works, ed. W. E. Gladstone, Oxford, 1896, 2 Vols.

Calamy, Edmund, Nonconformist's Memorial, ed. S. Palmer, 2nd ed., London, 1802, 3 Vols.

Cambridge History of American Literature, New York, 1917-23, 4 Vols.

Cambridge History of English Literature, New York, 1932, 15 Vols.

Carlisle, H. H., Honour to Whom Honour, London, 1874.

The Christian Disciple and Theological Review (Boston), new series, Vol. II (1820), pp. 461-72: A Review of the 1816 Edition of Watts's "Faithful Enquiry."

The Christian Observer (London), Vol. XXXII (1832), p. 648: Unpublished Pastoral Letter of Dr. Isaac Watts.

The Christian Observer for the Year 1835 (London), pp. 17 ff. and 143: Letters on Dr. Watts's Imitation of Sir John Denham.

Christian Observer, Conducted by Members of the Established Church (London), Vol. XII (1818), pp. 719-30: A Review of Nine Sermons Preached in the year 1718-19, by the late Isaac Watts.

The Christian Reformer; or Unitarian Magazine and Review (London), Vol. II (1835), p. 164: Review of Milner's Life of Watts.

Clark, Henry W., History of English Nonconformity, London, 1911-13, 2 Vols.

Colligan, J. Hay, Eighteenth Century Nonconformity, London, 1915.

Conder, Josiah, The Poet of the Sanctuary, London, 1851.

Congregational Historical Society, Transactions (London), Vol. (1901) *et al.*

Congregational Magazine, N.S. Vol. XI (May, 1835), pp. 189-93: Catalogue and Sale of Dr. Watt's Manuscripts.

Cornthwaite, Robert, An Essay on the Sabbath, London, 1740.

Courthope, W. J., A History of English Poetry, London, 1905, 6 Vols.

Cowper, Wm., Letters, ed. J. G. Frazer, London, 1912, 2 Vols.

Crane, R. S. and Prior, M. E., "English Literature, 1660-1800: A Current Bibliography," *Philological Quarterly,* Vol. XI (1932), pp. 167-314.

Crosby, Thomas, The History of the English Baptists, from the Reformation to the Beginning of the Reign of George I, London, 1738-40.

Dale, R. W., History of English Congregationalism, New York, 1907.

Damon, S. F., William Blake, his Philosophy and Symbols, London, 1924.

Darton, F. J. Harvey, Children's Books in England, Cambridge, University Press, 1932.

Defoe, Daniel, An Enquiry into Occasional Conformity, London, 1702.

Dictionary of National Biography, ed. Leslie Stephen, New York, 1885.

Doddridge, Philip, The Correspondence and Diary, ed. John D. Humphreys, London, 1830, 5 Vols.

——— ———, Free Thoughts on the Most Probable Means of Reviving the Dissenting Interest, London, 1730.

——————, The Principles of the Christian Religion, Expressed in Plain and Easy Verse, London, 1743.

——————, The Rise and Progress of Religion in the Soul, 2nd ed., London, 1745.

Draper, John W., The Funeral Elegy and the Rise of English Romanticism, New York, 1929.

Dunton, John, Life and Errors of John Dunton, Citizen of London, London, 1818, 2 Vols.

Eames, Wilberforce, "Early New England Catchisms," *Proceedings of the American Antiquarian Society* (Worcester), new series XII (1897-8), pp. 76-182.

Edwards, Jonathan, Works of President Edwards, Worcester, 1808, 8 Vols.

Emerson, Joseph, Questions and Supplement, to Watts on *The Improvement of the Mind,* Boston, 1831.

Evans, Charles, American Bibliography, Chicago, 1903-34, 12 Vols.

Evans, Rev. J., A Compendious View of the Proofs of the Authenticity and Inspiration of the Old and New Testaments . . . a Companion to Watts's Scripture History, Oxford, 1831.

Fairchild, H. N., Religious Trends in English Poetry, New York, 1939.

Faust, C. H. and Johnson, T. H., Jonathan Edwards, New York, 1935.

Fay, Paul J., "Isaac Watts—An Unsung Singer of Education," *School and Society,* Vol. XXVIII (New York, Aug. 25, 1928), pp. 217-24.

F. J., "Dr. Isaac Watts," *The Christian Witness* (London), Vol. XV, No. 178 (Oct. 1858), pp. 470 ff.

Fleming, Caleb, A Letter to a Friend, containing select Remarks upon the Rev. Dr. Isaac Watts's Treatise, entitled, the Glory of Christ as God-Man, London, 1746.

Fleming, Sanford, Children and Puritanism 1620-1847, New Haven, 1933.

Fletcher, Giles and Phineas, Poetical Works, Cambridge, 1908-9, 2 Vols.

Ford, Paul L., The New England Primer, New York, 1897.

Four Letters of Dr. Isaac Watts (Published by Mass. Historical Society), 1898.

Foxcroft, Thomas, An Apology in Behalf of the Rev'd Mr. Whitefield: . . . The Second Edition, To which is Prefixed Dr. Watts's Opinion of Mr. Whitefield, Boston, 1745.

Gardiner, Dorothy, English Girlhood at School, London, 1929.

General Advertiser (London), Nov. 26, 1748: Notice of Watts's death and eulogy.

Gentleman's Magazine (London), Vol. XVIII (1748), p. 525: Death notice of Isaac Watts; Vol. LVII (1787), p. 99: Genuine Copy of a Letter from Dr. Samuel Johnson; pp. 75-6: Letter on Dr. Watts's Religious Views; Letter protesting Unitarian Mutilation of Watts's *Divine Songs;* Vol. LX (1790), pp. 1085-6: Two Letters from Watts to Doddridge; Vol. LXV (1795), p. 321: Review of a *Collection of Hymns and Psalms* by Andrew Kippis and others; Vol. LXVI (1796), pp. 925 and 1068: Letters on Unitarian treatment of Watts's hymns; Vol. LXVII (1797), p. 655: A Letter from Watts to Lardner; Vol. LXXXVI (1816), pp. 10-11: Watt's letters to Joseph Highmore.

George, M. Dorothy, London Life in the Eighteenth Century, London, 1925.

Gibbons, Thomas, Juvenilia: Poems on Various Subjects of Devotion and Virtue, London, 1750.

————, Memoirs of the Rev. Isaac Watts, D.D., London, 1780.

Gibson, Edmund, The Peculiar Excellency and Reward of Supporting Schools of Charity, London, 1716.

Gill, Thomas H., "Isaac Watts," *The Congregationalist* (London), Vol. III (1874), pp. 432 ff.

————, "Watts in his Dealings with the Psalms," *The Congregationalist* (London), Vol. V (1876), pp. 424-38.

————————, "Watts and Wesley Compared," *The Congregationalist,* Vol. VII (1878), pp. 129 ff.

Gordon, Alexander, Addresses Biographical and Historical, London, 1922.

Gough, Strickland, An Enquiry into the Causes of the Decay of the Dissenting Interest, London, 1730.

Gray, B. Kirkman, A History of English Philanthropy, London, 1905.

Haller, William, The Rise of Puritanism, New York, 1938.

Haller, William, Tracts on Liberty in the Puritan Revolution, Vol. I, New York, 1934.

Hamer, Enid, The Metres of English Poetry, New York, 1930.

Harder, Johannes Hendrik, Eighteenth Century Tendencies in Poetry and Essay, Amsterdam, 1933.

Harsha, D. A., The Life and Choice Works of Isaac Watts, D.D., New York, 1857.

(Hastings, A Member of the Houses of Shirley and), Life and Times of Selina Countess of Huntingdon, London, 1844, 2 Vols.

Havens, R. D., "Changing Taste in Eighteenth Century," *P. M. L. A.,* Vol. XLIV (1929), pp. 501-37.

———————— "Romantic Aspects of the Age of Pope, *P. M. L. A.,* Vol. XXVII (1912), pp. 297-325.

————————, The Influence of Milton in English Poetry, Cambridge (U. S. A.), 1922.

Hearnshaw, F. J. S. and Clarke, F., A Short History of Southampton, Oxford, 1910.

Hood, E. Paxton, Isaac Watts; His Life and Writings, London, 1875.

Hood, George, A History of Music in New England, Boston, 1846.

Horder, W. G., The Hymn Lover, 2nd ed. revised, London, (n.d.).

Housman, A. E., The Name and Nature of Poetry, Cambridge, 1933.

Hughes, John, Correspondence, Dublin, 1773, 2 Vols.

Janeway, James, A Token for Children, Leeds, 1793.

Jennings, David, A Sermon Occasioned by the Death of the Late Reverend Isaac Watts, D.D., London, 1749.

Johnson, Samuel, Works, Troy, N. Y., 1903, 16 Vols.

Johnson, Thomas H., "Jonathan Edwards' Background of Reading," *Publications of the Colonial Society of Mass.* (Boston), Vol. XXVIII (1935), pp. 193-222.

Julian, John, A Dictionary of Hymnology, revised edition, London, 1907.

Kell, Edmund, A Lecture on the Life, Character, and Religious Opinions of the Reverend Isaac Watts, D.D., London, n.d.

Krutch, J. W., Comedy and Conscience after the Restoration, New York, 1924.

Lecky, E. W. H., History of England in the Eighteenth Century, London, 1878, 8 Vols.

Lee, Umphrey, Historical Backgrounds of Early Methodist Enthusiasm, New York, 1931.

Legouis, E., and Cazamian, L., History of English Literature, New York, 1930.

Lindsey, Theophilus, A Second Address to the Students of Oxford and Cambridge, London, 1790.

Lyell, Jas. P. R., Mrs. Piozzi and Isaac Watts, London, 1934.

MacLachlan, H., English Education under the Test Acts. Manchester, 1931.

Mandeville, Bernard, The Fable of the Bees, ed. F. B. Kaye, Oxford, 1924, 2 Vols.

Marks, Harvey B., The Rise and Growth of English Hymnody, New York, 1938.

Massachusetts Historical Society. Collections, 1st series, Vol. V (Boston, 1798), p. 200: Letter from Watts to Mather; 2nd series Vol. X (Boston, 1823), pp. 39-40: Letter from Dr. I. Watts to a Friend in New England, May 8, 1734; 5th series, Vols. V (1878), VI (1879), VII (1882): Diary of Samuel Sewall; 6th series, Vols. VI (1894) and VII (1895): The Belcher Papers; 7th Series, Vols. VII (1911) and VIII (1912): Diary of Cotton Mather.

Massachusetts Historical Society, Proceedings (1855-58), Boston, 1860, pp. 285-329: The Belknap Donation.

Massachusetts Historical Society, Proceedings, 2nd series, Vol. IX (Boston, 1895), pp. 331-410: Letters of Dr. Watts; 2nd series, Vol. X (Boston, 1896), p. 429: Edwards' Church and Watts's Hymns.

Mather, Samuel, The Life of the late Reverend and Learned Dr. Cotton Mather of Boston (New England), Phila., 1829.

Miller, Perry, The New England Mind, New York, 1939.

Miller, Perry, and Johnson, T. H., The Puritans, New York, 1938.

Milner, John, The Rest and Reward of Good Men at Death. A Sermon Preached . . . Dec. 11, 1748. Being the next Lord's-Day after the Interment of . . . Dr. Isaac Watts, London, 1749.

Milner, Thomas, The Life, Times and Correspondence of the Rev. Isaac Watts, D.D., London, 1834.

Missing, John, A Poem to the Memory of Isaac Watts, D.D., London, 1749.

Mitchell, W. F., English Pulpit Oratory from Andrewes to Tillotson, London, 1932.

The Monthly Repository of Theological and General Literature, Vol. VIII (Hackney, 1813), p. 322: A Review of Belsham's *Memoirs of Lindsey;* pp. 683-776: A Review of Samuel Palmer's *Dr. Watts no Socinian;* pp. 706 ff.: Essay on The Relation between Protestant Nonconformity and Nonconformity to the World.

Monthly Review, or Literary Journal, Vol. X (London, 1754), p. 93; A Review of Watts's authorized Works: Vol. LXVI (1782), p. 170: Lardner's Letters.

Moore, C. A., "Shaftesbury and the Ethical Poets in England (1700-60)," *P. M. L. A.,* Vol. XXXI (1916), pp. 264-326.

Nation (New York, Mar. 16, 1927), p. 280, "Homage to Isaac Watts."

Neal, Daniel, The History of New England, London, 1720.

————, The Method of Education, in the Charity Schools of the Protestant Dissenters, London, 1723.

Nelson, Robert, An Address to Persons of Quality and Estate, London, 1715.

New England Historical and Genealogical Register, Vol. I (Boston, 1847).

Nichols, John, Literary Anecdotes of the Eighteenth Century, London, 1812-16.

Ninde, Edward, A Story of the American Hymn, New York, 1921.

Notes and Queries (London), Ser. 4, Vol. VIII (1871), p. 414: Letter from Watts to Dr. Byles of Boston.

Otis, Philo A., The Hymns You Ought to Know, Chicago, 1928.

Overton, J. H., The Evangelical Revival in the Eighteenth Century, London, 1886.

The Oxford Book of English Mystical Verse, Oxford, 1916.

Palmer, Frederic, "Isaac Watts," Harvard Theological Review, Vol. XII (Oct. 1919), pp. 371-404.

Palmer, Samuel, Defense of the Dissenters' Education in their Private Academies, London, 1703.

Palmer, Samuel, The Life of the Rev. Isaac Watts, D.D. by Samuel Johnson, L.L.D. with Notes, London, 1785.

Parker, Percy L. (ed.), The Heart of John Wesley's Journal, New York, 1903.

Parker, Irene, Dissenting Academies in England, Cambridge, 1914.

Pattison, Mark, "Tendencies of Religious Thought in England, 1688-1750," Essays and Reviews, London, 1860.

Paul, H. G., John Dennis, New York, 1911.

Perdeck, A. A., Theology in Augustan Literature, Groningen, Den Haag, 1928.

Perronet, V., A. Second Vindication of Mr. Locke, . . . To Which are added Reflections on some Passages of Dr. Watts's Philosophical Essays, London, 1738.

Philip, Robert, The Life and Times of the Reverend George Whitefield, M.A., New York, 1838.

Pinto, V. de Sola, "Isaac Watts and His Poetry," Wessex, Vol. III, No. 2, (Southampton, 1935), pp. 27-36.

Pratt, Anne Stokeley, Isaac Watts and His Gifts of Books to Yale College, New Haven, 1938.

Priestley, Joseph, Dr. Watts's Historical Catechisms, with Alterations, 2nd ed., Birmingham, 1788.

Prior, Matthew, Poetical Works, London, 1907, 2 Vols.

Quincy, J., History of Harvard University, Cambridge, 1840, 2 Vols.

Ralph, James, Miscellaneous Poems, London, 1729.

R. E., "Inconsistency of Several Passages in Doctor Watts's Hymns with Scripture and with Each other," American Unitarian Tracts, (Phila., 1807).

Reed, Amy, L., The Background of Gray's Elegy, New York, 1924.

Reeves, J. B., The Hymn as Literature, New York, 1924.

Reid, H. M. B., "Watts and Wesley: A Contrast," *Good Words* (London, 1900), pp. 658-662.

Register of the Bury Street Chapel [MS. fragment in Memorial Hall Library, London].

Rix Manuscript Collection [Property of the Rev. Mr. Wilton Rix, Ealing, London].

Robertson, John M., A Short History of Free Thought, London, 1915, 2 Vols.

Romaine, William, An Essay on Psalmody, London, 1775.

Saintsbury, George, A. History of English Prosody, London, 1908, 3 Vols.

Salzman, L. F., "The Little Busy Watts," *Cornhill Magazine,* new series, Vol. XLIX (London, 1920), pp. 472-78.

Seybolt, Robt. F., "Student Libraries at Harvard 1763-4," *Publications of the Colonial Society of Mass.,* Vol. XXVIII (Boston, 1935), pp. 449-461.

Shepherd, T. B., The Children's Verse of Dr. Watts and Charles Wesley, *London Quarterly and Holborn Review* (London, April 1939), pp. 173-84.

Shoffler, Herbert, Protestantismus und Literatur: neue Wege zur Englischen Literatur des achtzehnten Jahrhunderts, Leipzig, 1922.

Shuster, George N., The English Ode from Milton to Keats, New York, 1940.

Sickels, Eleanor M., The Gloomy Egoist, New York, 1932.

Skeats, H. S., A History of the Free Churches in England, 2nd ed., London, 1869.

Smith, H. F. R., The Theory of Religious Liberty in the Reigns of Charles II and James II, Cambridge, 1911.

Smith, Jeremiah, The Magistrate and the Christian, . . . Exemplified in the Character of Sir Thomas Abney, . . . with an Elegiac Poem by the Reverend Mr. Isaac Watts, 2nd ed., London, 1722.

Southey, Robert, The Sacred Classics, Vol. IX, London, 1834.

Southey, Robert, Specimens of the Later English Poets, London, 1807, 3 Vols.

Stainer, S., History of the Above Bar Congregational Church, Southampton, Southampton, 1909.

Stanhope, George, Danger of Hard-heartedness to the Poor, London, 1705.

Steele, Richard, The Religious Tradesman, Bath, 1802.

Stephen, Sir Leslie, History of English Thought in the Eighteenth Century, New York, 1927, 2 Vols.

Stephenson, J., Sacred History, London, 1836.

Stone, Wilbur M., A Brief List of Editions of Watts's Divine Songs Located since 1918 . . . . [Dated Oct. 1929—a MS. in the Harvard Library].

————, The Divine and Moral Songs of Isaac Watts, New York, 1918.

Stoughton, John, Religion in England under Queen Anne and the Georges, London, 1878, 2 Vols.

Tawney, R. H., Religion and the Rise of Capitalism, New York, 1926.

Thayer, Vivian T., "The Misinterpretation of Locke as a Formalist in Educational Philosophy," University of Wisconsin Studies in the Social Sciences and History, No. 3 (Madison, 1921).

Thompson, A. Hamilton, "The Mystical Element in English Poetry," Essays and Studies, Vol. VIII (Oxford, 1922), pp. 90-108.

Tindall, William York, John Bunyan Mechanick Preacher, New York, 1934.

Tomkins, Martin, A Sober Appeal to a Turk or an Indian, concerning the Plain Sense of Scripture, relating to the Trinity. Being an answer to Mr. J. Watts's late Book, entitled, The Christian Doctrine of the Trinity, London, 1722.

Toplady, Augustus, Works, 2nd ed., London, 1794, 6 Vols. (Vol. IV, pp. 107-17: "Some Outlines of the life of Dr. Isaac Watts").

Toulmin, Joshua, An Historical View of the Protestant Dissenters in England, . . . from the Revolution to the Accession of Queen Anne, London, 1814.

Trevelyan, George M., England under Queen Anne—Blenheim, London, 1930.

Trimmer, Mrs. Sarah, A Comment on Dr. Watts's Divine Songs for Children with Questions, London, 1789.

————, Reflections upon the Education of Children in Charity Schools, London, 1792.

Twenty-Five Sermons Preached at the Anniversary Meetings of the Children Educated in Charity-Schools . . . From the year 1704, to 1728 inclusive, London, 1729.

Tyerman, Rev. L., The Life of the Rev. George Whitefield, London, 1876, 2 vols.

Waterland, Daniel, Religious Education of Children, London, 1723.

Watts, Doct., A Wonderful Dream, New London, 1766.

Watts, Isaac, Correspondence between The Rev. Dr. Isaac Watts, and the Rev. Martin Tomkins, concerning The Worship of the Holy Spirit, London, 1803.

Watts, Isaac, Faith and Practice Represented in Fifty-four Sermons on the Principal Heads of the Christian Religion; Preached at Berry-Street, 1733, 2nd ed., London, 1739. 2 Vols. (By Watts, Guyse, Neal, Price, Jennings, and Hubbard).

——————, A Faithful Enquiry after the Ancient and Original Doctrine of the Trinity Taught by Christ and His Apostles, ed. Gabriel Watts, Bath, 1802.

——————, A Funeral Discourse preached in two Sermons the 12th and 19th July 1724 on occasion of the Death of Mr. John Dent . . . Taken in Short Hand and Transcribed by T. H. [MS., Memorial Hall Library, London].

——————, Nine Sermons, Preached in the years 1718-19, by the late Isaac Watts, D.D., ed. John Pye Smith, Oxford, 1812.

——————, A Manuscript Copy of a Sermon at Mr. Richier's Anniversary, Aug. 27, 1726 [Dr. Williams' Library].

——————, A Manuscript Sermon on Sight vs. Hearing [Mass. Historical Society Library, Boston].

——————, The Posthumous Works . . . Adjusted and Published by a Gentleman of the University of Cambridge, London, 1779, 2 Vols.

——————, The Religious Improvement of Public Events, London, 1727.

——————, A Solemn Address to the Great and Blessed God, London, 1840.

——————, Some Cursory Remarks on Reading the Book of Common-Prayer, . . . Written in the year 1704, Bath 1801.

—————, To His Excellency, Jonathan Belcher, Esq., Boston, 1730.

—————, The Watchful Christian Prepared for Early Death. A Sermon on Occasion of the Decease of Mrs. Sarah Abney, . . . London, 1732.

—————, The Works of the Late Reverend and Learned Isaac Watts, D.D. Published by himself, and now Collected into Six Volumes, ed. D. Jennings, D.D. and P. Doddridge, DD., London, 1753 (Authorized Works).

—————, The Works of the Rev. Isaac Watts, D.D. in Seven Volumes, Leeds, (n.d.). (Preface signed by Edward Parsons, Leeds, and dated Aug. 25, 1800).

—————, The Works of the Reverend and Learned Isaac Watts, D.D., ed. George Burder, London, 1810, 6 Vols.

—————, The Works of the Rev. Isaac Watts, D.D. in Nine Volumes, Leeds, 1812-13.

Weber, Max, The Protestant Ethic and The Spirit of Capitalism, London, 1930.

Welsh, Charles, A Bookseller of the Last Century, New York, 1885.

Wesley, John, The Journal of the Rev. John Wesley, A.M., ed. N. Curnock, London, 1913, 7 Vols.

—————, The Heart of John Wesley's Journal, ed. Percy L. Parker, New York, 1903.

Wesley, Samuel, A Letter from Country Divine to his Friend in London concerning the Education of the Dissenters in their Private Academies, . . . 3rd ed., London, 1706.

—————, Poems on Several Occasions, 2nd ed., Cambridge, 1743.

Whelan, Sister M. Kevin, Enthusiasm in English Poetry of the Eighteenth Century, Washington, 1935.

Whitney, Lois, Primitivism and the Idea of Progress, Baltimore, 1934.

Willson, Jas. R., Dr. Watts, an Anti-Trinitarian; Demonstrated in a Review of Dr. Miller's Letter to the Editor of the Unitarian Miscellaney, Phila., 1821.

Wilson, F. W., The Importance of the Reign of Queen Anne in English Church History, Oxford, 1911.

Wilson, W., Memoirs of the Life and Times of Daniel Defoe, London, 1830, 3 Vols.

Wilson, Walter, The History and Antiquities of Dissenting Churches . . . in London, London, 1808, 4 Vols.

Wright, J. P., "Some Forgotten London Benefactors," *Congregational Historical Society, Transactions,* Vol. X (1927), pp. 73-77.

Wright, Thomas, The Life of Isaac Watts, London, 1914.

Wright, Thomas G., Literary Culture in Early New England, New Haven, 1920.

Young, Edward, Works. Charlestown, 1811.

INDEX

Starred (*) titles are the works of Watts.

Abney, Lady, 31, 34, 54, 65, 66-7, 71, 77

Abney, Sir Thomas, 31, 32, 33, 34, 36, 37, 39, 67

Abneys, the, 23, 31, 64, 67, 84

Above Bar Church, 2, 4, 6

Academies, 10-12, 17, 19

Achates to Varus, 216, 222

Adams, Rev. M. J., 141

Addison, Joseph, 16, 127, 141, 152, 211

Akenside, Mark, 162

Anglican divines, 42

Anglican preaching, themes of, 132

Anglicans, hymnody of, 208-10

Anti-Jacobin, 180

Anti-Trinitarianism, 41, 110

Arian Invited to the Orthodox Faith, 51, 113

Arianism, 40, 109, 110

Aristotle, 86

Arminianism, 40

Arnold, Matthew, 212

Art of Prophecying, 134

Art of Reading and Writing English, 73, 84-5

L'Art Poétique, 159-60

Ashworth, Caleb, 71

Assembly Shorter Catechism, 89

Auden, Wystan Hugh, 185

Austin, John, 193

Authentic Account of Dr. Watts's Last Avowed Sentiments, 124

Author's Solemn Address, 120

Baptists, hymn-singing among, 195-6

Baptists, hymn-writers among, 210-11

Barbauld, Mrs. Anna L., 20-1, 56, 81, 122, 211

Barker, John, 65

Barker, Rev. Mr., 115-16

Barrington, Lord, 13, 23, 54, 55, 59

Barrow, Isaac, 150

Barton, William, 190-1

Baxter, Richard, 127, 134, 141, 193, 194, 217

Bayle, Pierre, 146

Bay Psalm Book, 189

Beard, John R., 208

Beattie, James, 162

Beauties of Watts, 229

Belcher, Jonathan, 56

Belsham's Memoirs of Lindsey, 125

Bendish, Bridget, 23

Benson, Louis F., 194, 196

Bernard, Richard, 134

Beveridge, Bishop William, 189

Biathanatos, 141

Blackmore, Sir Richard, 135, 160, 162, 225

Blair, Robert, 170, 186, 228

Blake, William, 228

Blank verse, 178, 180-1

Boileau, 159-60

Book for Boys and Girls, 76-78

Book of Common Prayer, 91, 209

Book of Discipline, 3

Bowes, Mr., 31

Brackstone, Betty, 83

Brackstone, James, 64-5

Brackstone, Sarah, Watts's sister, 6

Bradbury, Thomas, 25, 30, 40, 58-61, 66, 112, 114, 216, 217, 220

Brief Scheme of Ontology, 73, 87-8

Browne, Isaac Hawkins, 162

Browne, Moses, 71, 227

Browne, Simon, 210

Budgell, Eustace, 141

Bunhill Fields, 70

Bunyan, John, 76-8, 103, 195

Burder, George, 117

Burnet's funeral sermon on Tillotson, 130

Bury, Arthur, 110

Bury Street Chapel, 29-30, 40, 59, 135

Bury Street Chapel, Deacons' Record Book of, 71

Busy Bee, The, 81, 83

Caffyn, Matthew, 110

Call to the Unconverted, 217

Calvinism, 15

Calvinism, poetic influence of, 163-8

Calvinism, Watts's type of, 163

Calvin, John, 10, 14, 108-9, 188, 189

Cambridge, 73, 87

Campion, Dr. Thomas, 191-2

Canticles, The, 15

Carroll, Lewis, 83, 156

Cartwright, Thomas, 132

Caryl, Joseph, 3, 54, 139

Casimire, 9, 174, 175

Catechisms, 73, 74, 89-90, 122

Cave, Edward, 225-6

Caveat against Infidelity, 105

Cazamian, Louis, 158

Century of Select Hymns, 190-1

Century of Select Hymns and Portions of Psalms, 190

Chandler, Samuel, 71, 144

Chappell, William, 134

Characteristics, 149-50

Charity school sermons, 41, 94

Charity schools, origin of, 92-8

Chauncy, Charles, 52

Chauncy, Isaac, 22, 23, 24, 25, 26

Cheare, Abraham, 75, 76

Child's Week's Work, 75

Christian Directory, 134

Christian Disciple and Theological Review, 125

Christian Doctrine of the Trinity, 111, 113

Christian Psalmist, 215

Christian Reformer, 126

Christian Register, 125

Christ's Death and Victory, 160

Clarke, Samuel, 111

Collection of Hymns for Public and Private Use, 208

Collection of Psalms and Hymns, 208

Collection of Sermons Preached at Berry Street, 53, 127

Colligan, J. Hay, 63

Collins, William, 162

Colman, Benjamin, 46, 47, 48, 49, 50, 51, 52, 65, 114, 218

Commentaries, The, 108-9

Comment on Dr. Watts's Divine Songs for Children, 81

Conder, Josiah, 208

Conduct of the Understanding, 88

Congregational Fund Board, 60, 63, 100

Congregational Hymn Book (1836), 208

Congregationalists, 215; *see also* Independents

Corneille, 160

Cotterill, Thomas, 209

Courthope, W. J., 171

Coward Trust Fund, 49, 52, 63, 100

Coward, William, 53, 54

Cowley, Abraham, 160, 162, 178, 186

Cowper, William, 34, 72, 156, 179-80, 228, 229

Cradle Hymn, 79-80

Crashaw, Richard, 15, 185, 193

Creation, The, 162

Croft, William, 206

Cromwell, Oliver, 3, 4

Cromwell, Richard, 4, 23, 30

Crossman, Samuel, 192-3

Crouch, Nathaniel, 75

Curll, E., 222

Damon, S. Foster, 228
Darton, F. J. Harvey, 83
Davideis, 160
Day of Doom, 167
Day of Judgment, 166
De Arte Poetica, 154
*Death and Heaven, 127, 129, 135-6
De Doctrina Christiana, 137
*Defence against the Temptation to Self-Murther, 141
Defoe, Daniel, 33, 59, 99
Deism, 104, 105-9
Dennis, John, 162
Descartes, 148, 140
Devotions, in the Ancient Way of Offices, 193
Devout Exercises of the Heart, 45, 55, 57, 177, 226
Dickinson, Emily, 185
*Discourse of the Love of God, 141-2
*Discourse on the Education of Children and Youth, 74, 98-100
Dissent, 3, 20-1, 39-41, 52
Dissenting Doctors, 30
Dissenting Gentleman's Answer, 104
Distinguishing Marks of the Spirit of God, 142
Divine Emblems: see A Book for Girls and Boys
Divine love, poems on, 175-6
*Divine Songs, 36, 73, 74, 76, 78-84, 90, 122, 163, 181, 192, 229
Dr. Watts no Socinian, 125
Doctrine of Original Sin, 44
Doctrine of the Blessed Trinity, 110
*Doctrine of the Passions, 141-2
Dod, John, 127, 134
Doddridge, Philip, 38, 48, 49, 50, 51, 53, 61-4, 65, 67, 69, 70, 81, 187, 207, 210, 219, 223-4, 226, 228
Donne, John, 141
Dooms-Day Thought, 167
Doxology controversy, 115
Draper, J. W., 168, 186

Dryden, John, 179
Dunciad, The, 156
Dunton, John, 30
Dyche, Thomas, 85
Dykes, John B., 206

Eames, John, 86, 87
Economy of Charity, 98
Edwards, Jonathan, 50, 51, 52, 104, 142, 147, 148, 230
Elegiac Poem to . . . Isaac Watts, D.D., 227
Emblems, 168
English hymnody, origin of, 188
English Primer, 83
Enquiry into the Causes of the Decay, 40, 63, 142
Enquiry into the Occasional Conformity . . ., 33
Enquiry into the Original, . . . of Evangelical Churches, 147
Erskine, Ralph, 211, 227
Essai Politique sur le Commerce, 95
*Essay Against Uncharitableness, 30, 141
Essay concerning Self-Murther, 141
Essay on Charity and Charity Schools, 94
Essay on the Education of Children, 8
*Essay on the Freedom of Will, 147
*Essay towards the Encouragement of Charity Schools, 73, 92, 95-8
*Evangelical Discourses, 128, 138
Evangelical Movement, 42, 43, 228
Evangelical Revival, 208-9
Evans, Dr. John, 13
*Exhortation to Ministers, 131, 134, 222
Experimental preaching, 15, 62, 132, 133, 147

Fable of the Bees, 95
Fairchild, H. N., 157, 186, 227
*Faith and Practice: see A Collection of Sermons Preached at Berry Street

*Faithful Enquiry, 117, 120, 121, 125

Faithful Narrative of the Surprizing Work of God, 51

Faithful Shepherd, 134

Father's Blessing . . ., 75

Feast for Worms, 168

Firmin, Thomas, 110

Flatman, Thomas, 167

Flavel, John, 119, 139

Fleming, Caleb, 118

Fletcher, Andrew, 95

Fletcher, Giles, 160

Fletcher, Phineas, 191

Fountain of Life Opened, 119

*Four Dissertations relating to the Christian Doctrine of the Trinity, 114

Franke of Halle, 42

Free Philosophy, 13

Free Thoughts on the Most Probable Means of Reviving the Dissenting Interest, 63

Friendly Epistle by way of Reproof . . . to T. B., 59

Funeral elegies, 167-70

Future State, 135

Gale, Theophilus, 3, 12, 13

Gardiner, Dorothy, 100

Garrett, George M., 206

General Advertiser, 70

Geneva Psalter, 206

Gentleman's Magazine, 53, 72, 225-6

Gibbons' Diary, 58, 67

Gibbons, Thomas, 2, 6, 57-8, 65, 68, 72, 130, 210, 216, 219, 226

Gibson, Edmund, Bishop of London, 42, 46, 131

*Glory of Christ as God-Man, 118-9, 120

"Good godly books", 74-6, 102

Goodwin, John, 103, 145, 146

Goodwin, Dr. Thomas, 3, 119, 127, 139

Gordon, Alexander, 13

Gospel Canticles, 227

George, Thomas, 19, 89

Gough, Strickland, 40, 63, 142, 143

Grace Abounding, 103

Grave, The, 228

Graveyard themes, 186

Gray, Thomas, 170, 186

Great Awakening, 52

Great Christian Doctrine of Original Sin Defended, 105

Greenham, Richard, 127, 134

Grove, Henry, 13, 52

*Guide to Prayer, 36, 73, 90-1, 138, 222

Guide to the English Tongue, 85

Guyse, Dr. J., 51

Haller, Wm., 3, 132, 133

Hallet, Joseph, 111

Hamer, Enid, 179

Handel, George Friedrich, 206

Happy Union, 110

Harder, J. H., 141

*Harmony of all the Religions which God ever Prescribed, 146

Harrison, Thomas, 227

Hartcliffe, John, 150

Hartopp, John, 21-2, 34

Hartopp, John, the younger, 22, 86

Hartopp, Lady, 30

Harvard, 49, 50

Havens, R. D., 180

Henry, Matthew, 89, 194

Herbert, George, 185, 192, 229

Hertford, Frances, Countess of, 43, 44-5, 57, 64, 207, 219

Hervey, James, 42, 43, 153, 207, 227

Hildersam, Arthur, 134

Hill, Aaron, 162, 167

Historical Preface, 111

History of New England, 50, 52

History of the Puritans, 52

*Holiness of Times, Places, and People, 143

Hollis, Thomas, 29, 30

Hopkins, John, 53, 54

Horace, 154, 161, 174

*Horae Lyricae, 9, 15, 22, 30, 52,

159-62, 163, 164, 175, 177, 186, 200, 201, 203, 221, 229

Hort, Josiah, 10, 13, 17, 42

Housman, A. E., 157

Howe, John, 19, 33, 103, 110

Hughes, John, 10, 13, 15, 16, 17

*Humble Attempt towards the Revival of Practical Religion, 40, 92, 104, 142

*Humility Represented in the Character of St. Paul, 143

Hunt, Dr. Jeremiah, 13

Huntingdon, Countess of, 31-2, 43

Hymnals, Watts in recent, 213-14

Hymns Ancient and Modern, 209

*Hymns and Spiritual Songs, 30, 122, 188, 194, 200, 201-2, 203, 205, 207, 221, 228, 230

Hymns and Spiritual Songs (Browne), 210

Hymns and Songs of the Church, 192

Hymns for Infant Minds, 82

Hymns for Social Worship, 49

Hymns founded on Various Texts, 210

Hymns in Commemoration of . . . our Blessed Savior, 195

Hymns in Prose for Children, 81

Hymn tunes, 206

Hymn-writing, School of Watts in, 210-11

*Improvement of the Mind, 22, 74, 88-9, 92, 154

Imputatio Fidei, 103

Independents, 3, 4, 49, 208

Independents, church discipline among, 26, 27

Independents, hymn-singing among, 196

Indwelling scheme, 111, 117

Inner light, 137, 138, 145, 146

Institutes, The, 108-9

Inward Witness, 69, 105, 137-9

James I, 189, 192

Janeway, James, 75

Jennings, David, 51, 65, 71, 104, 129, 220

Jennings, John, 63

Jessey, Henry, 75

Johnson, Samuel, 52, 58, 86, 87, 88, 122, 130, 154, 156, 171, 175, 217, 226

Jole, William, 75

Jonah, 227

Jonson, Ben, 191

Judgment Day, 167

Julian, John, 209

Juvenilia (Gibbons), 226

Kaye, F. B., 95

Keach, Benjamin, 75, 76, 195

Ken, Thomas, 193

Kippis, Andrew, 208

*Knowledge of the Heavens and the Earth, 73, 87

Lamb, Charles, 180

Lardner, Dr. Nathaniel, 41, 55, 123-5

Last Day, The, 167

Law, William, 105

Leclerc, 12, 86

Legalistic preaching, 147, see also moralistic preaching

Leland, John, 105

Letter from a Country Divine, 17

Letters from the Dead, 55

Letters of Religion between Theophilus and Eugenia, 135

Letter to a Friend, 119

Letter to a Gentleman Dissenting, 104

Letter to the Rev. Mr. Barker, 115

Lindsey, Theophilus, 121

Little Book for Children, 75

"Little Busy Watts", 156

Locke, John, 13, 88, 101, 110, 148-9, 150

*Logic: or, the Right Use of Reason, 22, 55, 86-7, 88, 89

London Congregational Board, 41, 52

Longueville, David, 62

Looking Glass for Children, 75
Love and Friendship: A Pastoral, 56
Lugubres Cantus, 227
Luther, Martin, 188

MacLeish, Archibald, 185
Magnalia, 50
Mandeville, Bernard, 92, 94-6
Manual of Prayers, 193
Mark Lane, 21, 22, 23, 24, 27, 28, 29
Marlowe, Christopher, 185
Mason, John, 193, 194, 197, 199
Mather, Cotton, 50, 51, 89, 113, 114, 200
Mather, Samuel, 51
Mayjor, Dorothy, 4
Meditations and Contemplations, 43
Melancholy, themes of, 164, 186
Melon, J. F., 95
Memorable Affairs in My Life, 5, 6, 22, 29, 30
Methodist program, 41, 48, 49
Methodist Revival, 49, 207-8, 230
Methodists, 41, 43, 46, 49, 215
Miller, Perry, **146**
Milligan, H. V., organist, 213
Milner, John, 71
Milner, Thomas, 126
Milton, John, 17, 110, 137-8, 160, 179, 180-1, 182, 186, 218
Minstrel, The, 162
Miscellanea Sacra, 55
Missing, John, 72
Mitchell, Joseph, 227
Montgomery, James, 215
Monthly Repository, 125
Monthly Review, 124, 155
Moral Essays, 53
Moralistic preaching, 130-2, 147
Moral sense, 149
Moral Songs for . . . Children, 82

Naked Gospel, 110
Nation, The, 157
Neal, Daniel, 13, 50, 52, 59, 123

Neo-classic compromise, 158-9, 187, 230
Newbery, John, 84
New England, 49-52
New England Academies, 87
New England Primer, 91
New Essay on Civil Power in Things Sacred, 144-6
Newton, Sir Isaac, 72, 135, 148, 149
New Version of the Psalms of David, 189
New York *Herald-Tribune*, 213
Night Thoughts, 152
Nye, Philip, 3, 110

Oakman, John, 82
Ode on the Poetical Character, 162
Ode to Fancy, 162
Of the Calling of the Ministerie, 134
Olney Hymns, 209
On Design and Beauty, 162
On the General Conflagration, 167
On the Harmony, Variety and Power of Numbers, 17
On the Numbers of Paradise Lost, 17
Original genius, 170-1
Orthodoxy and Charity United, 109, 146, 217
Orton, Job, 63
Otis, Philo A., 214
Owen, John, 3, 21, 23, 40, 89, 139, 147
Oxford, 73, 87
Oxford Movement, 209

Pamela, 225
Palgrave, 155
Palmer, Frederic, 215
Palmer, Samuel, 12
Palmer, Samuel (1741-1813), 124-5
Paradise Lost, 180, 218
Paraphrase, . . . upon the Song of Solomon, 227
Pardies, Father, 86
Parker, Joseph, 66, 67, 69, 70
Patrick, John, 61, 190, 197, 198, 199

*Pattern for a Dissenting Preacher, 147

Peirce, James, 111

Penn, William, 75, 110

Perkins, William, 127, 134

Perdeck, A. A., 186

Perronet, Vincent, 150

Phillips, Edward, 162

*Philosophical Essays on Various Subjects, 87, 148-51

Pilgrim's Progress, 195

Pindaric folly, 178-9, 185

Pindarics, 9, 15, 186

Pinhorne, Rev. John, 8, 9, 174, 175

Pinners' Hall, 19, 29

Pinto, V. de Sola, 157

Piozzi, Mrs., 151

Playford, Henry, 194

Playford, John, 194

Pleasures of the Imagination, 162

Pocyon, 14

Poems on Divine Subjects, 227

Poems on Several Occasions, 227

Poems on Subjects Chiefly Devotional by Theodosia, 210

Poems on Various Subjects, 227

Poem to the Memory of Isaac Watts, D.D., 72

Poetical Fragments, 193

Polhill, David, 13, 172

Political Works, 95

Pomfret, John, 167

Pope, Alexander, 16, 53, 141, 156, 178, 225

*Posthumous Works, 60, 163, 239-42

Powell, Vavasor, 195

*Prayers Composed for . . . Children, 73, 91

Preacher, or the Art and Method of Preaching, 134

Presbyterian Hymnal, 214

Presbyterians, 3, 40

Price, Richard, 41

Price, Samuel, 24, 29, 36, 59

Priestley, Joseph, 41, 122, 208

Primitive Christianity, 111

Prince, Thomas, 113, 125

Principles of the Christian Religion, 81

Prior, Matthew, 56

Prosody, 178-82

Psalms, accommodation of, 190

Psalms and Hymns for Public and Private Worship, 209

*Psalms of David Imitated, 50, 59, 188, 190, 199-200, 207, 230

Psalms of David Translated in Lyrick Verse, 189

Puritanism, 21, 23, 230

Puritanism, the new, 49, 230

Puritan preaching, 133-4

Puritans, children's literature of, 74-6

Quarles, Frances, 168, 192

*Questions Proper for Students in Divinity, 73, 92

Racine, 160

Ralph, James, 180

*Rational Foundation of a Christian Church, 147

*Redeemer and the Sanctifier, 106

Reed, Amy, 167

Reflections upon the Education of Children in Charity Schools, 98

Reformation Societies, 128

Reformed Pastor, 134

Register of the Bury Street Church, 24-9

Regium donum, 39

*Religious Improvement of Public Events, 127, 128

Religious Trends in English Poetry, 157

*Reliquiae Juveniles, 45, 57, 152-5, 163, 175, 180, 186, 202

*Remnants of Time Employed in Prose and Verse, 152-5, 163

Retirement theme, 164-66, 186

Revival, New England, 139

Richardson, Samuel, 225

Rippon, John, 210

Rise and Progress of Religion in the Soul, 62, 223-4, 226
Robinson, Nathaniel, 4, 5
Rogers, Richard, 127, 134
Romaine, William, 207
Ronksley, William, 75
Rous's Version, 189
Rowe, Benoni, 30
Rowe, Elizabeth (*née* Singer), 44, 45, 52, 55-7, 177, 226
Rowe, Thomas, 11, 13, 14, 27, 29, 30
Rowe's Academy, 12, 52, 54
*Ruin and Recovery of Mankind, 44, 104, 105, 107-9

Saintsbury, George, 156, 181
Salters' Hall Controversy, 30, 39, 40, 41, 50, 52, 54, 59, 111
Salzburgers, The, 41
Sandys, George, 189
Sapphics, 16, 179-80, 186
Sarbiewski, Matthew Casimir: *see* Casimire
Say, Giles, 3, 4, 5
Say, Samuel, 13, 15, 16, 17, 136
Schöffler, Herbert, 186
Schumann, Robert, 206
Scripture Doctrine of Original Sin, 104
Scripture Doctrine of the Trinity, 111
Scriptural songs, making of, 190
Secker, Archbishop, 31, 42
Second Vindication of Mr. Locke, 150
Selection of Hymns from the best Authors, 210
Selection of Psalms and Hymns, 209
*Self-love and Virtue Reconciled only by Religion, 107
Serious Call, 105
Serious Considerations, 44
*Sermon Preached at Salters' Hall, to the Societies for Reformation of Manners, 30, 127, 128
*Sermons on Various Subjects, Divine and Moral, 115, 127, 129, 202

Shaftesbury, Earl of, 107, 149-50
Shakespeare, William, 185
Shallet, Arthur, 19, 30, 93
Shallet, Arthur, the younger, 86
Sheriffhales, 11, 12
Sherlock, T., 110
Shortest Way with the Dissenters, 33
*Short View of the Whole Scripture History, 92
Shuster, George N., 179
Shute, John: *see* Lord Barrington
Sickels, Eleanor, 164
Sidney, Sir Philip, 16, 179, 186
Singer, Elizabeth: *see* Elizabeth Rowe
Sluggard, The, 81, 83-4
Smith, Henry, 134
Smith, Jeremiah, 37
Snowden, Benjamin, 72
Sober Appeal to a Turk or an Indian, 112-13
Socinianism, 14-15, 40, 109, 110, 118
Songs of Innocence, 228
South, Robert, 110
Southey, Robert, 122, 156, 180, 218-19, 222
Spectator, 52, 93, 152, 220, 225
Speed, Dr. John, 9, 10
Spender, Stephen, 185
Spirit, extraordinary visitation of, 52, 138-9
Spiritual Bee, 75
Spiritual preaching, 132
Spiritual Songs, or Songs of Praise, 193-4
Steele, Anne, 210
Steele, Sir Richard, 127, 152
Stennett, Joseph, 19, 30, 195-6
Stennett, Samuel, 210
Stephen, Sir Leslie, 140, 149
Sternhold and Hopkins, 16, 189, 190, 196, 197
Stone, Wilbur Macey, 81, 83
Strasburg Psalter, 206
*Strength and Weakness of Human Reason, 106
Sufficiency of reason, 106-8, 136-9

Sunday School Movement, 82, 90, 102

Supplement to the New Version of Psalms, 194

Swift, Jonathan, 54, 127

Sylvae, 179

"System of Praise", 49, 90, 105, 158, 188, 202, 206-15, 229

Tate and Brady, 189-90, 195, 199, 207

Taunton, Alderman Richard, 1

Taunton, Sarah, Watts's mother, 2, 7

Taylor, Jane and Ann, 82, 84

Taylor, John, 104, 105

Tenison, Archbishop, 93

Theatrum Poetarum, 162

Theobalds, 31

Theomachia, 145

Thompson, A. Hamilton, 177

Thomson, James, 162

Thorner's Charity, 4

Three Dissertations relating to the Christian Doctrine of the Trinity, 112

Tindall, William York, 76, 195

Token for Children, 75, 82

Tomkins, Martin, 112-13, 115, 116, 122, 208

Toplady, Augustus M., 65, 209

Toulmin, J., 11

Towgood, Michaijah, 104

Treatise of Moral and Intellectual Virtues, 150

Trimmer, Sarah, 81, 98

Trinitarian Controversy, 109-121

Trinitarianism, 104

True Nature of a Gospel Church, 147

Turner, Daniel, 72

Two Bookes of Ayres, 192

Unitarian Controversy, 208

Unitarians, 41, 82

Unitarians claim Watts, 122-26

Useful and Important Questions, 117-18, 119

Vision of the Daughters of Albion, 228

Wallis, John, 110

Walpole, Sir Robert, 144

War with the Devil, 75

Warton, Joseph, 162

Was Dr. Watts a Believer in the Supreme Divinity of Jesus?, 125

Waterland, Daniel, 80

Watts, Enoch, 6, 66, 197-8, 201

Watts, Gabriel, 117

Watts, Isaac, birth, 1; family, 6; early verses and studies, 7-8; conversion, 8; academy life, 11-15; first hymn, 19; to Hartopps, 21; call to pastoral office, 24-9; first publications, 30; to Abneys, 31; Wesley and Whitefield, 43-9; New England friends, 50-2; Bradbury and Doddridge, 58-64; family quarrels, 64-6; will, 71; influence of Bunyan, 76-8; influence of Locke, 101; place as educator, 100-2; Deistic controversy, 105-9; his Calvinism, 108-9, 168-9; Trinitarian controversy, 109-21; Doxology controversy, 115-6; Trinity beliefs, 120; as preacher, 129-32; appearance, 129; evangelicalism, 135-40; theory of disestablishment, 144-6; as stylist, 154-5; as mystic poet, 175-8; prosody, 178-80; position and influence as poet, 183-7; influence of hymns among denominations, 207-11; position as hymnwriter, 211-15; character, 216-23; his inconsistencies, 222-3; contemporary religious influence, 223-4; literary and general influence, 225-30.

Watts, Isaac, letters of, 231-8

Watts, Isaac, the elder, 2, 4-6, 19, 240

Watts, "Jemmy", 66

Watts, Richard, 6, 65, 66

Watts, Sarah, "Sarissa", 6, 181

Watts's Geometry, 86

*Watts's *Shorthand*, 86
Watts, Thomas, grandfather of Isaac, 1
Weber, Max, 37
Wesley, Charles, 43, 46, 208, 209, 211, 212-15
Wesley, John, 42, 43, 44, 46, 209, 211, 221, 223, 230; the *Journal* of, 43, 221, 223
Wesley, Samuel, 10, 17, 18
Westminster Assembly, 3
Whig panegyrics, 6, 171-3
Whiston, William, 110, 111
White, John, 104
White, Thomas, 75
Whitefield, George, 42, 43, 45-49, 63, 230
Whole Booke of Psalmes, 189
Wiche, John, 123

Wigglesworth, Michael, 167
Williams, Elisha, 49
Williams, Roger, 146
Wilson, Walter, 207
Winter, 162
Wither, George, 76, 189, 192
World to Come, 127, 129, 136
Wotton, Sir Henry, 8
Wylie, Elinor, 185

Yale, 49, 51
Young, Edward, 55, 152, 167, 170, 186, 225
Young Man's Calling, 75
Young Man's Monitor, 193

Ziegenhagen, F. M., 41
Zinzendorf, Nicolaus, 41